College Business Communications

Second Edition

Kansas City)

Dear Ms. Inverness:

Congratulations on your election as presi[d]
of Practicing Engineers. I read the announ[
morning's Detroit News.

Our organization has an interesting year a[
leadership I know we will be successful i[
the goals we've been discussing during th[
and I have both attended.

Since the article in the News is more th[
announcement, I am sending you a copy w[
looking forward to our convention in Co[

Sincerely,

Ms. Lucia Katz
Administrative Assistant

pd

[En]closure

by Mary Anderson Bogle

THE H. M. ROWE COMPANY

Baltimore

College Business Communications, Second Edition
List No. 130-2
ISBN 0-88294-200-X
9008-1

© The H. M. Rowe Company 1991
Printed in the United States of America

Except for the names of major cities, organizations,
and newspapers, the names and addresses used in
this book are fictitious.

Director of Publications: Lyn M. Tisdale
Editor: Mark A. Slater
Cover designer: Jane F. Powell

Contents

Your Communications Course   v

PART ONE   Basic Elements of Good Writing   1

Unit 1 Structural Elements of Writing   3
Parallel Construction
Agreement
Placement of Modifiers
Verb Forms

Unit 2 Vocabulary   11
Concise Vocabulary
Specific Vocabulary
Accurate Vocabulary
Contemporary Vocabulary

Unit 3 Style Development   23
Courteous Writing
Positive Writing
Specific Writing
Natural Writing

Unit 4 Organization   31
Determining Your Purpose
Assembling Facts
Arranging Material
Organizing for Emphasis
Formal Outlining
Paragraphing

Unit 5 Verifying and Proofreading   39
Using a Dictionary
Using an Almanac
Using an Atlas
Using a Thesaurus
Using Etiquette Guides
Using Other References
Choosing a Reference
Proofreading
Word Processing

PART TWO   The Form of a Letter   49

Unit 6 Letter Formats and Parts   51
Business Letter Formats
Heading Address
Date
Inside Address
Salutation
Attention Line
Special Headings
Complimentary Close
Company Name
Signature Block
Items Following the Signature Block
Continuation Pages

Unit 7 Memos   67
Memo Formats
Preparing Memos

Unit 8 Paper and Envelopes   73
Quantity
Weight
Color
Finish
Size
Continuation Sheets
Copy Sheets
Paper for Memos
Envelopes
Folding Stationery for Envelopes
Addressing Envelopes

Unit 9 The Body of the Letter   79
Dynamic Entrance
Logical Development
Graceful Exit

PART THREE   Types of Letters, Memos, and Reports   85

Unit 10 Orders and Acknowledgments   87
Placing Orders
Acknowledging Orders

Unit 11 Inquiries   97
Consumer Inquiries
Inquiries Between Organizations
Inquiries Within an Organization

Unit 12 Responses to Inquiries   107
Form Letters
Responses to Consumers
Responses Between Businesses
Responses Denying Information
Responses Within a Company

Unit 13 Credit Letters   115
What Is Credit?
Who Is Creditworthy?
Credit Application Letters
Requests for Credit Information
Credit Information Responses
Letters Granting Credit
Letters Refusing Credit
Guide for Writing

Unit 14 Collection Letters   123
Purpose of Collection Letters
The Customer's Position
The Writer's Attitude
The Collection Letter Series
Writing the Letter
The One Who Owes Money
Language and Tone

Unit 15 Adjustment Requests   131
Reasons for Adjustment Requests
Making Adjustment Requests
Problems Within a Company
Getting Help

Unit 16 Adjustment Responses   141
Reasonable Requests
Unreasonable Requests
Favors to the Customer
Writing Adjustment Responses

Unit 17 Employment Communications   151
Application Forms
Cover Letters
Resumes
After the Interview
Other Employment Letters
Resignation Letters

Unit 18 Sales and Fund-Raising Letters   165
Style and Format
Form Letters

Unit 19 Good Manners Letters   171
Business Manners
Appreciation Letters
Apology Letters
Congratulations Letters
Invitation Letters
Acceptance or Refusal Letters
Condolence Letters
Reference Letters
Purchased Cards

Unit 20 A Business Writer's Workshop   181
Reservations Letters
Press Releases
Other Announcements
Agendas
Minutes
Resolutions
Telegrams and Electronic Mail

Unit 21 Reports   191
Purpose of Reports
Organization
Introduction and Conclusion
Short Reports
Formal Reports
Transitions
Letters of Transmittal

PART FOUR Other Forms of Communication   197

Unit 22 Oral Communication   199
Speaking Style and Vocabulary
Telephone Basics
Telephone Uses
Employment Interviews
Informal Occasions
Speaking to a Group

Unit 23 The Positive Listener   203
Listening Skills
Listening Techniques
Listening in Business Situations

Unit 24 Communicating Without Words   205
Attitude Toward Ourselves
Attitude Toward Situations
Attitude Toward Others
Other Nonverbal Messages

APPENDIX   211
200 Words Often Misspelled
Mail and Distribution Services
State and Territory Abbreviations
Time Zones and Area Codes
Military Time
Glossary

INDEX   217

Your Communications Course

Your business communications course will help you become a competent and effective business writer. You will also develop other important communications skills.

Writing. You review the basics of English grammar and punctuation through clear instruction with examples. You then check your skills by completing worksheets that focus on business writing applications.

Organizing. No business writer can produce effective materials without planning. You practice gathering information and organizing your points into an outline to make the desired impression on your reader.

Verifying and Proofreading. Checking reference books to verify facts is an important part of the business writer's job. This course provides you with a guide to reference sources. You also learn important procedures for proofreading your work.

Formatting. This course provides a handy reference for formatting business letters, memos, and reports.

Composing. A useful three-step guide to composing your own letters helps you write effectively in any business situation.

Understanding Business Writing Situations. You compose letters and memos in many typical business writing situations. These categories include inquiries, inquiry responses, credit letters, and the all-important employment communications.

Reviewing Other Communications Needs. You consider the role of speaking, listening, and nonverbal communications in three helpful units.

Your communications course provides **over 80 sample letters** for use as models for your own correspondence. The worksheets offer a wide variety of **business writing situations** that will keep your interest as they help build your communications skills.

Build your communications skills! Your ability to communicate effectively in writing and in speaking will be a real advantage to you in the years ahead.

Part One
Basic Elements of Good Writing

Many people feel a sense of panic when faced with the need to express their thoughts in writing. These same people may not hesitate to speak freely, and they may do so fluently and effectively. Somehow writing seems different.

Writing *is* different. In conversation there are many opportunities to add to our words with gestures, tone of voice, and facial expressions. If our meaning is misunderstood, we often know at once because we see or hear a response from those who are listening to us.

A written message is usually intended to be read when its author is not present. The words must stand alone to convey the message. Moreover, those words are in a form that has some permanence and that may even become a legal record.

Precise use of language in writing requires good grammatical structure, a specific vocabulary, and careful organization. Effective use of language also requires a style that is forceful and appealing. These basic elements—structure, vocabulary, organization, and style—are the background for all our written expression.

1
Structural Elements of Writing

In this course you will write many kinds of business letters. You will also write business memos and reports. Your ability to write clear, accurate sentences will be essential for every letter or memo you compose.

This unit focuses on four essential elements of sentence structure. Reviewing these elements will help you write strong sentences.

PARALLEL CONSTRUCTION

Parallel construction means that equal ideas are expressed in equal terms. Business writers often use a *series* of nouns, verbs, adjectives, or other elements in a sentence. Each series must be parallel in structure.

To maintain parallel structure, connect equal ideas in equal terms. Connect verbs to verbs, nouns to nouns, and adjectives to adjectives:

Not: **The road is steep, narrow, and a danger.**

Danger, a noun, is not parallel in structure to the adjectives *steep* and *narrow*. *Dangerous* is an adjective, and it is parallel in structure to the other adjectives:

Write: **The road is steep, narrow, and dangerous.**

When a series consists of verb forms, such as gerunds or infinitives, be sure that all the items in the series have the same form. Use all gerunds or all infinitives.

Keep gerund forms parallel:

Not: **Your responsibilities include purchasing, operating, and to maintain the equipment.**
Write: **Your responsibilities include purchasing, operating, and maintaining the equipment.**

Keep infinitive forms parallel:

Not: **The auditors will arrive Monday to examine the books, to prepare the statement, and for completing the analysis.**
Write: **The auditors will arrive Monday to examine the books, to prepare the statement, and to complete the analysis.**

If one verb form in a series has an object, it is usually a good idea to write that verb first in the series so that the sentence will not be misread:

Not: **We are ready to pack, move, and sign the contract.**

The preceding sentence might indicate that we are ready to pack and move the contract, in addition to signing it. Write the series in this order instead:

Write: **We are ready to sign the contract, pack, and move.**

Sometimes a writer mistakenly connects a clause to a series of nouns:

Not: **Mr. Wilson reviewed the regulations, the transcript, and what the jury said.**

What the jury said is a clause, and it is not parallel to the nouns *regulations* and *transcript*. *Jury's decision* is a noun, and it is parallel to the other nouns:

Write: **Mr. Wilson reviewed the regulations, the transcript, and the jury's decision.**

Occasionally we mistakenly write nonparallel sentences because we do not use as many words as we need. In compound verb phrases, be sure that all the helping verb forms fit the main verb. In the following sentence, the first helping verb doesn't belong with the main verb:

Not: **We have and will buy our supplies from Druffton Company.**

Will buy is correct, but *have buy* does not make sense. To make the sentence parallel, add the verb that should go with *have*:

Write: **We have bought and will buy our supplies from Druffton Company.**

3

In compound prepositional phrases, be sure that the prepositions are used appropriately. Add a preposition if necessary to maintain parallel structure:

> *Not:* **We want to express our confidence and appreciation for our advisers.**
> *Write:* **We want to express our confidence in and appreciation for our advisers.**

When writing comparisons, be sure to use enough words to make your meaning clear. *Than* can be used alone to connect ideas in a comparison, but *as* usually must be repeated:

> **This report is as long as the earlier study.**
> **This report may even be longer than the earlier study.**

If you want to combine these two ideas, be sure that you keep the entire comparison phrase. If you mistakenly write *as long* instead of the complete *as long as*, the new sentence reads like this:

> *Not:* **This report is as long or longer than the previous one.**

As long than does not make sense. To make the sentence parallel, keep the entire phrase, *as long as*:

> *Write:* **This report is as long as or longer than the previous one.**

Correlative conjunctions are always used in pairs:

either ...... or	not only .... but also
neither..... nor	both .... and

To maintain parallel structure, be sure that the same sentence element follows each part of a correlative conjunction. If a clause follows *either*, then a clause must follow *or*. If the sentence sounds better when a phrase follows *or*, then reword the sentence so that a phrase also occurs after *either*:

> *Not:* **Either we can send you a different article or a copy of the old one.**
> *Write:* **We can send you either** *a different article* **or** *a copy of the old one.* **(phrases)**
> *Or write:* **Either** *we can send you a different article* **or** *we can send you a copy of the old one.* **(clauses)**

Items in a series should be equal in meaning. If a series consists of names of cities, every item in the series should be the name of a city. To make a series parallel, express all items in equal terms:

> *Not:* **I have lived in Chicago, Denver, and Missouri.**
> *Write:* **I have lived in Chicago, Denver, and St. Louis.**
> *Or write:* **I have lived in Illinois, Colorado, and Missouri.**

Parallel structure is also important when we separate ideas into lists or make outlines. Itemized lists are often used in memos, letters, and reports. The following list of items in an agenda is not expressed in parallel terms:

1. **Welcome speech from Mike Hadley**
2. **Fill out income tax forms**
3. **To explain vacation procedures**
4. **Sick leave**

The simplest change is usually the best one. In this case, change all items to match the first item on the list:

1. **Welcome speech from Mike Hadley**
2. **Completion of income tax forms**
3. **Explanation of vacation procedures**
4. **Discussion of sick leave**

Maintaining parallel structure will make your writing easier to read and understand.

AGREEMENT

Careful writers pay attention to subject-verb agreement and to agreement between nouns and the pronouns that refer to them.

The subject and predicate verb of a sentence must agree in number. Both should be either singular or plural:

> *Singular:* **The leaf falls.**
> *Plural:* **The leaves fall.**

A pronoun must always agree in number (either singular or plural) with its *antecedent*, the noun to which it refers:

> *Singular:* **The manager trains his (or her) assistant.**
> *Plural:* **The managers train their assistants.**

Indefinite pronouns ending in *one* (*everyone*), *body* (*everybody*), and *thing* (*everything*) are always singular. Use singular verbs with singular indefinite pronouns:

> *Not:* **Everyone like apples.**
> *Write:* **Everyone likes apples.**

Some indefinite pronouns are always plural:

both	**few**	**many**	**several**

Use plural verbs with plural indefinite pronouns:

> *Not:* **Both likes peaches.**
> *Write:* **Both like peaches.**

A pronoun must agree in number with the indefinite pronoun it refers to:

> *Singular:* **Everyone likes his (or her) gift.**
> *Plural:* **Both like their gifts.**

Sometimes a sentence can be rephrased to avoid awkwardness:

Not: **Anyone is welcome to attend if they speak French.**
Write: **Anyone is welcome to attend if he or she speaks French.**
Or write: **Anyone who speaks French is welcome to attend.**

Another way to rephrase sentences with awkward indefinite pronouns is to change the awkward word to a noun:

Not: **Nobody is interested in adding to their responsibilities without increasing their income.**
Write: **The workers are not interested in adding to their responsibilities without increasing their income.**

Sometimes it is possible to use the indefinite article *a* or *an* in place of a possessive pronoun:

Not: **Someone offered their chair to the visitor.**
Write: **Someone offered a chair to the visitor.**

Collective nouns such as *company*, *staff*, *organization*, and *department* are almost always singular. Use the singular form when you add a pronoun:

That company has a beautiful new building at its headquarters in Tulsa. (not *their* headquarters)
This organization expects to win an award for its outstanding research. (not *their* outstanding research)

The singular pronoun *its* is correct because the antecedents, *company* and *organization*, are singular.

Be sure that the subject agrees with the predicate verb even when the subject is separated from the verb:

Not: **The list of our credit customers are on the desk.**
Write: **The list of our credit customers is on the desk.**

The verb must be *is* because the subject, *list*, is singular. The list, not the customers, is on the desk.

PLACEMENT OF MODIFIERS

Modifiers—adjectives and adverbs—may be single words, phrases, or clauses. The relationship of the words will be clear only if the modifiers are placed correctly. Be sure that all modifiers refer to a word in the sentence, and try to place modifiers as close as possible to the word they modify.

Misplaced modifiers can create humorous sentences:

Sold at neighborhood stores, all children enjoy these cookies.

To make the meaning clear, rephrase the sentence:

All children enjoy these cookies, sold at neighborhood stores.

Be sure that all modifying phrases are properly placed in a sentence. A *misplaced modifier* is a phrase that is too far from the word it modifies. In the following sentence, the placement of the phrase *in the file cabinet* suggests that Bob wrote the report while inside a file cabinet:

We found the report Bob wrote in the file cabinet.

Place the phrase near the verb it modifies—*found*:

In the file cabinet we found the report Bob wrote.

In the following sentence the placement of the phrase *after robbing the bank* suggests that the police robbed the bank:

The thief was pursued by the police after robbing the bank.

Place the phrase next to *thief* so that the meaning is clear:

After robbing the bank, the thief was pursued by the police.

A *dangling modifier* is a phrase that doesn't modify anything in the sentence. The following sentence doesn't tell who is *driving across the bridge*:

Driving across the bridge, the Statue of Liberty is visible.

Reword the sentence to make the meaning clear:

To visitors driving across the bridge, the Statue of Liberty is visible.

Modifying clauses should be placed close to the words they modify. When an adverb clause follows a verb other than the one it modifies, a sentence could be interpreted in more than one way:

I want to know what has been done because I was not at the meeting.

Do you want to know because you weren't there, or are you concerned about what was done as a result of your absence? Moving the clause closer to the word it modifies clarifies the meaning:

Because I was not at the meeting, I want to know what has been done.

A sentence might be misinterpreted when an adjective clause follows a noun other than the noun it modifies:

For lunch we had sandwiches that had been wrapped in plastic that tasted delicious.

The sandwiches, not the plastic, tasted delicious. The simplest way to avoid this problem is to change the clause to a single word:

For lunch we had delicious sandwiches that had been wrapped in plastic.

Pay special attention to the modifiers *only* and *almost*. In the following sentences, the placement of *only* and *almost* affects the meaning:

We have planned only one meeting.
(We don't expect to have additional meetings.)

We have only planned one meeting.
(The meeting has been planned but not held.)

We drove almost to Chicago.
(We didn't quite get to Chicago, but we did go part of the way.)

We almost drove to Chicago.
(We considered driving there, but we didn't.)

VERB FORMS

Active verb forms are important in business writing. Passive forms have their uses, but business writers normally avoid them:

Active: **We sent the shipment last week.**
Passive: **The shipment was sent last week.**

Active: **Six packages arrived today.**
Passive: **Six packages were received today.**

Active: **Mr. Valdez told me to wait here.**
Passive: **I was told by Mr. Valdez to wait here.**

Usually the active form produces a stronger sentence.

When you write a compound sentence, avoid shifting from active to passive:

Not: **We ordered three reams of letterheads, but they have not been received.**
Write: **We ordered three reams of letterheads, but we have not received them.**

A sentence that begins with *Thank you* should not be part of a compound sentence:

Not: **Thank you for taking such care to fill our order correctly, and we are enclosing our check.**
Write: **Thank you for taking such care to fill our order correctly. We are enclosing our check.**

Verbs must be used logically. Use the present tense for something that continues to be true in the present:

Not: **Mrs. O'Brien told me yesterday that her department intended to begin a new schedule tomorrow.**
Write: **Mrs. O'Brien told me yesterday that her department intends to begin a new schedule tomorrow.**

If a condition is permanent, use the present tense. The verb used to state the permanent condition should be in the present tense, even if another verb in the sentence is in the past tense:

Not: **I learned that Trenton was the capital of New Jersey.**
Write: **I learned that Trenton is the capital of New Jersey.**

Avoid using *I would* when you mean *I do* or can use a simpler form:

Not: **I would expect the price to rise next month.**
Write: **I do expect the price to rise next month.**
Or write: **I expect the price to rise next month.**

Not: **I would hope to see you at the meeting.**
Write: **I do hope to see you at the meeting.**
Or write: **I hope to see you at the meeting.**

Parallelism, agreement, correct placement of modifiers, consistent and logical verb forms—all these structural elements contribute to the smoothness and clarity of your writing.

1
Worksheets

Name _____ Date _____

Class _____ Score _____

A. Each of the following sentences contains an error in parallel structure or in agreement. Rewrite each sentence to eliminate the flaws and improve the sense.

1. You will like our new camera because of its low price, simplicity, and it is convenient to use.

2. Either send the material to Mr. Jones or Ms. Barber.

3. The new plan is sure to be approved because it is clear, effective, and its usefulness.

4. Responding to inquiries, processing orders, and to open new accounts are handled by the customer service staff.

5. Mrs. Bordini explained that our next projects are painting, polishing, and to hang new draperies.

6. Mr. Frandell assigned me to reorganize the files, requisition new desks, and preparing the conference agenda.

7. Customers should have confidence and respect for their advisers.

8. That problem has not only been concerning us for several weeks but also our accountants.

9. You must either fill out new forms, or the report must be rewritten.

10. We do not and never have sold wallpaper.

11. These certificates are as valuable or more valuable than the ones that were stolen.

12. We visited Amsterdam, London, and Italy.

13. We have not only received an invitation to the dinner but also to the concert.

14. Our firm has offices in Houston, Atlanta, and Mississippi.

15. Every worker deserves praise for their efforts on this project.

16. The Loganville government is well known for their economical operation.

17. If everyone does their part, we will be able to finish the work on schedule.

18. In a situation like this, each person is entitled to plan their own work.

19. Anyone who wants to have their vacation in June should sign up before the end of this week.

20. The list of address changes have been proofread carefully.

21. This presentation, along with those from the other departments, indicate the strength of Powerscourt Industries.

22. The June and August reports, as well as the report for October, reveals a change in our sales figures.

23. Somebody who visited the new laboratories left their raincoat in the closet.

24. That chapter, in addition to the three that preceded it, are now ready for review.

25. Nobody was willing to shift their lunch hour to 2 p.m.

B. Each of the following sentences contains an error in placement of phrases or in consistency of verb forms. Rewrite each sentence to eliminate the errors and improve the sense.

1. The names of the winners will be posted on the bulletin board by Tuesday in the employees' lounge.

2. Made of Southern hardwood, our decorators are pleased to offer these tables as fashionable accents for your home.

3. We placed our order for the new workstations, but they have not been received by us.

4. We have received your request for information about Sylvia Heston in today's mail.

5. The members of the board explained the plan to have only 20 students in a group at last Tuesday's board meeting.

6. This morning the director announced that next month's speaker was Father O'Rourke from the Hospice Committee.

7. I have been reading about the people who are campaigning against unsanitary food in the newspaper.

8. Andrew's son was born when he was eighteen.

9. Mr. Smithson heard about the new bridge over the radio in his office.

10. Entering the tunnel, the river will be on your right.

11. Refrigerated for four hours, you will be pleased with the taste of these pastries.

12. Removing her hat and coat, the cat watched Jessica carefully.

13. The car accelerated suddenly when Karen put her foot on the pedal at the gas pump.

14. These doors will be gracious additions to your home, made of solid steel.

15. Having read your letter, the situation is much easier to understand.

16. The Nolan Animal Hospital had a reputation for good service and wins the veterinarians' award.

17. Pablo's request seems reasonable, and it is being approved by us.

18. Thank you for your suggestions, and they will be very helpful.

19. Yesterday the agency announced that the new product was selling well this month.

20. We would hope that the lack of rain doesn't damage the trees.

21. We are out of green shutters, and they are expected to be in soon.

22. In a news conference today, the Mayor announced that the new budget was ready for the council.

23. We ordered fourteen cases of spiced pumpkin, but they have not been received yet.

24. Thank you for the assistance you gave Mr. Pym, and we look forward to receiving your report.

25. I would hope that the staff will accept the changes readily.

2
Vocabulary

The quality of a piece of writing is not judged by how long it is or by how many long words it contains. Contemporary business letters, memos, and reports must get to the point. Time is valuable in business, and it takes less time to read material that is straightforward and direct. In addition, a concise message is likely to have a strong impact.

CONCISE VOCABULARY

A good business writer aims for clarity and replaces wordy expressions with direct language.

Study your writing carefully to be sure that you haven't added extra words just to fill space. Sometimes we mistakenly use two words or phrases that mean the same thing. Think about the *meaning* of the words you use so that you won't inadvertently say the same thing twice:

> *Not:* **I am in the process of planning the next step.**
> *Write:* **I am planning the next step.**

The words *in the process of* can almost always be cut from any sentence without affecting the meaning.

> *Not:* **This procedure is a new innovation.**
> *Write:* **This procedure is an innovation.**

If the procedure is an *innovation*, it is *new*. Use one word or the other, but not both.

> *Not:* **In my opinion I think we should meet at noon.**
> *Write:* **I think we should meet at noon.**

Write either *in my opinion* or *I think*, but never both.

> *Not:* **He made a precise, clear-cut distinction.**
> *Write:* **He made a clear-cut distinction.**

Possibly *distinction* could stand alone, but it isn't necessary to write both *precise* and *clear-cut* since the terms have the same definition.

Avoid using extra words that add nothing to the meaning of a sentence:

> *Not:* **That article will help to fill up the page.**
> *Write:* **That article will help to fill the page.**

Extra, unnecessary words sometimes convey an idea that is unintentionally humorous:

> *Not:* **I will be more than happy to help you.**
> *Write:* **I will be happy to help you.**

More than willing is a reasonable description of a good business attitude. However, the expression *more than happy* is too extreme for a business letter.

Avoid unnecessary words or phrases that tell readers something they already know:

> *Not:* **I visited the city of San Francisco in the month of July 1988.**
> *Write:* **I visited San Francisco in July 1988.**

Your readers know that San Francisco is a city and that July is a month.

> *Not:* **Our staff meetings are always held at 9 a.m. in the morning.**
> *Write:* **Our staff meetings are always held at 9 a.m.**

9 a.m. is always *in the morning.*

By careful editing, you can eliminate repetitious or unnecessary words from your writing. Sometimes you can condense a two-page document to one page, a useful saving of time when many copies of the material are needed.

SPECIFIC VOCABULARY

Using a specific vocabulary is easier if you think about the meaning you want to convey and if you have a reasonably good vocabulary. Often the simplest word is the best one, but a specific word can make your writing more clear. Consider a simple word like *said*:

> **Mr. Bishop said that he had not received the order.**

Notice the effect of replacing *said* with a more specific verb, as in these sentences:

Mr. Bishop explained that he had not received the order.
Mr. Bishop mentioned that he had not received the order.
Mr. Bishop claimed that he had not received the order.
Mr. Bishop complained that he had not received the order.

Each change of verb conveys a different attitude toward Mr. Bishop's statement. By selecting the word that is most specific, you can be more precise.

Consider all the meanings *indicated* might have in the following sentence:

My supervisor indicated her approval.

She might have stated her approval, failed to say that she didn't approve, or signed a commitment of some sort.

A common usage that adversely affects the clarity of business writing is the use of *feel* in place of *think* or *believe*. Since *feel* conveys an emotional response, use *feel* and *felt* in situations involving emotions. When you are referring to thoughts rather than feelings, use *think* or *believe*:

Not: **I *feel* we should increase our insurance coverage.**
Write: **I *think* we should increase our insurance coverage.**

Some other verbs that work well to convey thoughts are *consider*, *judge*, *estimate*, and *suppose*.

Take special care with *feel* when you are reporting someone else's response. You know what the person *said*, maybe what he or she *thought*, but not what the person *felt*:

Not: **Mr. Henry O'Neill *felt* that we should support the program.**
Write: **Mr. Henry O'Neill *said* that we should support the program.**

Other common words can often be replaced by more specific words. Instead of the verb *contact*, choose the appropriate word—*write*, *telephone*, or *visit*.

Option means *right to choose* or *legal right to purchase*. When you mean *choice*, *possibility*, or *alternative*, avoid writing *option*.

A *document* can be a specific item such as a *will*, *deed*, *certificate*, or *lease*. When you can, use the exact word that shows your meaning. In word processing terminology, a document is usually a specific file on a disk.

ACCURATE VOCABULARY

Writers sometimes confuse words that are pronounced alike or almost alike. Such words present a particular problem to secretaries who are transcribing from shorthand or from tape and must rely on the sound. You might also misspell a word or use a word incorrectly because you have confused it with another word.

Study the following words and definitions. Be sure that you use the correct word in your business correspondence.

Addition/Edition. *Addition* is a noun that means *something extra* or *the process of adding*. *Edition* is a noun that means *version of a book, magazine, or newspaper*:

The addition has increased the value of the house.
The previous edition of the book is still in print.

Affect/Effect. *Affect* is a verb that means *to influence*. *Effect* is usually a noun that means *result*. *Effect* may also be a verb that means *to bring about*:

The weather affects the voter turnout.
What effect will the new policy have on production?
Paul will effect these changes next week.

Cite/Sight/Site. *Cite* means *to quote*. *Sight* refers to vision. Occasionally *sight* is used as a verb to mean *to have within a range of vision*. *Site* is a noun meaning *location*:

Mrs. Smith cites John F. Kennedy in her report.
The operation should improve her sight.
The construction site hasn't been decided.

Detract/Distract. *Detract* means *to take away from*. *Distract* means *to draw attention from*:

Too many flowers will detract from the comfort of the room.
We were distracted by the sound of the fire engines.

Farther/Further. *Farther* is an adjective or an adverb that refers to measurable distance. *Further* is an adjective or an adverb that refers to a figurative distance or that means *additional*:

Winston walked farther each day.
Give us further identification.

Fewer/Less. *Fewer* is an adjective meaning *not as many* (used with plural nouns). *Less* is an adjective that means *not as much* (used with singular nouns):

Accounting has fewer employees than advertising.
Mr. Young does less work than his colleagues.

Imply/Infer. *Imply* means *to suggest indirectly*. *Infer* means *to draw conclusions*:

Try not to imply that we will be uncooperative.
He tends to infer lack of confidence from casual actions.

Ingenious/Ingenuous. *Ingenious* is an adjective that means *clever* or *resourceful*. *Ingenuous* is an adjective that means *naive* or *unsophisticated*:

An award was given for the ingenious design.
It would be ingenuous of me to believe your story.

Oral/Verbal. *Oral* means *spoken, not written*. *Verbal* means *in words, either spoken or written*:

An oral contract is valid if it is properly witnessed.
We need a verbal response, not just a nod of the head.

Perquisite/Prerequisite. *Perquisite* means *special privilege because of rank or position*. It is often shortened to *perk*. *Prerequisite* means *a requirement that must be met in advance*:

Reserved parking is one of the perquisites of this position.
Typing I is a prerequisite for the word processing course.

Right/Rite/Wright/Write. *Right* may mean *correct*, *fair*, or *the opposite of left*. *Rite* is a noun that refers to a *formal ceremony*. *Wright* means *worker* and is used in compound words like *playwright*. *Write* is a verb that means *to put words on a surface* or *to compose*:

Only one answer is right.
Everyone there witnesses the marriage rites.
That playwright owns six theaters.
I shall write the letter of recommendation today.

To/Too/Two. *To* indicates *direction toward*. *Too* means *also*. It may intensify the meaning of an adjective or another adverb. *Two* is a number:

We ran to the end of the pier.
I too have read the proposal.
The light is too dim for reading.
Marie planted two bushes in the courtyard.

Suffixes change the meaning of some words. The endings *-ance* and *-ence* designate *a condition*. The endings *-ants* and *-ents* indicate *persons who perform a certain task*. Remember which suffixes indicate a condition and which refer to people:

Condition: assistance, attendance, correspondence, residence

People: assistants, attendants, correspondents, residents

Consult a dictionary to be sure you are using these words accurately:

accept	eminent	precede
except	imminent	proceed
access	finally	principal
excess	finely	principle
advice	its	respectfully
advise	it's	respectively
capital	know	stationary
capitol	no	stationery
complement	passed	there
compliment	past	their
council	perspective	your
counsel	prospective	you're

CONTEMPORARY VOCABULARY

Modern usage allows a writer to use a relaxed, informal writing style. Avoid using formal expressions. Try also to avoid unnecessary use of legalistic language. For example, *on or before* is accurate as a legal term. For other purposes, *by October 1* serves as well as *on or before October 1*.

Omit formal expressions that do not add to the meaning of a sentence. Compare these examples of formal and informal writing:

Not: Please be advised that we are holding your reservation for late arrival.

Write: We are holding your reservation for late arrival.

Not: I would like to inform you that your credit application has been approved.

Write: Your credit application has been approved.

Not: I would like to thank you for writing a letter of reference for me.

Write: Thank you for writing a letter of reference for me.

Not: May we take the liberty of informing you that the April meeting will be held at the Boxwood Hotel at noon on April 12.

Write: The April meeting will be held at the Boxwood Hotel at noon on April 12.

Avoid using a long formal word or phrase if there is a short, clear way to write the same thing. In the following examples, the formal words or phrases have been replaced by simple, direct words or phrases to create more readable sentences:

Not: Enclosed herewith please find your tickets for the fall season.

Write: We are enclosing your tickets for the fall season.

Not: We require your signature on the contract.

Write: Please sign the contract.

Not: The required form is attached hereto.

Write: We are attaching the required form.

Not: Please forward your payment.

Write: Please send your payment.

(*Forward* means to send on to another place something you have received. Do not use *forward* to mean *send.*)

Not: Please phone the undersigned.

Write: Please phone me.

Not: Return the questionnaire to my attention.

Write: Return the questionnaire to me.

Not: Subsequent to our conversation, I looked up your account.

Write: After I spoke with you, I looked up your account.

Not: Pursuant to your instructions, we are sending you three copies of the owner's manual.

Write: Following your instructions, we are sending you three copies of the owner's manual.

Not: In accordance with your request, we have canceled your subscription.

Write: As you requested, we have canceled your subscription.

Not: Kindly advise us of Miss Lavery's flight number.

Write: Please tell us Miss Lavery's flight number.

Sometimes an entire sentence should be replaced by more up-to-date wording:

Not: Your cooperation is greatly appreciated.

Write: We appreciate your cooperation.

Not: Please remit by return mail.

Write: Please send your payment at once.

Both men and women work at all levels of business. You may risk offending your reader if you assume that a manager is male and a secretary is female. Here are a few outdated words, with suggested replacements:

Instead of	*Write*
businessmen	managers or executives
workmen	workers or employees
salesman	sales representative or salesperson
mailman or postman	postal worker or letter carrier
man hours	worker hours
man the office	staff the office

Whatever your business—research, sales, consumer services, manufacturing, government, entertainment—your writing should be direct and informal. Remember these guidelines for using the right word:

- Be concise.
- Be specific.
- Be accurate.
- Be up to date.

Worksheets

A. Rewrite each of these sentences to avoid the use of unnecessary words or phrases.

1. He has committed a numerous number of infractions of the law.

2. The Pasquale Pizza Palace will have its grand opening in the month of April.

3. Thank you for your recent letter which you wrote us recently.

4. The salespersons need relief from standing on their feet all day.

5. In my opinion I think the conference should be canceled.

6. Gino Tevalli was born in the city of New Orleans.

7. All the time I was thinking in my own mind that the plan would never work.

8. Be sure to place the date up at the top of the page.

9. In your letter, be sure to state the true facts of the case.

10. First I will begin with an outline of the plan.

11. If you need more time, please call us collect at our expense.

12. We will be happy to reciprocate at some time in the future.

13. My attorney and my doctor both have the same name.

14. If you need further information, please write us a letter or call us on the telephone.

15. We are more than happy to receive your order.

16. Ms. Fox placed her signature down at the bottom of the page.

17. Your house that you own on Georgia Avenue has an unusually large lot.

18. In his explanation Mr. Willard explained how the machine works.

19. This recommendation is based on our past experience.

20. This situation is previously unprecedented.

21. We are looking forward to serving you again in the future.

22. We are always more than pleased to welcome new clients.

23. Your account will be paid in full if you send us your check for the amount of $457.

24. We are in the process of preparing a new edition of our handbook.

25. Please be on time for our meeting tomorrow afternoon at 2 p.m.

B. For each of the words or phrases in italics, write a more specific expression.

1. He *indicated* his disapproval.

2. Write a *paper* about the equipment failure.

3. Ms. Johnson *said* she had not been told about the meeting.

4. We will sign the *documents* today.

5. Consider your *options*.

6. *Contact* our office next week.

7. Josie *feels* that the price is too high.

8. I think Dave *felt* we should close the office early.

9. We are enclosing three *pieces of information* about our cruises.

10. *We had some trouble with the machine*.

C. The following paragraphs contain errors in the accurate use of words. Correct the errors.

Thank you for you're order for too reams of white stationary, Stock No. 333. One advantage of ordering from our company is service. We can advice you about the paper you need and give you assistants in your selection.

For the passed three years the residence of Rose City have asked the City Counsel to consider a new civic center. We are pleased to tell you that we have finely raised enough capitol to purchase the land for the building. Thank you for your help.

2
Worksheets

D. The following memo contains errors in the use of words that are often mistaken for other words. Correct the errors.

If everything precedes on schedule, we will open Oak Creek condominiums by May 15. That gives us six months to take care of any farther details. Our verbal agreement with the construction firm was in effect until the written contracts were signed last week.

Too problems have already been resolved. Their was only a slight delay in obtaining the rite of way for the edition of underground utility cables. Through the ingenuous planning of our landscaper, the road that provides excess to the recreation area has been redesigned so that traffic will not distract from the beauty of the picnic sight.

One perquisite to a successful opening in May is the completion of the patios and balconies that face the lake. The principle criterion for there design was that the private patios should complement the public gardens. We proceeded with that standard in mind, and we have been able to keep our prospective about such things as choice of tiles and railings so that the effect is just wright.

E. The following memo contains errors in the use of words that are often mistaken for other words. Correct the errors.

May is finely here, and the opening date for Oak Creek Condominiums is imminent. Attendants at the opening meeting of the owners of the condos at Oak Creek was high. With the assistance of Sarah Hayes, we are providing this edition to the material that was distributed at that meeting.

Since less buyers than expected have chosen the 3—bedroom units, we are offering the owners of those units the prerequisite of one year's free membership in the tennis club. Most of the residence have excepted the invitation, which will be in affect for the rest of the year.

It will be easy to find locations at Oak Creek. The condos on Jade Street, Topaz Road, and Garnet Lane will have 300, 400, and 500 numbers respectfully. Accept for Marble Circle and Stonewall Avenue, all the streets have numbers that increase as you go further east. In addition, each unit has it's own mailbox with the numbers painted clearly so that people who drive passed will be able to read them.

At the opening ceremony on May 15, several imminent guests will be in attendants. As one of the condo owners, your invited to the reception at the clubhouse following the ceremony. I hope you will be their.

F. Rewrite each sentence, using contemporary, concise language to replace outdated expressions. Omit unnecessary expressions.

1. Please be assured that we will be in touch with you as soon as we can.

2. Subsequent to our telephone conversation of this date, I checked the records on the Ingres account.

3. Kindly advise us of your arrival time.

4. We are writing to tell you that the meeting has been postponed.

5. I would like to express my appreciation to you for your help.

6. We have located the information you wanted, and you will find it enclosed.

7. After I talked with you, I took the liberty of speaking with Mrs. Parker about the plan.

8. We would like to inform you that your account is overdue.

9. Please be advised that your reservation will be held until noon.

10. In accordance with your request, we are sending you three sample kits.

11. Enclosed herewith please find a copy of the schedule for shipments to your plant.

12. Kindly refer to our letter for an explanation of the charges.

13. Your cooperation in this matter will be greatly appreciated.

14. We beg to inform you that we have renewed your lease as you requested.

15. Please return this reservation on or before August 30.

16. We will forward our check to you as soon as the work is completed.

17. Our booth at the exposition will be manned by Pat Corman and Lee Brittain.

18. The businessman's platter is the most popular item on our menu.

19. None of our salesmen were willing to move to the new branch office.

20. Attached hereto is the form your company requested this office to complete.

21. We would like to offer you our appreciation for the time you spent on the project.

22. Kindly mail the completed forms to the undersigned.

23. The project will require 100 man hours.

24. Please send your payment by return mail.

25. Send your reservation application to my attention.

3
Style Development

It may seem that only "creative" writers should be concerned with writing style. Business writing may be concerned with routine matters, but writing style is still important to business writers.

Your writing style may mean the difference between an effective letter and a letter that goes unread. It can also mean the difference between accurate, clear correspondence and a letter that misleads or confuses your reader. When you develop a good writing style, you ensure that your message will be understood easily and accurately.

COURTEOUS WRITING

The proper attitude for business correspondence is courteous, sincere, affirmative. Express your ideas so that they make a favorable impression on your reader.

To make a favorable impression, address your reader courteously. Say *please* and *thank you* when appropriate. Writing courteously shows respect for your reader and builds good will. A discourteous tone never improves a situation.

Your writing will always convey a courteous tone if you write with your reader's interests in mind—with a *you attitude*. Let your writing demonstrate that you understand your reader's point of view and that you care about your reader's concerns, convenience, and comfort.

POSITIVE WRITING

A positive attitude in a letter, memo, or report leaves a good impression on your reader. Positiveness makes you sound capable and confident, and it shows that you approach a situation in a constructive manner.

Remember, don't say what you can't do. Say what you *can* do. Rephrase negative-sounding statements into positive messages:

Negative: **We won't be able to answer your request until you give us more information.**

Positive: **As soon as you send us the information we need, we'll be able to answer your request.**

Negative: **Unless the Gorgon Company sends its bid by April 1, we won't be able to consider that company's contract.**

Positive: **If we receive the Gorgon Company's bid by April 1, we can consider that company's contract.**

Negative: **Mr. Leonidas is on vacation, and we can't do anything about your request until he returns.**

Positive: **As soon as Mr. Leonidas returns from vacation, we'll be able to take care of your request.**

Maintain a positive approach when referring to someone else's actions:

Negative: **You failed to explain what you want us to do when the advertisements are delivered.**

Positive: **Please tell us what you want us to do when the advertisements are delivered.**

Negative: **Failure to pay this bill by September 14 will result in the loss of your benefits.**

Positive: **Send your check by September 14 to protect your benefits.**

A positive tone shows an optimistic approach, even when the situation may clearly have some negative aspects. Avoid negative words like *not*, *no*, and *never*. You should also avoid using words like *however* and *unfortunately*.

You will make a favorable impression if you make your company sound competent. If your writing shows a lack of regard for your reader's company, your message will lose its impact. For effective positive communication, present yourself, your company, and your reader in as favorable a way as you can:

Negative: **I don't know how to handle the schedule for the meeting.**

Positive: **I need your help in planning the schedule for the meeting.**

Negative: **Your company will just have to wait its turn for delivery.**

Positive: **Your are on our list to receive shipment on November 16.**

Negative: **We have never heard of Floss Swimming Pools before.**

Positive: **We are pleased to have our first order from Floss Swimming Pools.**

Negative: **I don't know how you can get away with such poor service.**

Positive: **I'm sure you didn't intend to neglect my order for so long.**

Negative: **The merchandise you shipped us was no good.**

Positive: **Some of the items in the shipment were not up to your usual standards.**

In business situations it is sometimes necessary to apologize. Avoid such expressions as *we are sorry this situation had to happen*. Your reader certainly knows that the situation *did not* have to happen. Focus on correcting the error or finding a solution for the problem.

The best apology is a simple one that conveys a positive image of your company:

Negative: **I don't see how I made such a stupid mistake.**

Positive: **The error was my fault.**

Negative: **We are sorry we gave you such poor service.**

Positive: **We apologize for the mistake in your bill.**

Negative: **I regret that you had to be inconvenienced by the strike that occurred in our factory.**

Positive: **We are sorry that we had to delay the shipment until the strike was settled.**

Negative: **It is too bad that our company couldn't fill your order properly.**

Positive: **We shipped you the correct items today, and we apologize for the error.**

SPECIFIC WRITING

When you must state a negative idea, make a complaint, or express a criticism, try to do so in an objective way. Frequently pieces of business communication must stand as legal evidence of actions taken.

In business writing, state what you know is true and avoid casual conclusions. Give facts. Avoid opinions unless the opinions are based on solid information:

Vague: **Mrs. Walker doesn't care about being on time.**

Specific: **Mrs. Walker has been late to work twice this week.**

Vague: **The department's report was incomplete.**

Specific: **The figures we need for the time survey are missing.**

Vague: **I didn't like the looks of the employees' cafeteria.**

Specific: **The employees' cafeteria had trash on the floor and leftover coffee in cups on the tables.**

Vague: **While Mr. Jamison worked for us, he was a good employee.**

Specific: **While Mr. Jamison worked for us, he developed three valuable procedures to improve safety in our shops.**

Vague: **Mr. Gregory is a troublemaker.**

Specific: **Mr. Gregory often leads groups that protest the decisions of management.**

Vague: **We are not comfortable with the plan you suggested.**

Specific: **We want to make several changes in the plan you suggested.**

When you are writing about a sum of money or a period of time, use specific details. Vague references seem indecisive. Use exact figures and exact amounts whenever possible:

Vague: **We placed the order several weeks ago.**

Specific: **We placed the order on July 12.**

Vague: **This account is two or three months overdue.**

Specific: **This account is 60 days overdue.**

Vague: **We paid almost $400 for the service.**

Specific: **We paid $380 for the service.**

Vague: **I telephoned your office in June or July.**

Specific: **I telephoned your office on June 30.**

Vague: **Mr. Johanssen worked here for several months in 1985.**

Specific: **Mr. Johanssen worked here from January 27 to August 22, 1985.**

Whether you want to praise or criticize, specific details will increase the power of what you write.

NATURAL WRITING

Effective business writing should be easy to read and understand. Most awkward writing can be avoided if you use a simple, straightforward way of saying something. Study your writing carefully to make sure you haven't included phrases and sentences that will be hard for your reader for follow.

Keep the words of a sentence or a clause in natural order:

Not: **Old and rusty was the lock on the storeroom.**

Write: **The lock on the storeroom door was old and rusty.**

Not: **Concerned about the rise in prices were all our clients.**

Write: **All our clients were concerned about the rise in prices.**

Keep a subject and its verb as close together as possible. Place modifying phrases so that they do not interfere with the smooth flow of the message:

Not: **The samples of cosmetics that we distribute free of charge to department stores and drugstores each year are an important part of our promotion.**

Write: **An important part of our promotion is the distribution of free cosmetics samples to department stores and drugstores.**

Not: **Mr. Jennings, hoping to avoid the long lines that are likely to occur at the bank's main office on Friday afternoons, went to the automatic teller's window.**

Write: **Hoping to avoid the long lines that are likely to occur at the bank's main office on Friday afternoons, Mr. Jennings went to the automatic teller's window.**

Not: **Two vans driven by employees of the Victoire Hotel that were en route to the airport had flat tires.**

Write: **En route to the airport, two vans driven by Victoire Hotel employees had flat tires.**

Not: **The airplane with its precious cargo of vaccines landed safely.**

Write: **The airplane landed safely with its precious cargo of vaccines.**

Sometimes it is necessary to make a long modifying phrase into a separate sentence to make the message clear:

Not: **The committee appointed by the Mayor to study ways of meeting the needs of the homeless will meet Thursday, March 12.**

Write: **The Mayor has appointed a committee to study ways of meeting the needs of the homeless. The committee will meet Thursday, March 12.**

Not: **The soundproofing panels placed in our office to minimize the noise from the printers and the typewriters are not effective.**

Write: **Soundproofing panels were placed in our office to minimize the noise from the printers and the typewriters. The panels are not effective.**

Voice indicates the relation of the action of a verb to its subject. Business writers use the active voice more than the passive voice because the active voice produces stronger sentences:

Passive: **The decision to postpone the meeting was made by Ms. Moss.**

Active: **Ms. Moss made the decision to postpone the meeting.**

Passive: **Several buildings in the downtown business district are owned by Branigan and Whitmore.**

Active: **Branigan and Whitmore owns several buildings in the downtown business district.**

In certain situations, however, the passive voice is needed to convey meaning accurately. Use the passive voice when the source of the action is unknown or unimportant:

The mail had been opened before noon.

The documents were delivered yesterday.

Use the passive voice to focus on the result of an action:

The contracts were destroyed by the fire.

The context for writing sometimes determines whether the active or passive voice is more appropriate. Notice that the following sentences in active and passive voice convey the same idea:

Active: **The proposal impressed the new client.**

Passive: **The new client was impressed by the proposal.**

To emphasize the effect of the proposal, the active voice would be more appropriate. To emphasize the reaction of the new client, the passive voice would be more appropriate.

Avoid passive verbs except in circumstances when the passive voice is necessary to express ideas clearly.

You can often use several short sentences in place of one long sentence to help make your writing easier to read. It is difficult to follow a conversation in which the speaker seldom pauses. Written material that contains long sentences is also difficult to follow, even when the sentences are well constructed.

Several short sentences often convey ideas more clearly than one lengthy sentence:

> *Not:* **Having met Ms. Rocco while she was in college studying forensic medicine, Mr. Rutherford was pleased to learn that she has been appointed chief counsel for the Londres Company.**
>
> *Write:* **Mr. Rutherford met Ms. Rocco while she was in college studying forensic medicine. He was pleased to learn that she has been appointed chief counsel for the Londres Company.**

> *Not:* **Although the procedure we have just described is complicated and time-consuming, we are convinced that the benefits your organization will receive will far outweigh the problems because the result will be a superior service.**
>
> *Write:* **The procedure we have just described is complicated and time-consuming. We are convinced that the benefits outweigh the problems. The result will be a superior service.**

Business writers who develop a good writing style are able to write with vitality, even when the material is routine. Whenever possible, use a conversational tone and a style suited to your reader.

Most awkward writing can be avoided if you use a simple way of saying something without trying to sound formal. Don't clutter your business letters and memos with lengthy words and complicated sentences.

3
Worksheets

A. Rewrite these sentences so that they reflect a more positive attitude and have a more natural style.

1. The new tax information has not been received by us.

2. Your failure to supply us with details of the procedure will result in delay.

3. I don't think these reports can be completed by this department on time.

4. Many absences have been experienced in this department, and a new method of having someone who is here cover for someone who is absent is needed by us before the winter sets in.

5. I don't understand why so many absences have occurred in your department this month.

6. Ms. Bellini, in an effort to promote the sale of the new hand lotion to high school and college students, distributed samples.

7. Mr. Tanko was to have handled your account, but now I shall have to do it because he is too busy.

8. I will not be able to appear as a speaker on your program because I have something important on my schedule for that day.

9. The inconvenience you suffered as a result of the inability of this office to serve you in a timely manner is a source of great concern to me.

10. The foregoing statements are not to be construed by you to signify that we are going to be unwilling to cooperate.

11. During his employment with us, Mr. Emmett never failed to be punctual.

12. We cannot prepare the newsletter by May 15 unless you send us your article by April 30.

13. We are apologetic that such an unfortunate delay had to happen to your order.

14. If a repeat of the failure of the equipment to operate properly is experienced by us, you will be expected to make repairs.

15. The rise in oil prices is believed by Mr. Leonard to be the cause of the increase in the cost of our product.

16. We are not able to understand what problems occurred that you were writing about.

17. The deduction you requested from your bill cannot be allowed by us.

18. Mrs. Hernandez was not, unfortunately, available at the time you telephoned.

19. Improved methods of cleaning the floors of the reception area in our main building are needed.

20. There are no problems with these machines that are caused by faulty circuits.

3
Worksheets

B. Rewrite these paragraphs so that they are more positive in attitude and more natural in style.

1. We are instituting in an effort to alleviate the excessive volume of traffic in the cafeteria area a staggered program of times for eating lunch. Please be good enough to observe the schedule that has been posted in each department to that attention to normal work patterns will not be unduly disrupted by the absence from the desks of too many people at any given same time period. It is to be hoped that by not having more than 200 employees eating lunch at any one time, a smoother flow of traffic in the cafeteria will be actuated.

2. It has been brought to my attention that personal telephone calls have been taking place on the office telephones during office hours. I would like to call your attention to the fact that our telephones exist for the purpose of being used as instruments of business communication. No one needs to be told that if a customer of ours cannot get through on the telephone to us, he or she will direct his or her order to another company, probably one of our competitors. Hopefully, all employees are able to recognize that this situation must be altered by some changes in the pattern of making and being receivers of personal calls during office hours. To implement a plan for limiting such calls is what we are going to do as soon as a meeting has been held to discuss the situation.

3. This is to announce that Ms. Gwendolyn DeStefano, of our Localli branch, will be in this office all day on Thursday, April 7. Her visit will have as its purpose the demonstration of procedures needed to be followed when filling our forms expected to accompany material that is being sent to the Word Processing Department. Incomplete and inadequate information on these forms will have the likely result of impeding the prompt and efficient flow of work issuing from the Word Processing Department back to the originating individuals. Attendance at the demonstration by all persons who use the interoffice forms for such processing will be required. See your individual supervisor to ascertain at what particular time you are anticipated to be at the demonstration.

4. Wormwood Industries is at last ready to implement the operation of the Child Care Center, which has been in the process of being developed for several years. Mothers who have children needing to be left in the Child Care Center are hereby instructed to fill out the forms provided by the Personnel Department and which are now available. Attention is called to the fact that failure to supply complete information on the above-mentioned forms may result in a delay in actuating the services of the center. It is expected by this department that the full operation of the Center can be anticipated on or not later than July 22. All interested parties can facilitate the early operability of the center by total cooperation with the Center's staff.

4
Organization

Before you begin to write, consider how you will organize your material. Some subjects are best arranged in chronological order. Others can be arranged by the relative importance of individual items. Always make some kind of plan before you begin to write.

DETERMINING YOUR PURPOSE

The first step in organizing is to determine your purpose. What is the reason for the letter, the memo, or the report? What do you expect to accomplish with this piece of writing?

Imagine that you are moving to another city to begin a new job. You will have limited time to find a place to live, and you have decided to write a letter to a realtor in the city to which you are moving. You are asking the realtor to select several possible residences for you to see.

First, determine your purpose for writing. You are writing to explain what you are looking for in your new home. You want to give the realtor a clear idea of your needs and resources so that he or she can give you useful advice.

ASSEMBLING FACTS

The next step is to assemble your facts. Make a list of all the information you want to include, just as the ideas occur to you. You might end up with this list:

1. Rent, not buy, at least for two years
2. Size of family: two adults, one child
3. Want three bedrooms, could manage with two
4. Storage for sports equipment (skis, golf clubs, canoe)
5. Near public transportation
6. Garage space for one car
7. Carpet and draperies needed
8. Small dog
9. Limitation on amount of rent
10. Quiet neighborhood
11. Shopping areas
12. Choice of house or apartment

The list provides the material from which you can begin to organize the letter.

ARRANGING MATERIAL

As you look at the list, you realize that the items are neither structured nor organized. Some items refer to existing conditions that are not likely to change soon. Others refer to circumstances that limit what you can consider. As you rearrange the list, you see that you have three kinds of information:

- Background
- Requirements
- Optional characteristics

When you set down these headings, almost every item in your list will fit into one of the three categories. Then you have a rough outline:

Background
> Family includes two adults, one child, one small dog
> Financial considerations limit cost to $600 a month and require renting, not buying

Requirements
> **Two bedrooms**
> **Public transportation**
> **Storage space**

Optional characteristics
> **Quiet neighborhood**
> **Garage space**
> **Carpet and draperies**
> **Shopping nearby**

The only item that doesn't fit into one of the three categories is the choice of renting a house or an apartment. What you do with an item that doesn't fit into the pattern of all the others depends on how important you think that item is. You could omit it if you consider it unessential. In this rough outline you could add another category:

Choice between house or apartment

After you have made a list of the information you want to include and have grouped that list into several categories, you might realize that your original list omitted some important elements. In the list about housing needs, for example, you might want to include two other items: nearness to schools and other kinds of rooms wanted or needed. Both could fit into the requirements category.

You might also realize that some of your raw data is not necessary and can be discarded. The selection of material to omit or to add will be determined by your purpose. Everything in your outline should serve your purpose in the letter, memo, or report.

For some messages, you may want to include only a few items. Make a brief list of the major points you want to make:

> **Memo about meeting change**
> **Friday instead of Thursday**
> **Same time and place as usual**
> **Important announcements to be made**

A list of items you want to include will keep you from omitting important details. A list may also give you a sense of perspective about the material you want to use.

ORGANIZING FOR EMPHASIS

Your writing will be more effective if you identify which relationships you want to stress, which similarities you want to emphasize, and which contrasts you want to point out before you begin to write. Ask yourself, "What are the parts of this subject?" Then you can develop an organizing concept—the focus that gives perspective to the ideas you are presenting.

Imagine that the coordinator of the Employees' Committee is making plans for redecorating the employees' lounge. He has asked you to submit your ideas in a written report.

What you want to emphasize will determine how you will organize the material. If you think comfort and convenience are most important, organize the material to emphasize these qualities. You might list these ideas:

- placement of tables
- size of chairs
- location of lamps
- ventilation

If you want to focus instead on appearance, your list of items would be different:

- color schemes
- pictures
- plants

Still another focus for such a report could be the cost of such renovations. Your list of items to be covered might be something like this:

- existing furniture that can be kept
- inexpensive replacements
- small changes that would make a big difference

You would include all factors in one report only if your report is intended to give an overview of all possibilities. Your point of view will determine how much information you need.

FORMAL OUTLINING

An outline is the pattern from which the report (or letter or memo) can be developed. When you prepare an outline before you begin to write, your report will develop smoothly and logically.

In a formal outline, all headings must be parallel in structure with other headings. All subheadings must be parallel in structure with other subheadings. Do not list subheadings unless you have more than one under a heading. Two or more subheadings are needed if they are used at all.

Writing an outline is simple, once you have gathered your ideas. This formal outline shows the plan for a letter about housing needs:

> I. **Background**
>   A. **Family characteristics**
>   1. **Two adults**
>   2. **One child**
>   3. **One small dog**
>   B. **Financial considerations**
>   1. **No money for buying a house**
>   2. **Limit of $600 for rent**
> II. **Requirements**
>   A. **Space**
>   1. **Two bedrooms**
>   2. **Storage space for sports equipment**
>   3. **Eating space in kitchen**
>   B. **Neighborhood facilities**
>   1. **Public transportation**
>   2. **Schools**
> III. **Desirable characteristics**
>   A. **On premises**
>   1. **Carpet and draperies**
>   2. **Garage for one car**
>   3. **Laundry facilities**
>   4. **Two bathrooms**
>   B. **In neighborhood**
>   1. **Shopping facilities**
>   2. **Friendly, quiet neighbors**
> IV. **Choice between house or apartment**

This sample can be a model for any formal outline you need to write. Some word processing packages offer an outline feature that inserts the numbering and spacing for you.

Another frequently used system for outlines is the legal numbering system. In this system, each main heading has a different Arabic numeral (1, 2, 3, etc.), and the subheadings are shown with decimal points:

1. **Background**
   1.1. **Family characteristics**
       1.1.1. **Two adults**
       1.1.2. **One child**
       1.1.3. **One small dog**
   1.2. **Financial considerations**
       1.2.1. **No money for buying a house**
       1.2.2. **Limit of $600 for rent**
2. **Requirements**
   2.1. **Space**
       2.1.1. **Two bedrooms**
       2.1.2. **Storage space for sports equipment**
       2.1.3. **Eating space in kitchen**
   2.2. **Neighborhood facilities**
       2.2.1. **Public transportation**
       2.2.2. **Schools**

Whatever style of numbering you use, be sure to be consistent. Always remember the need for parallel structure. Also remember that since you cannot divide anything into just one part, you must always have at least two subheadings if you have any at all. If one category seems to have too many subheadings, consider making a different kind of division.

PARAGRAPHING

A paragraph is a group of sentences combined to relate or develop one particular idea. In business letters and memos, as in any kind of writing, always begin a new paragraph when you change to a different idea. The most important point to remember about paragraphing is to make the material easy to read.

Paragraph lengths vary. A paragraph should be as long as it takes to develop an idea—usually two to five sentences. In letters and memos where the emphasis is on quick readability, occasional one-sentence paragraphs are not unusual and are often desirable.

This memo is hard to read as one long paragraph:

```
On Monday, April 8, we'll have a chance to pioneer
the new Fixitall computer system. Mr. Horace
Delvino, of the Fixitall Company, will be in our
Accounting Department to supervise the
installation of the new equipment. He will also
answer questions about how we can make the system
work for all our accounting procedures. When we are
all aware of the capabilities of the new system,
we'll be ready for the training course, "Computers
in Our Office," which begins May 12. The course is
free and will take two hours on Mondays and
Thursdays for six weeks. Mrs. Nicole Bell, Director
of Human Resources, has made arrangements for the
course to be conducted from 4 to 6 p.m. so that half
the time will be during the working day. When we
have learned how to operate this computer,
additional terminals will be available for our
work.
```

Divide the memo into short paragraphs for easier reading:

```
On Monday, April 8, we'll have a chance to pioneer
the new Fixitall computer system.

Mr. Horace Delvino, of the Fixitall Company, will
be in our Accounting Department to supervise the
installation of the new equipment. He will also
answer questions about how we can make the system
work for all our accounting procedures.

When we are all aware of the capabilities of the
new system, we will be ready for the training
course, "Computers in Our Office," which begins
May 12.

The course is free and will take two hours on
Mondays and Thursdays for six weeks. Mrs. Nicole
Bell, Director of Human Resources, has made
arrangements for the course to be conducted from 4
to 6 p.m. so that half the time will be during the
working day.

When we have learned how to operate this computer,
additional terminals will be available for our
work.
```

As a general rule, the body of a letter has three parts—an introduction, a main section, and a conclusion. The introduction should be a separate paragraph, as should the conclusion. The main section might have only one paragraph, but it could have any number, depending on the length of the letter.

Get into the habit of jotting down the main idea of each paragraph you intend to write. You might list these ideas for a letter explaining how to get to your office from a neighboring town:

- welcome to visitor
- directions to Interstate highway
- description of points along the Interstate
- directions from Interstate to Allicorn Building
- plans for time of meeting

Here is how the paragraphs written from the list might look in a well-organized business letter:

Dear Mr. Jones:

We at Allicorn Research are pleased that you and three members of your staff can be with us for the meeting on October 21.

The drive from Greenville to Springfield takes about one hour. From your Greenville plant, you can drive north on Goldby Road to I-255. Go north on I-255 for 13 miles to Exit 56. Take that exit to I-55.

On I-55 you will drive about 45 miles before you come to the first exit for Springfield. It is labeled South Springfield. Do not take that exit. About two miles farther, there is an exit marked Springfield Junction. This is Exit 23. Exit there and use the right lane of the ramp.

From the exit ramp, turn right onto Yardwick Street. At the third traffic light, turn left onto Method Lane. Our building is the only one now occupied in the new Method Research Center. Park in the lot wherever there is a space. The security guard can direct you to the entrance.

We plan to begin the meeting at 11 a.m. If you can get here a little earlier, there will be time for you to join our coffee break. We look forward to seeing you.

Each paragraph of the letter develops a separate idea. The introductory paragraph provides a welcome to the visitors. The next three paragraphs provide step-by-step directions from Greenville to Springfield. The concluding paragraph tells what time the meeting will begin.

Organizing before you begin to write ensures that your message will be complete and accurate. Careful organizing and skillful paragraphing are two ways to make your writing more effective.

Worksheets

A. Here is a list of items you have decided to include in a report on the characteristics of a good secretary. Some of the items should be main topics. Some should be subheadings. Form this list into an outline following the formal outline system:

Tact

Patience

Typing skill

Word processing ability

Spelling ability

Discretion

General knowledge

Cooperation

Professional appearance

Good health

Reliability

Attendance

Good humor

Shorthand skill

Punctuality

Competence

Personal Traits

Language skill

B. The supervisors in your office have decided to make some changes in the way personal telephone calls are handled. At the meeting at which the decision was made, you took the following notes as the discussion took place. Prepare an outline to show how you would organize the material for a written summary of the meeting.

Only emergency incoming calls will be allowed.

Outgoing calls can be made only from certain phones.

Incoming calls that are not emergencies will be logged in and reported to the person called, but not until the end of the day.

Commercial callers will be told that personal business cannot be transacted during working hours.

No long-distance calls to be charged to the company.

Maybe we should install pay phones on each floor?

What will the office workers think about these new procedures?

Home telephone numbers will not be given to any callers.

Too much time is wasted by employees talking on the telephone to nonbusiness callers.

There have been some instances of calls being made to long-distance numbers and charged to the company without a record of the name of the person who placed the call.

All employees will need to cooperate because there will be serious repercussions otherwise.

4
Worksheets

Name _____ Date _____

Class _____ Score _____

C. Using the outline on housing needs (page 32) as a guide, prepare an outline of what your own housing needs would be if you were in the situation described in the text.

D. Here is the body of a new letter to be sent to alumni to encourage honoring a retiring professor. Add a paragraph symbol (⁋) where each new paragraph should begin.

To those of us who have known him during the past 50 years, Dr. George Spelvin will always seem an active part of Northwest College. The years have passed, however, and Dr. Spelvin will be retiring in May. He came to Northwest as a drama coach and became director of the Drama Department 15 years later. We who are members of the Alumni Repertory Theater (ART) have made some plans for honoring Dr. Spelvin, and we hope you will join us in the festivities. Our planned events will begin on Friday, May 12, when ART will produce Dr. Spelvin's new play, <u>Winter Rain</u>. This will be the play's premiere. We'd like to see the house filled with members of ART for that evening, so that when the final curtain calls are taken and Dr. Spelvin joins the actors onstage, he will know that the entire audience consists of his former students. Later there will be the usual cast party in the theater, but this time the guests will include all the members of ART who are present that evening. On Saturday we plan to honor Dr. Spelvin with a picnic at the Grove, where all our outdoor performances have taken place for the past 16 summers. Remembering that he has always liked us to participate, we've drawn up a list of "pot luck" items. Look at the enclosed list and tell us what you will bring. The climax of our celebration will be Saturday night, when we will have our annual dinner at the Castle. Dr. Spelvin may guess that we will be honoring him that night, but we hope he doesn't get even a hint of what we are planning. All members of ART should be dressed in their finest—ready for the cameras. Thanks to the generosity of all ART members and to some special contributions from our celebrity grads, Paul Oakley, Dina Pinehurst, and Gigi Spruce, we will be ready to announce that construction of the Spelvin Playhouse will begin in June. You'll find the schedule of events and forms for making your reservations on the attached sheet. This occasion should be the most memorable of all of the special events we've had at Northwest.

5
Verifying and Proofreading

No matter how well informed some people may be, no one can know everything. To produce accurate written communications, we need to be able to verify information, jog our memories, and learn new facts as we proceed with the task of putting words on paper. We also need to be able to check our writing to be sure we've written exactly what we intended.

Reference material makes it possible for writers to enhance their ideas as they produce letters, memos, and reports. References also increase the ability of a writer to proofread for errors in facts, in spelling, and in usage.

A business writer needs to have a basic set of reference sources—those that are essential to the practice of good and accurate writing. These sources should be *on hand*, ready for use, to ensure that there is no temptation to skip checking for accuracy. A basic reference set should include a good dictionary, a recent atlas, a current almanac, a thesaurus (or a dictionary of synonyms), and an up-to-date etiquette book.

USING A DICTIONARY

The dictionary can supply a wide variety of information.

Definitions. The first purpose for which we use a dictionary is to learn what a word means. Often students are given assignments to find definitions. It is sometimes difficult for students to tell what a word means, since some elements of a definition, such as symbols, are not entirely understood. Finding what a word means should involve looking at the entire entry, especially noticing the phrases that show how the word is used.

Hyphenation and Pronunciation. For each word listed in the dictionary, the number of syllables and the correct place or places to hyphenate the word are indicated. In addition, the correct pronunciation of each main entry is given immediately after the word itself. Any letter or symbol used to indicate the pronunciation of a word is explained in a separate section on the page on which the word appears or in the introduction to the dictionary.

If more than one pronunciation for a word is acceptable, the dictionary lists the various possibilities. In Unit 22 we shall consider the importance of correct pronunciation in oral communication.

To make the best use of your dictionary, take a little time to read the introduction, both to learn what kinds of information are available in the volume and to learn the meaning of the various symbols.

General Information. Along with the definition, some dictionaries list synonyms and antonyms of entry words. For more thorough information about synonyms, consult a thesaurus.

Most good dictionaries contain several appendices with specific kinds of information, such as definitions of selected foreign terms. In a geographical appendix you will find much material that will serve your purpose if you do not have quick access to an atlas—correct spellings of place names; general locations of cities, rivers, and mountains; and population figures for countries and cities.

Your dictionary is only as good as your ability to use it. Beware of partial information. For example, how do you spell *Pittsburg*—does it end in *h* or not?

The spelling of the city name depends on what state it is in. The city in Pennsylvania is *Pittsburgh*, but there are at least two other cities or towns whose names are spelled *Pittsburg*.

Spelling. Another basic reason we use a dictionary is to verify the spelling of words. Almost everyone has had the experience of trying to find out how to spell a word and being unable to locate it in the dictionary. If you don't know at least the first two letters, you may not be able to find the word at all. Even so, the dictionary can help. Many dictionaries provide a list of *sound correspondences*. You can use this list to find other spellings for the sounds in the word you are looking up.

Style. Some dictionaries contain as a separate section a guide to proper ways of addressing various officials of the government and of religious organizations. Another special section may be a general summary of rules of spelling, punctuation, and grammar. Many dictionaries also include a manual of style, which serves as a reference for the format of manuscripts and letters.

A dictionary can also help solve the question of whether an expression is written as one word, two words, or as a hyphenated word. In this kind of situation, you should also beware of partial information. You will find that *makeup* is the correct form for a noun; *make up*, for a verb; and *make-up*, for an adjective, as in a make-up test.

USING AN ALMANAC

Each year many excellent almanacs are published. Besides being filled with interesting information for those who enjoy trivia, almanacs also contain easy-to-locate capsule summaries and useful explanations of various facts.

Colleges. Information about colleges includes the names, addresses, founding dates, type of support, and sometimes the names of the chief officers.

Countries. Information about nations includes size, population, chief cities, and names of main products. Even such facts as numbers of telephones, automobiles, and radios are sometimes provided.

Cities. Information about major cities includes size, population, names of officials, names of newspapers, and facts about commerce and industry.

Government. Information about the United States government includes names of governors, senators, and representatives; a copy of the Constitution and the Declaration of Independence; addresses and names of chief officials of major government agencies; election statistics; and census figures in various categories for several decades, with some information that goes back to 1790.

Finance. Information about money includes the names and values of currencies from around the world.

Business. Information about business includes a list of names, addresses, chief executive officers, and types of business of major firms.

History. Information about history includes a chronological listing of major events in the history of the world and a more detailed list of events of the past year.

Geography. Information about geography includes distances by land and air between major United States cities and between major world cities.

Entertainment. Information about entertainment and the arts includes the names of winners of major prizes, as well as the date and place of birth of individual artists.

USING AN ATLAS

When we consult an atlas, we are usually looking for a map. Atlases do contain maps, and often they contain more than one map of a given area to show topographical features as well as political features. An atlas usually includes a *gazetteer*—a list of the political entities with their populations. Since an atlas is specifically for geographical use, the list of places will be far more extensive than the lists you will find in a dictionary or an almanac. Even towns with only a few hundred people will be listed in an atlas and shown on the maps.

An especially useful aspect of an atlas is its information about time zones. Since many cities in Europe and in Asia are within areas with direct-dial telephone service, people in business have more reason than ever for being aware of the time in cities around the world. Even within the United States it is helpful to know what time it is in the city you are calling.

USING A THESAURUS

The word *thesaurus* is derived from a word meaning *treasury*. A thesaurus is a treasury of words, arranged so that the user will develop additional ideas about a subject as different associated words are presented. Most words have shades of meaning, or connotations. In a thesaurus the arrangement of words is likely to be such that the particular shade of meaning can be identified.

A synonym dictionary is usually set up in a more direct style. A word's various synonyms are listed under the entry for that word, along with an indication of where additional information can be found.

Use a thesaurus or a synonym dictionary to find an alternative way or a more specific way to express an idea.

In a report or letter, a particular idea is often expressed over and over. You would not want to repeat the same word several times in a sentence or paragraph. As you seek a synonym, you need to judge the suitability of a particular synonym for your purpose. If, for example, you are writing about *information*, you can use such words as *material*, *data*, *facts*, *knowledge*, or *statistics*. Each has a special kind of usage.

When you need a word to convey an idea, there are times when the word that comes to mind is not quite what you want. Recourse to a thesaurus gives you a wide range of possibilities. It could also jog your memory so that the word you need becomes apparent to you even if you have not found it in the book.

USING ETIQUETTE GUIDES

The requirements of etiquette in contemporary society are characterized by flexibility far more than by standard rules of behavior. Etiquette books are constantly being revised and new ones being written to meet the needs of our social structure. You may enjoy old etiquette books as curiosities, but for reference purposes, use the most recent one you can find.

One principal use of an etiquette book is to provide guidance in some of the formal situations that most of us do not encounter on a daily basis. How to respond to a formal invitation in a properly formal manner is not something we need to know every day. An etiquette book provides a description of the correct form, and the responder can then be sure of making the correct response. The most common formal occasions today are weddings and funerals. Some people also need to know about diplomatic and official government functions. Etiquette books give advice on ways of making introductions and on the acceptable forms of signatures and titles.

USING OTHER REFERENCES

Many business manuals give facts about industries and commercial endeavors. Which ones you use will be determined by the nature of the business in which you work. In many businesses there is a need for certain kinds of scientific data. In most companies a reference book of basic legal terminology is available.

Most businesses use one or more of the following general references regularly.

ZIP Code Directory. Any business firm that does much communication by mail must have access to correct ZIP Codes. These directories are updated regularly.

City Directory. The directory for the city in which your office is located will enable you to find the addresses of firms and individuals within your area. In the case of cities that are very close to other cities—Baltimore and Washington, New York and Newark, Fort Worth and Dallas, for example—access to the directories of the neighboring cities may also be useful.

Telephone Directory. This directory provides a source of information about addresses as well as about telephone numbers. It may also serve as a limited directory of goods and services.

Transportation Schedules. Your own city's schedule of buses, trains, or subways is useful for intracity travel. Schedules for airlines and for buses and trains that go from one city to another should also be available if that kind of travel is part of the planning you do.

Special Lists. The company for which you work may use a specialized vocabulary or certain set formats. For example, a company that manufactures containers for prescription drugs might need to know and use technical medical terms. These lists would vary from company to company.

CHOOSING A REFERENCE

The basic five references will give a good background for many of the situations you will encounter as you write for business. The information contained in the five basic references overlaps somewhat. For example, you will find forms of address in dictionaries, almanacs, and etiquette books.

The circumstances should dictate which reference you will consult if all are available. If you are dealing with a very fine point of formality, the etiquette book would be the best source. If you want the latest factual information, an almanac would be the book to use, since almanacs are updated annually. Population figures are available in almanacs, atlases, and dictionaries. An atlas will give figures for smaller towns, but an almanac might be more up to date for larger ones.

References make it possible for you to have available a wide range of information about many subjects. When the required books are ready at hand, you will not be tempted to take for granted something that you could check. Accuracy in language and in facts will make your written communications stand out as valid and authoritative. Inaccuracies will give a poor impression to your readers and will diminish both your status and the status of the company for which you work.

Symbol	Example	Meaning
ℐ	He gave a ℐ speech	take out
/	He ᶜᵍ͏ɦave a speech	change
⌒	He gave a spe⌒ech	close up space
ℐ	He gay⁊e a speech	take out and close up
∧	He gave ᵃ∧ speech	insert word
ⱽ̈ or ⋏	ⱽ̈He gave a speech⋎̈ she said⊙	insert punctuation
⊙	He gave a speech⊙	add period
∽	He ⌠a⌡gave speech	transpose
[	[He gave a speech	move left
]	]He gave a speech	move right
⌐ [	]He gave a speech[	center
¶	¶He gave a speech	paragraph
∫	He gave a speech.⌐ We were present.	no paragraph (run in)
#	He gave# a speech	space
≡	he gave a speech	capitalize
/	He gave a /peech	lowercase
◯	He gave a speech on ⟨soc.⟩ ⟨sec.⟩	spell out
↝	He gave a speech ⟨mistake⟩ Mark the ∧ in punctuation	move
∫	He gave a speech	run in
.....	He ~~gave~~ a speech	stet (leave as is)

PROOFREADING

After you have created a letter or a memo or a report, you will want to be sure that it contains as few errors as possible. There are several techniques that will help you as you proofread.

Meaning. First, read for meaning. Be sure that the words you have written convey the idea you intended. Often we write without considering how many times we are using the same word in a sentence or a paragraph. The smooth flow of your writing will be lost if the words are not well chosen.

Spelling. Second, look for errors in spelling. In typewritten messages, spelling mistakes often involve transposed or omitted letters.

Punctuation. Third, look for punctuation problems. If a sentence does not "read" right, even when the words are accurate, a comma may be missing or there may be too many commas. Look at marks that are used in pairs, such as parentheses, quotation marks, and commas that set off material. Be sure that the second mark of the pair has not been omitted.

Numbers. Fourth, when proofreading numbers, be careful of transposed numerals. Be sure that the number is reasonable. For example, if a date includes a recent year, check for accuracy to avoid writing *1877* instead of *1977*.

Final Check. Finally, reread the material, looking at each word. Be sure that all the words you think you wrote are there. Common errors that can be located in this step include repeating the last word of one line at the beginning of the next.

For many years people have been learning to read rapidly, seeing only important words in order to derive the meaning. We have learned to see a part of a phrase and then to conclude that the rest of the phrase is there. We do this kind of reading so automatically that we are not aware of the technique. Consider the following sentence:

He was appointed to the United States Supreme in 1950.

You know it is the Supreme Court, and you don't notice that a word is missing if you are using techniques that enable you to read rapidly. Such reading is invaluable as a reading skill. For proofreading, a much slower pace will bring better results.

For proofreading technical material or material that includes names of people, sometimes a team effort is effective. In that case, the person who wrote or typed the text should read it aloud while someone less familiar with it reads along on a separate copy, comparing what is read aloud with what appears on the page. Spelling of names should always be double-checked in such material.

Proofreading Marks. To ensure that the corrections you make are easily understood, use the standard proofreading marks provided in this unit.

WORD PROCESSING

The text-editing capabilities of word processors offer a wide range of possibilities for business writers, especially for those who write reports and other kinds of presentations. The ease of making revisions in words and phrases makes it possible for a writer to sharpen both style and tone. The capability of moving sentences and paragraphs gives a writer greater control over the logical development of any piece of writing.

Along with greater ease in making revisions, word processors have also brought us some types of errors that are not likely to be made with typewriters. When entering and editing material on a word processor, check your work closely to avoid the following kinds of errors:

When you move a sentence or a paragraph, be sure to delete it from its original place.

When you use a code to underline, boldface, or capitalize, be sure to turn off the code at the appropriate place.

If you rely on the word processor for page headings and page numbers in a report, be sure the headings and numbers actually appear where you want them.

Although machines are growing more and more sophisticated, those who use them must take care not to expect more from a machine than it has been programmed to do. Machines that have built-in dictionaries, for example, can correct inaccurate spelling. This sentence would be corrected:

The kat had kittens.

The following sentence would not be corrected because the inaccurate words are real words, correctly spelled:

The new statue will effect the kind of stationary we can use.

As you proceed with text editing, you will see that the need for recognizing parallel structure is great. If you want to replace a word or a phrase, you must take care that the new expression can do the same work as the one you are omitting:

I want to review *last month's* figures.

You want to name the month in place of the words *last month's:*

I want to review *October* figures.

The words *last month's* indicate possession, but *October* does not. A better way to express the revision is to write *October's figures* or *the October figures*.

Suppose you started with the following sentence:

The new program will begin *on April 14*, the anniversary of the founding of the company.

If you replace *April 14* with a less specific time, the rest of the sentence becomes nonsense:

The new program will begin *as soon as possible*, the anniversary of the founding of the company.

To produce a meaningful sentence, you'd have to omit *the anniversary of the founding of the company*.

Material can be added or updated so that there is a less frequent need for complete revisions of standard passages:

In January our sales were up 2% over the same month last year, and .45% over December.

If the rest of the sentence did not need to be changed for the next report, the months and percentages could be replaced with new ones.

Consider some of the situations in which one or two words might be changed:

The brochures will be ready *on Monday*.

Suppose that you want to say the time of day, rather than the day of the week. Be careful to change the entire phrase to avoid this kind of sentence:

The brochures will be ready *on two o'clock*.

No one would write such a phrase as an original part of a sentence. The problem arises when a change is made that doesn't include the entire original expression.

This sentence has parallel construction:

For this job we need a person who can type, take dictation, and use a computer.

If you decide that you want to replace the phrase *take dictation*, be certain that what you put in its place is equal in structure:

Not: **For this job we need a person who can type, *good shorthand*, and use a computer.**

Write: **For this job we need a person who can type, *has good shorthand*, and can use a computer.**

5
Worksheets

A. For each question tell what kind of reference you would use. If you have access to the references, write the correct answer and give the copyright date of the book you used.

Question	Reference	Answer	Date
1. What is a concierge?			
2. What is the population of New Zealand?			
3. When did Beethoven live?			
4. When it is 11 a.m. in your city, what time is it in London? in San Francisco? in Honolulu? in Athens, Greece? in Athens, Georgia?			
5. What are the three main uses for an executive's business card?			
6. What amendment to the Constitution established the income tax?			
7. What is the address of the Washington office of the Federal Trade Commission?			
8. What is the name of a newspaper published in San Diego, California?			
9. What is the main post office ZIP Code for Phoenix, Arizona?			
10. How should you address a letter to a senator?			
11. Give five synonyms for *careless*.			
12. What is the telephone number of your local police department?			

Question	Reference	Answer	Date
13. How far is it by air from New York to London?			
14. Who was the first Secretary of the Treasury?			
15. Where are the Plains of Abraham?			
16. Alburquerque Albuquerque Albaquerque Which is correctly spelled?			
17. What is a roble?			
18. In what state is the stadium of the Kansas City Chiefs?			
19. Which is a food—halyard or halvah?			
20. Who is the Prime Minister of Canada?			
21. Name five states that have a city or town named Springfield.			
22. How many electoral votes does your state have?			
23. Where is the lowest point in the 48 contiguous states?			
24. Where is the car rental agency that is nearest to your office?			
25. Name three items that are appropriate gifts in a business situation.			

5
Worksheets

B. Proofread the following report. If your teacher asks you to, submit it in final form.

THE THIRTEEN ORIGINIAL COLONIES

Colonization of what we now know as the United states began
in 1607 with the settlement of Jamestown, Virgina. There had
had been many explorers here before than, but fore them the aim
was exploration and the search for gold, for furs and for
adventure. A earlier colonization attempt, the Roanoke Island
colony, did not succeed

After the establishment of the Virginia colony, the next
permenant settlement was at Plymouth in Massachussetts in 1620.
Other colonies followed during the 1600's——including Connecticut, Rhode Island, Deleware, New Hampshire, Pennsylvania,
Maryland, and the Carolinas. The last of the 13 was Georgia,
which was founded in 732.

The states that developed from the 13 colonnies all lie
lie along the East coast, with some excess to the Atlantic Ocean.
The port cities of these states have always been prominent in the
trade of this country. The early waling harbors have lost that
part of their importants, but such cities as Boston, New York,
Philadelphia, Baltamore, Charleston, and Savannah remain as major
centers for import and export. The products that pass through
these ports include fish, naval stores, cotten, lumber, and
electonic products.

C. Proofread the following report. If your teacher asks you to, submit it in final form.

SOME FACTS ABOUT OUR NATIONAL PARKS SYSTEM

Alphabeticly, the National Parks System runs from <u>A</u> (Acadia in Maine) to <u>Z</u> (Zion in Utah. Geographically, it's scope extends from the Everglades in Flordia to Denali (formerly called Mt. McKinley National Park) in Alaska and on to Haleakala in Hawiai.

The oldest park is yellowstone; its area was set aside in 1872. Yellowstone includes parts of the states of Idaho, Montanna, and Wyoming. It is famous for its gysers.

Beside the National Parks, the system also includes some Historical Parks. many of which are located in the northeast:

1. Chesapeake and Ohio Canal—a canal that run form Washington, D.C. to Cumberland, Maryland
2. Harper's Ferry—a Civil War sight in Maryland and West Virginia where the Sheandoah and Potomac Rivers meets
2. Morristown, New Jersey—Washingtons' head quarters in 1779-80
4. Colonail Virginia—the area that inlcudes Jamestown and Yorktown

The National Historic Sites include the birthplaces or homes homes of most the United States presidents. They also include the birth place of Dr. Martin Luther King, Jr., in Atlanta, Georgia, Thomas Edison's laboratory in West Orange, New Jersey; and Georgia O'Keeffe's studio in Albaquerque, New Mexico.

Part Two
The Form of a Letter

A letter represents an entire company or organization. It may be the first contact between the reader and a particular firm. It may be only one link in a long chain of correspondence. No matter what, the person who receives your letter will form an impression even before a single word is read.

To make a good impression on your reader, give some thought to the routine matters that may seem unimportant—the envelope, paper, and format of the letter; accurate placement of the parts of the letter; and effective paragraphing.

Writing and sending letters is expensive; it is worthwhile to be sure you make a good impression.

6
Letter Formats and Parts

Where business correspondence is concerned, appearance is important. Business letters are an extension of a company's image and personality, and a company is judged by their appearance. You can prepare effective and attractive materials by following a few standard format rules.

This unit focuses on a review of letter formats and the parts of a business letter.

BUSINESS LETTER FORMATS

As office technology has advanced from manual and electric typewriters to electronic equipment such as word processors and computers, standards of efficiency in the office have changed. Businesses want their correspondence to be easy to produce and easy to read. At the same time, business managers want their letters to reflect the image of their firms.

Contemporary business writers have the flexibility of choice among several letter formats. Some companies believe that their values are best reflected by the uncluttered appearance of the block or simplified style. Other companies consider that their strength lies in tradition, as demonstrated by the modified block.

Letter formats reflect the attitudes of the organizations that use them. Just as there is no single appropriate attitude, so there is no single suitable letter format for all companies.

Most companies have a preferred style, or standard format, chosen to suit the image they want to project. Always use the style your company prefers, and be careful to follow one format throughout a letter.

A business writer should be familiar with the various acceptable letter formats. Four letter formats are currently used for business correspondence: block, modified block, modified block with indented paragraphs, and simplified.

Block Format. The *block format* is widely used (see Examples 1 and 2). In the block format, all lines of the letter begin at the left margin. The block format is the preferred style for many companies because it is simple and efficient. One advantage of the block style is that it saves time in keyboarding. Since all lines begin at the left margin, keystrokes for tabs and paragraph indentations are eliminated.

The block format can be used with two punctuation styles. In mixed punctuation, a colon appears after the salutation, or opening, and a comma appears after the complimentary close (see Example 1). In open punctuation, there is no punctuation after the salutation or the complimentary close (see Example 2).

Modified Block Format. The *modified block format* is also used often. This format is the same as the block format, except for the date line, the complimentary close, and the signature block (see Example 3). The date line begins at the center or is backspaced from the right margin. The complimentary close and the signature block begin at the center.

Either open punctuation or mixed punctuation may be used with modified block.

In *modified block format with indented paragraphs*, the complimentary close and the signature block begin at the center. The first line of each paragraph in the body of the letter is indented five spaces. Some companies prefer a ten-space indentation.

Modified block with indented paragraphs is the most conservative style in current use. Mixed punctuation is used with letters prepared in this style.

Miller & Williams Theatrical Publishers
444 West Ninth Street
New York, NY 10019

March 19, 19--

Mr. John Shaw, Drama Coach
Columbus Regional High School
Columbus, TX 75101

Dear Mr. Shaw:

I appreciate your letter of February 3, in which you asked for
our catalog of nonroyalty, one-act plays for consideration by
your freshman drama club.

The new edition of the catalog is not yet available. We expect
to receive our first copies by April 20, and we will send you a
copy at once. Meanwhile, I am enclosing two copies of the
previous edition, published in 1988. Some of the plays described
in the 1988 edition are still available. The new edition of the
catalog contains many more titles.

Please let me know if I can provide any additional help. You may
reach me at our toll-free number, 1-800-555-6789.

Sincerely,

MILLER & WILLIAMS

Jeri Hunt

Ms. Jeri Hunt
Customer Service Representative

kja

Enclosure

Example 1
Block Format with Mixed Punctuation

```
                        Rhine Jewelry, Inc.
                     Empire State Building, Suite 43
                       34th Street at Fifth Avenue
                         New York, NY 10038

   June 6, 19--


   Mr. Nelson Gray
   Tremont Jewelers
   415 Tremont Street
   Chatham, NJ 07928

   Dear Mr. Gray

   After I talked with you on the phone yesterday, I looked up
   the orders you have sent us in the past three months. You
   are right! We billed you twice for the March order.

   On March 19 we received your order for 13 gold zodiac
   charms. We filled the order and billed you $480 on April 1.
   On April 10 we received your check for $480 and an order
   for 6 gold sports pins. We filled that order and billed you
   $183.45 on April 15. The next order for 13 Pisces charms was
   shipped on April 22. On the bill for that order, we again
   billed you for the 13 zodiac charms you had received and
   paid for earlier.

   Please deduct the second charge and pay only for the charms
   you received at the end of April. All you owe us now is $240
   for the most recent order, shipped on April 22.

   We apologize for this double billing. We know you were
   inconvenienced by the need to call it to our attention.

   I am enclosing a brochure showing the new fashion jewelry
   available in September. You can use the handy order form
   enclosed to order your stock in time for the holiday trade.

   Sincerely yours

   Walter Wotan

   Walter Wotan
   Credit Manager

   js

   Enclosures
```

Example 2
Block Format with Open
Punctuation

Simplified Format. In the *simplified format*, all lines begin at the left margin (see Example 4). The salutation and complimentary close are omitted. The letter begins with a subject line in all capital letters. At the close of the letter, the writer's name and title are typed in uppercase on the same line and are separated by a dash.

The simplified format is the most modern of all letter styles. The advantage of this format is efficiency. Many companies find the simplified format convenient for certain situations, but few use it exclusively.

All business letters include certain standard elements. The following guidelines for usage and placement of letter parts will help you prepare business letters.

HEADING ADDRESS

Stationery imprinted with a heading address is known as letterhead stationery. Letterhead stationery conveys the official status of a business firm or organization, and it should be used only for company correspondence.

The heading address on printed letterhead always includes a company's name and mailing address. A company's telephone number is often included in the letterhead design:

Concordia Drapery Fabrics
P.O. Box 1199
Willard, Georgia 31111
912-555-5550

Rhine Jewelry, Inc.
Empire State Building, Suite 43
34th Street at Fifth Avenue
New York, NY 10038

June 6, 19—

Mr. Nelson Gray
Tremont Jewelers
415 Tremont Street
Chatham, NJ 07928

Dear Mr. Gray:

After I talked with you on the phone yesterday, I looked up the orders you have sent us in the past three months. You are right! We billed you twice for the March order.

On March 19 we received your order for 13 gold zodiac charms. We filled the order and billed you $480 on April 1. On April 10 we received your check for $480 and an order for 6 gold sports pins. We filled that order and billed you $183.45 on April 15. The next order for 13 Pisces charms was shipped on April 22. On the bill for that order, we again billed you for the 13 zodiac charms you had received and paid for earlier.

Please deduct the second charge and pay only for the charms you received at the end of April. All you owe us now is $240 for the most recent order, shipped on April 22.

We apologize for this double billing. We know you were inconvenienced by the need to call it to our attention.

I am enclosing a brochure showing the new fashion jewelry available in September. You can use the handy order form enclosed to order your stock in time for the holiday trade.

Sincerely yours,

Walter Wotan

Walter Wotan
Credit Manager

js

Enclosures

Example 3
Modified Block Format with
Mixed Punctuation

If the name of the organization does not indicate the nature of its business, then the letterhead may include an identifying line:

Markwell and Righter
Certified Public Accountants
199 Bunche Boulevard
Baltimore, Maryland 21217
301-555-4321

Letterheads may also include facsimile machine (fax) numbers, trademarks, company logos or slogans, illustrations of products, company or industry emblems, founding dates, or names of major officers:

Boulanger Cakes and Pies
760 Madison Lane
Chicago, Illinois 60616
312-555-3729
Quality Since 1930   **Lem Kite, President**

Although most business writers use printed letterhead, you may sometimes have to provide a heading for a letter on plain paper. A typed heading includes the company name, mailing address, and phone number. Extra information that might be included on the printed letterhead usually is not included in a typed heading.

Typed headings should be centered starting on the seventh line from the top of the page:

Castle Carriage Company
16 Front Street
Baltimore, Maryland 21290
(301) 555-8687

For personal business correspondence, some people use stationery printed with their name and address centered at the top of the page. For personal

Example 4
Simplified Format

business correspondence on plain paper, type a single-spaced return address at the top of the page. A phone number is optional:

61209 South Broad Street
Richmond, Virginia 23220
(804) 555-7894
May 8, 19--

Place the date on the line immediately following the phone number (if used) or immediately following the return address.

Another style in current use for personal business correspondence places the return address after the writer's identification line:

Sincerely yours,

Gregory Campbell
1123 King Street
Columbus, Ohio 43291

DATE

All items of written communication should be dated. A reader's interpretation of a letter, memo, or report can be greatly affected by the date of its origin.

The date in business correspondence is typed two lines below the heading. In block style and simplified style, the date line begins at the left margin. In modified block, the date line begins at the center or is backspaced from the right margin.

For business correspondence, spell out the month in full, write out the day without a suffix, and use a comma after the day:

Not: **12/12/--**
Not: **Dec. 12, 19--**
Not: **December 12th, 19--**
Write: **December 12, 19--**

The military or continental style is often used by international companies. The day is written before the month, and no commas are used:

12 December 19--

Unless you work for an international company or the military, use the standard form with the month, day, and year, in that order.

INSIDE ADDRESS

The inside address of a letter matches the envelope address. The inside address gives the name and exact address of the recipient.

The inside address includes the addressee's name, official title, company name, a street address or box number, and a city, state, and ZIP Code:

Ms. Dorothy Potter
Safety Director
International Communication
455 Genesee Avenue
Philadelphia, PA 19177-0183

The inside address in business correspondence begins on the fifth line below the date.

Courtesy and Professional Titles. The name of the addressee is always given with a courtesy or professional title. Use the title *Mr.* for a man. Use either *Ms.* or *Mrs.* for a married woman, depending on her preference. Use either *Ms.* or *Miss* for an unmarried woman, depending on her preference. The title *Ms.* should be used for a married or an unmarried woman if her preference is unknown.

Use the title *Dr.* for a man or a woman who holds a doctor's degree in any field, or use the abbreviation for the degree after the name. Never use both:

Not: **Dr. Phoebe Webster, Ph.D.**
Write: **Phoebe Webster, Ph.D.**
Or write: **Dr. Phoebe Webster**

The term *Esquire*, abbreviated *Esq.*, is used after the name of an attorney. Do not use a courtesy title before the name if you use *Esq.* after it:

Not: **Miss Laura Chen, Esq.**
Write: **Laura Chen, Esq.**
Or write: **Miss Laura Chen**
       Attorney at Law

Balance. The inside address should have a balanced appearance. To give a balanced appearance, select the best arrangement of name, title, and company. Sometimes each will need a separate line. At other times you can place the name and title or the title and company on the same line. Always keep balance as your objective when deciding:

Poor balance:
Dr. John MacGregor Douglas
Director of Student Activities, Walston College
P.O. Box 22305
Bartonsville, MN 56098

Good balance:
Dr. John MacGregor Douglas
Director of Student Activities
Walston College
P.O. Box 22305
Bartonsville, MN 56098

Street Addresses. Use numerals separated by a hyphen for street addresses that include several lot numbers:

122–128 Clermont Street
Milwaukee, WI 53211

For streets or avenues that have numbers as their names, write out words for numbers that can be written as one word:

Fifth Avenue   **Eighth Street**   **Sixtieth Terrace**

Use numerals for streets that require more than one word:

42 Street *or* **42nd Street**
116 Street *or* **116th Street**

Mail addressed to office or apartment buildings often goes to a room, suite, apartment, or some other unit designation number. Place any unit designation numbers after the street address on the same line or on the line above the street address:

Ms. P. V. Corey
Corey Insurance Company
1271 Old Dalton Road, Suite 54
Portland, ME 04106

Melanson and Pflieger, Inc.
Suite 1079
21204 East University Parkway
Columbus, OH 43201

When an address includes a building name, place the building name on the line above the street address:

Mr. Nicholas Callahan
Safford & Associates
Fergins Building
1522 E. Monroe Street, Suite 12
Springfield, IL 62706

Abbreviations in Addresses. Most words should be written out in business usage. You should avoid abbreviations because they are often subject to misinterpretation.

Always spell out names of persons, words used to designate streets, and names of cities:

Charles (*not* Chas.)
Street (*not* St.)
Los Angeles (*not* L. A.)

What should be abbreviated? On envelopes and for inside addresses, always use the two-letter state abbreviations recommended by the United States Postal Service (see the Appendix).

Compass directions (*S.* for South, *N.* for North, *E.* for East, and *W.* for West) are usually abbreviated in addresses:

113 S. Garden Street   88 E. Coleman Avenue

College degrees, such as Ph.D., M.A., and M.B.A., should be abbreviated. Courtesy and professional titles, such as Dr., Mr., Mrs., Ms., and Esq., are correct as abbreviations. Official titles, such as President, Manager, and Director, should be spelled out.

For abbreviations that are part of a company's name (Co., Inc., Ltd., etc.), follow the practice of the firm involved.

SALUTATION

The salutation in a letter should include the last name of the addressee with the same courtesy title used in the inside address:

Miss Lisa Boleyn
16 Hightower Road
Rose City, NJ 07955

Dear Miss Boleyn:

The salutation in business correspondence is typed two lines below the inside address.

Be cautious with the use of first names. Many persons in business consider the casual use of first names discourteous. On the other hand, it is suitable to use the addressee's first name in the salutation when the writer and the addressee are on a friendly first-name basis. If the addressee is someone the writer knows well and if the writer would use the addressee's first name on the telephone or in person, it is cold and impersonal to use the courtesy title and last name in the salutation.

Many business letters are addressed to a company rather than to an individual. When the addressee of a letter is not an individual, use *Gentlemen*, *Ladies*, or *Ladies and Gentlemen* as the salutation:

Creative Decorating, Inc.
345 Miller Road
Wheeling, WV 25705-8634

Ladies and Gentlemen:

Avoid using *Sir(s)*, *Dear Sir(s)*, *Madam*, or *Dear Madam* as a salutation.

Punctuation Style. For *mixed punctuation*, use a colon after the salutation and a comma after the complimentary close. For *open punctuation*, use no punctuation after the salutation or complimentary close:

Mixed:
Dear Mr. Jones:

Sincerely yours,

Open:
Dear Mr. Jones

Sincerely yours

Open or mixed punctuation can be used with letters in block or modified block format. Mixed punctuation is used with letters prepared in modified block with indented paragraphs.

ATTENTION LINE

An attention line directs the message to the attention of an individual while still leaving the company as the addressee. Always use a person's courtesy title, first name, and last name in an attention line.

An attention line is usually placed within the inside address, immediately after the name of the company:

Jeffrey and Rhodes Advertising
Attention: Mr. Alden McFee
433 Madison Avenue
New York, NY 10077

An attention line may also be placed two lines below the inside address:

Jeffrey and Rhodes Advertising
433 Madison Avenue
New York, NY 10077

Attention: Mr. Alden McFee

Gentlemen:

When an attention line is placed two lines below the inside address, type the salutation on the second line below the attention line.

With an attention line, do not use a person's name in the salutation. Use *Ladies and Gentlemen* as the salutation for a letter that has an attention line directed to a woman.

SPECIAL HEADINGS

Sometimes it is a timesaver to use a *subject line*. A subject line states the subject of the correspondence at the beginning of the letter. Place a subject line two lines below the salutation:

Ms. Theresa Lane
Telfari Consumer Products
402 Wabash Avenue
Omaha, NE 68122

Dear Ms. Lane:

Subject: Invoice No. 1236

The words *Subject* and *Reference* are equally acceptable in a subject line.

Some companies use the Latin *In re* or *Re* instead of the words *Subject* or *Reference*. These expressions are not abbreviations. No period is needed after *In re* or *Re* when used in a subject line:

Mr. Theodore Street
Marketing Coordinator
Plus Chic Fashions
3901 Bay Shore Boulevard
San Francisco, CA 94124

Dear Mr. Street:

Re: Purchase Order No. TPS-412

Using the English words is considered less formal than using the Latin expressions.

In the simplified style, the subject line is typed in all capital letters and the subject line notation (*Subject*, *Reference*, *In re*, or *Re*) is omitted:

Princeton Caterers, Inc.
455 Dallmine Road
Cincinnati, OH 45233-7543

PURCHASE ORDER NO. 2141

Remember that a letter prepared in the simplified style has no salutation. Place the subject line two lines below the inside address.

COMPLIMENTARY CLOSE

Business letters prepared in block or one of the modified block formats conclude with a complimentary close. Most writers use one of the following complimentary closes:

Sincerely	**Sincerely yours**
Very truly yours	**Yours very truly**
Cordially	**Cordially yours**
Best regards	**Kind regards**
Respectfully	**Faithfully**

Sincerely and *Sincerely yours* are the most commonly used. When selecting a complimentary close, remember that the closing should be consistent with the tone of the contents of the letter. A letter that contains no warmth should not end with *Cordially*. In general, *Very truly yours* and *Yours very truly* convey the greatest formality. *Best regards* is frequently the choice for letters that are going to people who are well known to the writer.

The complimentary close is typed two lines below the last line of the body of the letter. Capitalize only the first word in a complimentary close.

COMPANY NAME

In some companies it is customary to include the company name below the complimentary close to indicate that the sender is speaking for the company:

Sincerely yours,
KITE COMPANY INC.

When using the company name, type the company name in all capital letters two lines below the complimentary close.

SIGNATURE BLOCK

The signature block includes the writer's identification line (the writer's name and title) typed below the complimentary close. The signature block identifies the writer of the letter and informs the reader of how to address any future correspondence. Place the writer's identification line four lines below the company name (if used) or four lines below the complimentary close:

Very truly yours,
MASON & DIXON INC.

Miss Hilda Mason, Manager

The writer's title may appear on the same line as the writer's name or on the following line. Separate the name and title with a comma if they are on the same line.

Persons who want to be addressed as *Dr.* in future correspondence include a degree with their names:

Bill Smith, Ph.D.   **Amanda Jones, M.D.**

Men usually do not use courtesy titles in the writer's identification line. Some first names, however, are used by both men and women, and some men use initials in place of their names. In these cases, men may use a courtesy title in the writer's identification line to avoid any confusion:

Mr. Leslie Williams
Mr. J. F. Adsit

A woman may also omit the courtesy title from her signature. However, a correspondent who is replying to a letter may not know the writer's preference in courtesy titles. Unless a woman is prepared to accept whatever title a responder selects, she should make her preference clear in the writer's identification line. The following choices are acceptable.

Professional use for a married woman:

Lisa Carmichael MacGregor
Mrs. Lisa Carmichael MacGregor
Ms. Lisa Carmichael MacGregor

Personal use for a married woman:

Lisa Carmichael MacGregor
Mrs. Robert MacGregor

Professional or personal use for an unmarried woman:

Patricia Novaes
Miss Patricia Novaes
Ms. Patricia Novaes

The handwritten signature will be written in the space provided between the complimentary close and the typed signature line. If a courtesy title is used, it is typed in the signature line or written in parentheses in the signature itself:

Sincerely,

MASON & DIXON, INC.

Hilda Mason

Miss Hilda Mason, Manager

Sincerely yours,

(Ms.) Claudia Preston

Claudia Preston
Field Representative

In the simplified style, the writer's name and title are typed in capital letters on the same line, separated by a dash:

ALLISON DRAKE—DIRECTOR

A letter in simplified format has no complimentary close. Place the writer's name and title four lines below the last line of the body of the letter.

Remember these points about signatures:

1. Be sure to remember to sign the letter.

2. Provide essential information so that the reader knows how to address the writer in future correspondence.

3. The person who signs a letter is accepting responsibility for its contents, including the format and the message.

ITEMS FOLLOWING THE SIGNATURE BLOCK

Notations following the signature block all begin at the left margin.

Reference Initials. Reference initials indicate who typed the letter. For business correspondence reference initials are typed in lowercase two lines below the writer's identification line:

Arnold Quinn, Manager

fmr

Enclosure Notation. An enclosure notation indicates that other materials have been included in the envelope with the letter. The enclosure notation is typed two lines below the reference initials. The word *Enclosure* should be written out:

Arnold Quinn, Manager

fmr

Enclosure

Enclosure notations often name what additional material has been included. Use a colon or dash after the word *enclosure* when an enclosure statement is included, and capitalize the main words in the statement:

Enclosure: Check No. 3321
Enclosure—Check No. 3321

If there are several enclosures, give the number of enclosures or list the materials included:

Enclosures: 2
Enclosures—Catalog
Copy of Letter of October 29, 19--

Copy Notation. The copy notation indicates who will receive a copy of the letter. The copy notation is typed two lines below the enclosure notation (if used) or below the typist's reference initials. The names of those to whom copies are sent are listed, usually with the letters *cc* preceding the names. Unless there is an order of official ranking, list the names alphabetically.

Names in copy notation should be given in full with courtesy titles:

> cc Ms. Danielle Grouton
> Mr. Horace Wheeler

Instead of *cc* some writers use the phrases *Copy to* or *Copies to* in the copy notation:

> Copies to Ms. Danielle Grouton
> Mr. Horace Wheeler

A *blind carbon* is a copy not noted on the original letter. If you are sending a blind carbon, the copy notation should be omitted from the original.

Postscripts. A postscript adds a final thought to a letter. The postscript is typed two lines below the notation that precedes it:

> PS: Our office hours on Saturday are 9 a.m.
> to 1 p.m.

Postscripts are rarely used in business correspondence, except in sales letters.

CONTINUATION PAGES

Business writers try to keep their letters short. Brief messages are more attractive to the reader than long ones, and therefore they are more likely to receive attention. Sometimes, though, a letter must run to a second or even a third page. Pages after the first page are called *continuation pages*.

Continuation pages are typed on plain paper of the same quality as the letterhead. Headings on continuation pages include the name of the addressee, the page number, and the date. The continuation page heading begins on the seventh line from the top of the page. The heading may be presented as a single-spaced block or as one horizontal line:

Gray Publishers
Page 2
September 15, 19--

Gray Publishers   2   **September 15, 19--**

All lines begin at the left margin. In the horizontal style, the page number is centered and the date is backspaced from the right margin. In either style, the text of the letter then continues after three returns.

6
Worksheets

A. The following inside addresses and salutations do not conform to the guidelines in this unit. Rewrite each one correctly. Assume that all proper names should be capitalized. Add courtesy titles of your choice if they have been omitted. Follow the guidelines in this unit to determine which abbreviations may be used. Use mixed punctuation.

1. Guido & Tralla Company
   1667 So. Baltimore St.
   K. C. Missouri 64112

   Dear Mr. Guido

2. Ms. Stephanie Labelle
   Dean of Students
   Park University
   P.O. Box 772
   Seattle, Wash.98122

   Dear Mr. Labelle

3. Allan—Hershey Toys
   Attention Grace Dunwooody
   7777 Seventieth Terr.
   Omaha, NE 68101

   Dear Ms. Dunwoody

4. Doctor Andrew Carmody
   Chief Surgeon
   Avondale Hospital
   116 Avondale Parkway
   Cleveland, Ohio 44113

   Dear Dr. Andrew

5. Ms Lily Groover, Esq.
   Groover and Lawton
   Suite 16, Lawton bldg.
   116 El Pardo Road
   Los Angeles, Cal. 90077

   Dear Miss Groover

B. Rewrite the following closing items (complimentary close, signature block, and items following the signature block) to conform to the guidelines in this unit. Assume that all proper names should be capitalized. Add courtesy titles of your choice if they have been omitted. If a first name has been omitted, use any first name you choose. Use mixed punctuation.

1. Yours Very Truly

   Deirdre Murphy, Curator
   CHILDREN'S MUSEUM OF BOSTON

   grd

   Enc. Catalog

2. Cordially

   Dr. Kenneth Stark, D.V.M.

   Copy to Mr. Genret

3. Sincerely yours
   The Macadamia Company

   Miss Emily k. Fletcher, director

   fdd

   Enclosure: Check and Brochure

4. Best Regards
   ARRIGO TRACTORS

   Sam Arrigo

5. Respectfully

   Marcus Domingo, Treasurer, THE JONES CORPORATION

   HGS

   Copies to Maude Clematis and Mr. Kraig

C. Use the following information to set up letters in Block Style with open punctuation. Draw several lines to indicate the body of the letter. If a first name has been omitted, use any first name you choose. Include the salutation where needed, and use state abbreviations in inside addresses. State names may be spelled out in the heading address. Use today's date and your own choice of complimentary close. Use your own initials for reference initials.

1. From Mark Hugh MacPherson, President, Wiggins Electronics, 12 Wakefield Road, Kansas City, Missouri 64102-9321; To Mr. Luis Gomez, Manager, Dakin Travel Service, 61 Bay Road, Miami, Florida 33111-9834; Enclosure: Check for $450 as deposit for cruise.

2. From Mr. Clarence Chinchow, E. J. Goleb Pharmaceuticals Inc., 94 Madison Avenue, Boston, Massachusetts 02145-1243; To Hector & Sebastian, Inc., 835 Willow Street, Baltimore, Maryland 21278-6543, Attention: Ms. Liz Carmichael; Copy to Dr. Jefferson.

3. From Angela Perez, Assistant Buyer, Dabney & Clements, 498 State Street, Chicago, Illinois 60692-2145; To Robert Marlowe, Credit Manager, Riviere Sportswear, 899 Wolfe Street, Detroit, Michigan 48233-9077; Subject: Invoice No. 44566.

4. From Lincoln Hanks, Office Manager, Springfield Products, Inc., Massey Building, Room 94, Cleveland, Ohio 44133-4141; To Willoughby Inn, 22 Main Street, Rose City, Ohio 44321.

5. From Miss Laura DiCapo, Security Director, Gordon Paper Products, 82 Industrial Parkway, Memphis, Tennessee 38122; To Trumbull Lock Company, Seville Avenue, Louisville, Kentucky 40213-0198, Attention: Mrs. Carmen Zuniga; Copies to Gregory Baldwin and Anna Lucas; Enclosure: Copy of letter to Trumbull dated two months ago.

6. From Simon Black, Nomad Van Lines, 1896 King's Highway, Augusta, Maine 04109; To Mrs. Maria Ducas, 825 Penrose Drive, St. Paul, Minnesota 55577; Subject: Plans for shipment of Mrs. Ducas's furniture from Augusta to St. Paul.

7. From Mrs. Georgiana Williams, Monroe Public Library, Monroe Plaza, Monroe, SC 29687; To Bixby Publishers, Accounting Department, 13322 North Stetson Street, Minneapolis, Minnesota 55467, Attention: Mr. Kevin Ames; Subject: Billing error in invoice 33444.

8. From Ms. Whitney Melton, President, Melton & Sharpless Realtors, 452 Eighth Avenue, New York, NY 10055-9518; To Mr. Jorge Antony Dantes, Amara Data, Inc., 1962 Peachtree Street, Atlanta, GA 30399-7753; Enclosures: Copy of lease for Mr. Dantes to sign and copy of Maintenance Contract.

9. From Edgar Ashton, Manager, Scottish Wool Products, 408 Ravenswood Road, Denver, Colorado 80296; To Anderson's Department Store, 401 Forsyth Street, Greenville, West Virginia 25020, Attention: Miss Isabel Tomaso.

10. To Charles Ling, Supervisor, New Way Electric Company, P.O. Box 440, Inwood, Nevada 89597; From Miss Lucia Katz, Director of Consumer Affairs, City of Inwood, Inwood, Nevada 89599; Enclosure: Copy of letter received from Inwood citizens' committee; Copy to Mayor Lee Beauregard.

D. Use the following information to set up letters in Modified Block Format. Each letter should have a heading address, centered like a letterhead. Use mixed punctuation, today's date, and a traditional complimentary close. Draw several lines to indicate the body for a three-paragraph letter.

These letters all originate from Corona Air Lines, 8 University Plaza, Minneapolis, Minnesota 55467.

1. To Thomas Rainwater, L. B. Blue Surveillance Systems, 999 Hennipen Road, Minneapolis, Minnesota 55666.

   Written and typed by you as the chief of office security.

2. To JHG Printers, 444 St. Ambrose Road, St. Paul, Minnesota 55126, Attention: Mr. Felix Yohannes; Subject: New flight schedules.

   Typed by you for the signature of Mr. L. C. Monroe, Director of Publications; Copy to Ms. Arvalene Hada, Flight Manager.

3. To Mr. Friedrich Wagner, Sales Manager, Norberg Motors, 788 Hillton Highway, Minneapolis, Minnesota 55643.

   Typed by you for the signature of Ms. Margot Van Braunn, Customer Service Representative; Enclosure: Signed sales contract.

4. To Colonel Fairbanks Wallace, USAF, Washington, DC 20045.

   Written and typed by Ms. Jessica Dowling, Training Director; Copy to Mr. Arvan Svanholm, Vice President Human Resources.

5. To Miss Yolanda Akanah, 465 Radcliff Road, Barnswell, Maine 04122; Subject: Employment interview (use suitable date in recent past).

   Typed by you for the signature of Mr. Arvan Svanholm, Vice President Human Resources; Enclosure: Employment benefits brochure.

6. To Ms. Mary Prentice, 345 West 70th Terrace, Kansas City, Missouri 64113; Subject: Employment interview (use suitable date in future).

   Typed by you for the signature of Mr. Arvan Svanholm, Vice President Human Resources; Enclosure: Employment application forms.

7. To Follensbay Gourmet Foods, 1988 Hillsdale Road, Chicago, IL 60677, Attention: Mr. Luke Enyo.

   Written and typed by you as director of in-flight meal service; Enclosure: Proposed menus; Copy to Ms. Sally Kramitz, Supervisor.

8. To Ms. Lucinda Gatto, Accounts Supervisor, Minneapolis Light and Power, 789 Wayzata Highway, Minneapolis, MN 55490; Subject: Error in billing.

   Typed by you for the signature of Josiah Woodedge, Office Manager; Enclosure: Copy of check #14235 for $4589.

9. To Mr. Alan Adzed, Director, Twin Cities International Airport, P.O. Box 12981, Minneapolis, MN 55489; Subject: Cleaning service.

   Typed by you for the signature of Ms. Ellen Jones Whiteman, Vice President.

10. To Dr. Gregor Ivanov, 234 Rowan Road, Chicago, IL 60678; Subject: Dr. Ivanov's letter dated 10 days earlier than this one.

    Typed by you for the signature of Ms. Margot Van Braunn, Customer Service Representative.

6

Worksheets

E. Use the following information to set up letters in Simplified Format. The heading address should begin at the left margin. Use today's date. Draw several lines to indicate the body for a three-paragraph letter.

All these letters originate from Amara Data, Inc., 1962 Peachtree Street, Atlanta GA 30399-7753.

1. To Richland Clinic, Attention: Ms. Geneva Como, Office Manager, 4400 Grafton Road, Knoxville, TN 37988; Subject: Demonstration of new equipment.

   Typed by you for the signature of Jason Winsell, Sales Manager; Enclosures: 40 copies of sales brochure.

2. To Andrew Hilkdion, Esq., Hilkdion & Widone, 1783 Hanover Place, Boston, MA 02145-1783; Subject: Bankruptcy claim of G. L. Oldham, Inc.

   Written and typed by you as secretary to Amara's general counsel.

3. To Highland Hospital, Kansas City, MO 64112, Attention: Fleming J. Peterson, M.D., Medical Director; Subject: System 122 for medical records.

   Typed by you for the signature of Dr. Lee Medina, Research Director.

4. To Michael M. Minsko, President, Thorton Electronics Inc., 557 Holland Road, Spencer, IA 51301; Subject: Patent for No. 765142.

   Typed by you for the signature of Dr. Lee Medina, Research Director.

5. To Potter and Spruce Office Supplies, Spruce Building, 887 Walker Highway, Salt Lake City, UT 84118, Attention: Ms. Francesca Zandon; Subject: Purchase order no. 45901.

   Written and typed by you as office manager for Amara Data.

6. To Mrs. Inez Hidalgo, 89 Calle Madrina, San Juan, PR 00911; Subject: Plans for September conference.

   Typed by you for the signature of Ms. Violetta Dumas, Training Director; Enclosure: List of participants; Copies to Mr. Lincoln Dobbs, Miss Mary Eason, Ms. Karen Whiggin, and Dr. Dorio Yung.

7. To Sandstone Inn, Jekyll Island, GA 31520; Subject: Confirmation of plans for September conference.

   Typed by you for the signature of Ms. Violetta Dumas, Training Director; Copies to Mr. Lincoln Dobbs, Miss Mary Eason, and Dr. Dorio Yung.

8. To Crossgates Food Service, 890 National Highway, College Park, GA 30337; Subject: Contract for coffee break service.

   Written and typed by you as office manager for Amara Data.

9. To Volunteers for Literacy, 778 Peachtree Colony Circle, Atlanta, GA 30319-1987; Subject: Financial contribution.

   Typed by you for the signature of Dwayne Archisa, Treasurer; Enclosure: Check for $1200.

10. To Mr. and Mrs. Walter Chesterfield, 56 Allegro Towers, Norcross, GA 30099; Subject: Appreciation for flowers sent to opening of Norcross office.

    Typed by you for the signature of Amara's president, Dr. Leslie Mahaso.

F. All the exercises in this worksheet originate from E. J. Goleb Pharmaceuticals Inc., 94 Madison Avenue, Boston, Massachusetts 02145-1243. The company uses a style manual for the preparation of correspondence. The following excerpt from the manual shows the company's policy for letter formats:

> All letters addressed to individuals by name should be in block format with open punctuation. Letters addressed to an organization or having an attention line should be in simplified format.

Set up the following letters, using the format required by Goleb's style manual. Use a centered letterhead, today's date, and a suitable complimentary close where needed. Draw several lines to indicate a three-paragraph letter.

1. To State Representative Hampton Adams, Massachusetts State House, Boston, MA 02145-0001.

   Typed by you for the signature of Laura Mason, Esq., General Counsel.

2. To *The Boston Daily Bugle*, 19 Tremont Street, Boston, MA 02144-1919; Subject: Revision of state sales tax laws.

   Written and typed by Mr. Art Page, Distribution Manager; Copy to *Concord Gazette*.

3. To Ms. Jennifer Grant, 1123 Kennedy Parkway, Apartment 41, Newark, NJ 07199.

   Typed by you for the signature of Noah Rivers, Vice President Human Resources; Enclosures: Employee benefits brochure and schedule for training sessions.

4. To Dr. Stephan Alexis, Department of Microbiology, Arcadia University, Cambridge, Pennsylvania 16711.

   Typed by you for the signature of Noah Rivers, Vice President Human Resources; Enclosure: Employment application form.

5. To Garibaldi Chemicals, Attention: Ms. Melissa Wolpert, 3345 Brent Avenue, Denver, CO 80211; Subject: Invoice #123401.

   Typed by you for the signature of Adam Jennings, Purchasing Director.

6. To Nomad Van Lines, Attention: Mr. John Weyman, 789 Bracken Boulevard, Cleveland, OH 44189; Subject: Corporate move for Mr. L. M. Craig.

   Typed by you for the signature of Mr. Roberto Santos, Assistant Personnel Director.

7. To Mrs. Andrew Pennington, Willow Towers, 223 Central Park South, Apartment 56, New York, NY 10091.

   Written and typed by Miss Shirley Faust, Consumer Service Representative.

8. Greene and Billings, Certified Public Accountants, Suite 55, Revere Building, Boston, MA 02134; Subject: New tax forms.

   Typed by you for the signature of Payne Caldecott, Tax Consultant; Copy to Laura Mason, Esq.

9. To Ms. Barbara Huff, Darnell College, Avondale, ND 58144.

   Typed by you for the signature of Ms. Amanda Strian, Information Officer; Enclosures: 4 brochures.

10. To Brooks Marchbanks, M.D., Medical Director, Cabot Hospital, 677 Zebulon Pike, New Lowell, VT 05555.

    Typed by you for the signature of Dr. Andrea Goldsmith, Director Quality Control; Enclosure: Copy of government report; Copy to Laura Mason, Esq.

7
Memos

Memos are frequently used for communication within a business. Some offices use the formal term *memorandum* and its plural *memoranda* or *memorandums*. The less formal term *memo* is more widely used.

This unit will help you prepare effective memos.

Communications within a company are essential to the effective operation of any business. Internal matters can often be settled immediately, either in person or by telephone.

Memos are used to exchange and disseminate written information. Memos are usually brief and limited to one subject.

Most people are on informal terms with their immediate peers in a business situation. Memos to your co-workers can be informal in style. Very brief memos are sometimes handwritten.

When you write a memo to someone whose position in the company is higher than yours, the tone of your memo is likely to be more formal than the tone of a memo to your co-workers. Formal memos should always be typed.

Within the message of a formal memo, refer to individuals by their first and last names:

> *Not:* **Bob and Sara will make the arrangements.**
> *Write:* **Bob Clemento and Sara Alloca will make the arrangements.**

Write a formal memo for a *memo to file*—a memo intended to serve as a record of action you've taken or recommendations you've made.

Whether formal or informal, memos should conform to the company's guidelines for interoffice communications. If there is a printed form, be sure to use it.

MEMO FORMATS

A good business writer should be familiar with the two acceptable formats used for interoffice memos: the standard format and the simplified format.

The *standard format* is the most widely used. The heading of the standard format includes guide words that indicate the recipient, the originator, the date, and the subject of the memo.

Some companies use the *simplified format* for memos. In the simplified format, the heading guide words are omitted.

PREPARING MEMOS

A memo can be prepared on a printed memo form, on plain paper, or on letterhead stationery. Since your memo may become part of the records of your organization, be sure that in every way it reflects your highest standards.

Standard Format. Many companies use a printed form for memos (see Example 1). A printed form includes a heading (**MEMO** or **MEMORANDUM**) with guide words (**TO:**, **FROM:**, **DATE:**, and **SUBJECT:**).

If there is no official form, create your own and use it consistently (see Example 2). You can store the form on a word processor.

On a plain sheet of paper, center the heading in uppercase letters on the seventh line from the top of

LOMBARDI CLEANING SUPPLIES
MEMORANDUM

TO: Kent Wiggins

FROM: Marlo Cathcart

DATE: January 27, 19--

SUBJECT: Planning for October Convention

Now that the date and place for the October convention have
been set, I'd like to meet with you to plan the schedule for
our speakers and special events.

I'll be free on February 2 from 1:30 until 5 p.m. Check your
schedule and let me know what time that afternoon you can come
in to work on these plans.

                              MC

ref

Example 1
Standard Format Memo on Printed Form

```
                    MEMORANDUM

     TO:       Clerical Support Staff

     FROM:     Dr. Lionel Rush

     DATE:     June 2, 19--

     SUBJECT:  New Security System


     Since the break-in at our office last week, Dr. Baxter,
     Dr. Evans, and I have decided to install an electronic
     security system.

     The system will be installed by The Kerberos Company on
     June 7. After that date the alarm system will be operating
     whenever the office is closed to the public. Unauthorized
     entry will set off the alarm. Authorized entry will be
     possible through the use of identification cards that will
     be issued to our employees on June 7.

     The new system should help prevent illegal entries into our
     building. Please use your identification card whenever you
     need to enter the building outside of normal office hours.

                             LR

     ref

     cc  Adrian Bartow
         Celeste Delino
         Miguel D'Osta
         Farley Eason
         Grant Farike
         Henrik Klaus
         Anna McNair
```

Example 2
Standard Format Memo on
Plain Paper

the page. Block the guide words at the left margin, two or three lines below the heading. Leave one blank line between the guide words.

For memos on letterhead stationery, begin the heading three lines below the heading address. In the heading, always use first and last names:

TO: Jim Barber

FROM: Calvin Farmer

Some companies also use official titles:

TO: Jim Barber, General Counsel

FROM: Calvin Farmer, Office Manager

Courtesy titles usually are not necessary.

Give the complete current date (month, day, and year):

DATE: April 23, 19--

Use a brief informative phrase for the subject:

SUBJECT: New Training Procedures

Begin the body of the memo three lines below the guide words. Set margins for a six-inch line of writing. Single-space the body of the memo in block paragraphs. Double-space between paragraphs.

Keyboard the initials of the originator of the memo two lines below the body of the memo, beginning two spaces to the right of center. Keyboard your reference initials at the left margin two lines below the originator's initials.

Simplified Format. A memo in the simplified format can be prepared on a printed memo form, on a plain sheet of paper, or on letterhead stationery. A

```
September 20, 19--

Graciela Martinez
Edmond Fremont


COMPUTER INSTRUCTION CLASSES


The new computers for the auditing department will be
installed on September 24. We will begin the instructional
classes on September 25 at 9:30 a.m. Please plan to attend
the classes in the auditing office from 9:30 to 11:30 a.m.
on September 25, 26, and 27.

Lydia Emerson, Training Coordinator

cs
```

Example 3
Simplified Format Memo on
Plain Paper

memo prepared in the simplified format provides the same information as a memo prepared in the standard format (see Example 3).

In the simplified memo format, all lines begin at the left margin. On a plain sheet of paper, keyboard the date on the seventh line from the top edge of the sheet. On a printed form or letterhead, place the date on the third line below the heading or heading address.

Keyboard the name of the recipient three lines below the date.

Three lines below the name of the recipient, keyboard the subject of the memo in uppercase letters.

Begin the body of the memo three lines below the subject line. Set margins for a six-inch line of writ-ing. Single-space the body of the memo in block paragraphs. Double-space between paragraphs.

Keyboard the name of the originator of the memo two lines below the body of the memo. Keyboard your reference initials at the left margin two lines below the originator's name.

Memos to a Group. Occasionally a memo is sent to all the members of a particular group—the employees of a department, for example. A memo to several members of a group is addressed to the group, and the names of the individuals are listed alphabetically at the end of the message in a copy notation (see Example 2). The person who distributes the memo uses the list of names as a checklist to be sure the memo reaches everyone who should have it.

Worksheets

A. Use the following information to keyboard memos to be prepared on plain paper in the standard format. Include all elements that belong in a memo. Draw three lines to represent the body of the memo.

1. The Barber Medical Group

   A memo dated April 14 from Norma Greene to her supervisor, Leonore Black, requesting two personal days on June 4 and 5.

2. Leonore Black's reply to Norma Greene, dated April 16, approving the leave.

3. Orlando and Aurora, Silversmiths

   A memo dated May 12 to Martha Colfax from her supervisor, Paul Devereaux, asking Martha to work overtime on May 26.

4. Martha Colfax's reply to Paul Devereaux, dated May 13.

5. Carrigna and Highland, Attorneys

   A memo dated August 22 from Mac Carrigna to his partner, Sam Highland, explaining Mr. Carrigna's travel plans for October 4–5.

Exercises 6–10 are memos within the Stewart Township Parks System.

6. On March 24, 19--, a memo from Barry Haywood, Director of Student Staff Members, to Hugh Cavanaugh regarding interviews for summer employees.

7. On April 18, 19--, a memo to Jane Durwood Markwell from Tomas Eloco, Grounds Superintendent, about Purchase Order No. 11987.

8. On May 19, 19--, a memo to Barbara Whittier and Tonya Washington from Parks Director Leslie Davis to express appreciation for work done on scheduling and organizing the parade during the May festival.

9. On July 22, 19--, a memo from Barry Haywood, Director of Student Staff Members, to Anna Herossa about the need for additional lifeguards for a swimming meet on August 12.

10. On September 12, 19--, a memo from Jerry Holzworth, Director of the Equestrian Team, to Manuel Ferro regarding the Fall Equestrian Show on October 23.

B. Use the following information to keyboard memos to be prepared on plain paper in the simplified format. Include all elements that belong in a memo. Draw three lines to represent the body of the memo.

1. Diaz, Caballe, and Enzio Consultants

   A memo dated March 1 to Miguel Caballe from his secretary, Lee Fine, asking for the January travel vouchers.

2. A reply to Lee Fine from Miguel Caballe, dated March 3.

3. Katzweise Control Systems

   A memo dated September 12 from Lucia Anthony, Research Chemist, to Manuel Chabrier, Public Affairs Officer, asking for media coverage for Ms. Anthony's speech to the Chamber of Commerce on October 1.

4. B & J Consultants

   A memo dated November 5 to George Pembroke, President, from Taylor Simerio, General Counsel, requesting a meeting to discuss the Behring account.

5. Andrews Office Supplies

   A memo dated July 19 from Pierre Auclois, Personnel Advisor, to Janet Jerrios, a recently hired secretary, asking her for completed tax forms.

Exercises 6–10 are in-house communications from Hector & Sebastian, a firm of consulting engineers.

6. On May 14, 19--, a memo to members of the word processing staff from Olivia Magda, Word Processing Supervisor, concerning plans for redecorating the Word Processing Center. Copies to be sent to Mavis Walters, H. J. Grant, Billie Grassman, Violet Winters, Joris Page, and Ursula Graham.

7. On March 3, 19--, a memo from Alton B. Wakefield, Esq., to employees hired since January 1 of current year regarding required income tax forms. Copies to George Interro, S. R. Ivey, M. Wilkes Ortega, Jeremy Jenkins, Mitchell Thyme, Beth Cunardo, Michael Chairman, and Grace Chester.

8. On June 12, 19--, a memo from Hildegarde Mueller to members of the Accounting Department about new equipment. Copies to go to Forest Bracewell, Hinton Lovett, Elena Marcusi, and Jack Rievers.

9. On November 12, 19--, a memo from Sylvia Trinidad to members of the Decorating Committee regarding the Annual Holiday Dance. Copies to be sent to Jim Dawes, Ann Bass, Lee Enrico, V. N. Dade, Zack Lowe, Karen Davies, and Anna Bassolino.

10. On November 13, 19--, a memo about the Annual Holiday Dance from Arnold Whiteside to members of the Refreshments Committee. Copies to go to Josh Franks, Douglas Franklin, Mellita Maha, Iris Franken, Joanne Maynes, and Sybil Franham.

8
Paper and Envelopes

Choosing paper for business correspondence may seem like a simple task, but that choice can have a strong effect on the reader. The paper used for envelopes and letterheads affects the reader's impression of a letter, even before the message is read.

The weight, color, finish, and size of the paper on which a message is written all contribute to the first impression a reader gets.

QUANTITY

Business firms usually order their letterhead paper and continuation sheets in reams. A *ream* is 500 sheets, and suppliers usually package paper in 500-sheet units. The designation M is often used in business to mean 1,000 units of a product. Two reams of paper equal 1M sheets. Be careful not to interpret M as meaning one million. M is the Roman numeral for 1,000.

For personal use you can buy paper in packages of 100 or 200 sheets.

Specialty paper used in small quantities (for example, cover sheets for reports) may be purchased by the quire. A *quire* is a unit of 24 or 25 sheets.

WEIGHT

The weight of paper is sometimes designated simply as light, medium, or heavy. Often the designation is given in numbers:

> **Heavy—Substance 24**
> **Medium—Substance 20**
> **Light—Substance 16**

The substance numbers are derived from the weight of four reams of a particular paper, $8\frac{1}{2}$ by 11 inches in size. Business letterheads are usually printed on paper that is Substance 20 or 24. The weight of such paper gives a good sense of *body* when you handle it.

When a lighter weight is needed to save postage, Substance 16 might be used. Postage is computed on the basis of one ounce as a minimum weight. Unless your mailing is several pages long, the weight of the paper will not be a crucial factor.

COLOR

Most businesses choose white paper for their correspondence. The crisp and efficient look of black type on white paper cannot be matched. Such writing is easily read. A practical advantage of white paper is that corrections made on it with erasures or correcting tape have a neater appearance than those made on any other color of paper.

Other colors sometimes used for business letterheads include ivory, pale gray, and pale blue. Ivory (or ecru or cream) paper has an elegant appearance, especially when the paper is suitably heavy. Occasionally a business firm chooses gray or blue to make its correspondence stand out from that of others.

Avoid strong colors that distract the reader's attention from the message. Colors such as yellow, pink, or lilac diminish the serious nature of the correspondence.

FINISH

The finish of paper affects the reader's impression of written communications. Most business paper is bond finish paper. Originally *bond paper* meant paper on which bonds and other official documents were printed. Today bond paper is simply high-quality paper. It is often used for business letterheads.

Bond paper often has a watermark—a design faintly visible on the paper when it is held to the light. The watermark is put into the paper during the manufacturing process. You can read the watermark only from the front of the paper. The heading address on the letterhead paper will always be printed on the front, or watermark, side of the sheet. If you're using plain paper that is erasable, the front is the side that has been prepared so that erasures can be made.

Paper that is unusually shiny or porous is not suitable for business correspondence. Readability is the most important element to consider when choosing a paper finish.

SIZE

The standard size for business letterheads and for reports is $8\frac{1}{2}$ by 11 inches. Business executives sometimes use monarch stationery for short, personal messages. Monarch paper measures $7\frac{1}{4}$ by $10\frac{1}{2}$ inches.

CONTINUATION SHEETS

Continuation sheets (for pages of a letter after the first page) should be exactly the same as the letterhead paper, but without the heading at the top of the page. Some firms use continuation sheets with their name printed at the bottom of the page.

COPY SHEETS

Sheets of paper used to produce typed copies may be part of carbon sets, or manifolds. Carbon copy sets or sets with specially treated paper are sold either in quires or in reams. Copies may also be produced by using NCR (no carbon required) copy paper. NCR paper is specially treated to reproduce the original without carbon. Such paper is frequently used for forms such as bank deposit slips.

If separate paper is used for making carbon copies, it should be lightweight—Substance 12 manila or onionskin.

In addition to making carbon copies, most businesses have a photocopying machine, or copier. A business office usually has a stated policy about how copies of letters are to be made.

Most photocopying machines are *plain paper copiers*. In a plain paper copier, any type of paper can be used to make copies. Some copiers require specially treated paper.

PAPER FOR MEMOS

A business firm may have memo paper printed with the name of the company and the heading guide words. Memo sheets are often lightweight, Substance 16 or lighter. Sometimes the sheets are smaller than standard size.

For memos not going into files, half sheets or even quarter sheets may be used. For memos to be filed with standard-sized sheets, it is convenient to use standard paper.

ENVELOPES

The envelopes used with letterhead paper should match the letterhead exactly in weight, color, and finish. The company's name and address should appear as the return address on the envelope and should be in the same format used on the letterhead.

For paper $8\frac{1}{2}$ by 11 inches, most companies use a No. 10, or business size, envelope. A No. 10 envelope measures $9\frac{1}{2}$ by $4\frac{1}{8}$ inches.

Occasionally a No. $6\frac{3}{4}$ envelope is used with standard letterhead paper. A No. $6\frac{3}{4}$ envelope measures $6\frac{1}{2}$ by $3\frac{5}{8}$ inches.

Use a No. 7 envelope for monarch, or executive, paper. A No. 7 envelope measures $7\frac{1}{2}$ by $3\frac{7}{8}$ inches.

FOLDING STATIONERY FOR ENVELOPES

To fold a standard sheet to fit a No. 10 envelope, fold the bottom third toward the top. Then fold the top third down to about one-quarter inch from the first fold. Be sure that the fold is straight before making a crease. Insert the letter into the envelope with the last fold at the bottom (see Example 1).

For monarch paper and a No. 7 envelope, use the same three-part fold as you use for standard paper and a No. 10 envelope.

If you are using a No. $6\frac{3}{4}$ envelope for standard letterhead paper, fold the bottom half of the sheet up to about one-quarter of an inch from the top edge of the sheet. Fold the left third toward the center, and fold the right third over to about one-quarter of an inch from the first fold. Insert the paper into the envelope with the last fold at the bottom (see Example 1).

The use of window envelopes is increasing. Time and money can be saved by using such envelopes. The letterhead can be folded in such a way that the typed inside address also serves as the *superscription*, or envelope address. Many companies use window envelopes for billing.

For a window envelope, fold the bottom third of the letter toward the top. Then turn the letter face down and fold down the upper part of the sheet to the first fold. Insert the letter in the envelope with the letterhead at the top facing the front of the envelope (see Example 1).

Fold in thirds for a No. 10 Envelope

1 Place the letter face up on your desk. Fold the bottom third toward the top. Make sure that the fold is straight; then crease the sheet.

2 Fold down the upper part of the sheet to bring the top edge to ¼ inch from the first fold. Check that the fold is even and then make a second crease.

3 Insert the letter in the envelope with the second crease toward the bottom of the envelope.

Fold in half for a No. 6¾ Envelope

1 Place the letter face up on your desk and fold the bottom edge of the sheet to within ¼ inch of the top edge.

2 Fold the right-hand third in toward the center.

3 Fold the left-hand third toward the center to within ¼ inch of the other fold.

4 Insert the letter in the envelope so that the last fold is at the bottom.

Fold accordion style for a Window Envelope

1 Place the letter face up on your desk. Fold the bottom third toward the top. Make sure that the fold is straight; then crease the sheet.

2 Pick up the letter and turn it face down on your desk. Fold down the upper part of the sheet to the first fold and make a second crease.

3 Insert the letter in the envelope so that the letterhead is at the top and is facing the front of the envelope.

4 Make sure the complete address shows through the window.

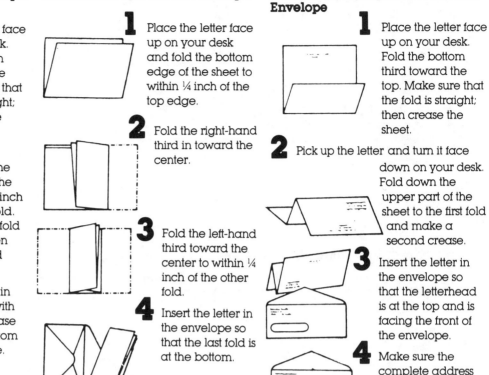

Example 1
Folding and Inserting Standard Letterhead Paper

ADDRESSING ENVELOPES

The United States Postal Service provides specific instructions on how to address an envelope for maximum efficiency in delivery.

Delivery Information. Addresses should be typewritten or machine printed. The address block should be single-spaced and have a uniform left margin.

The city, state, and ZIP Code should always be the last line of the address block. Always use the standard two-letter state abbreviations (see Appendix) and the ZIP Code or ZIP + 4 code.

The next-to-last line is the delivery address line. The delivery address line should show the street address, post office box number, or rural route and box number.

The lines above the delivery address should include the recipient's name (whether an individual or an organization) and any additional information needed to ensure accurate delivery to the recipient.

Any non-address data should appear above the address block. Do not type any information below or to the side of the address.

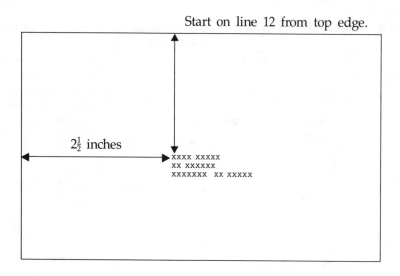

Start on line 12 from top edge.

$2\frac{1}{2}$ inches

```
xxxx xxxxx
xx xxxxxx
xxxxxxx  xx xxxxx
```

No. $6\frac{3}{4}$ and No. 7 envelope and postcard

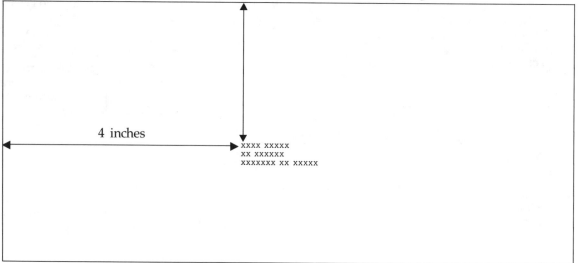

Start on line 14 from top edge.

4 inches

```
xxxx xxxxx
xx xxxxxx
xxxxxxx xx xxxxx
```

No. 10 envelope

Example 2
Address Block Placement

Placement of the Address Block. For a No. 10 envelope, begin the address on line 14 from the top of the envelope, four inches from the left edge. For No. $6\frac{3}{4}$ and No. 7 envelopes, begin the address on line 12 from the top of the envelope, $2\frac{1}{2}$ inches from the left edge (see Example 2).

Careful preparation of envelopes shows that the business firm takes pride in its correspondence. Following the Postal Service guidelines helps the mail move more efficiently and reach its destination quickly.

8
Worksheets

Answer the following questions about the paper and envelopes used for business writing.

1. Why is white the preferred color for business paper?

2. What colors besides white are sometimes used for business paper?

3. What is the size of standard letterhead paper?

4. How is a standard letterhead folded for a No. 10 envelope?

5. What is the advantage of using window envelopes?

6. How is a standard letterhead folded for a window envelope?

7. What is the significance of substance designations for paper?

8. What is a ream of paper?

9. How many sheets are in a quire?

10. What kind of paper or stationery would be purchased in quires?

11. Describe the kind of paper that should be used for the pages of a letter after the first page. What are these pages called?

12. What are copy sheets?

13. What are two ways of making copies of material as you type, without using single carbon sheets?

14. What is a watermark?

15. What does M mean as a measurement?

16. What color and finish would you choose for envelopes to be used with letterhead paper?

17. What are the four considerations that influence the choice of paper for business letterheads?

18. How might memo paper differ from letterhead paper?

19. What should determine the quality of the envelopes you use?

20. What is the purpose of the Postal Service guidelines for typing envelope addresses?

9
The Body of the Letter

The most important aspect of a letter is the message it contains. Brevity is important and can be accomplished through good organization and concise writing. Clarity is vital. We have already seen how being specific and using good grammatical structure can ensure a clear message. Strong beginnings and endings are also important for effective business letters.

A dynamic entrance gets the reader's attention. Logical development ensures that the message is clear. A graceful exit leaves the reader with a favorable impression.

DYNAMIC ENTRANCE

Dynamic means *powerful*. *Dynamic* also means *energetic* and *active*. The beginning of a business letter should be dynamic, but never abrupt. A dynamic entrance gets the reader's attention and makes the reader want to read the rest of the message.

There are times when you can write an opening sentence or paragraph that has dramatic impact, but not all writing situations provide such an opportunity. The important thing is to begin in such a way that your reader will have some idea of what to expect and will want to continue reading.

At one time business letters opened with expressions so routine that no one paid any attention to them. Today some writers continue to begin letters with phrases that are out of date and uninteresting.

How can you avoid such beginnings? Try to come to the point quickly to keep from wasting time and space. Be brief in your dynamic entrance, but try to write in such a way that the reader will want to read what you have written. From the beginning, link your reader's interests with your own by using words like *you* and *we*:

Not: **Enclosed herewith please find three copies of our price list.**
Write: **We are pleased to send you three copies of our price list.**

Not: **This will acknowledge receipt of your letter of February 20.**
Write: **We appreciate your letter of February 20.**

Not: **Please be advised that there are some problems that must be resolved.**
Write: **Some problems have arisen that I believe you can help us solve.**

A courteous *thank you* is always a good way to begin a letter. *Thank you*, like *please*, serves a purpose that can rarely be filled by other expressions. Sometimes you may write *we appreciate* or *we are grateful* or *it was kind of you*. Often the simple *thank you* or *please* will serve your purpose best.

The opening of your letter need not be long—perhaps only one sentence in which you set the stage for what is to come. Your first paragraph should not contain your entire message.

LOGICAL DEVELOPMENT

In Unit 4 you read about ways to put ideas into logical order for easy understanding by your reader. When you begin the development of your main idea, think of the order in which you will present your facts. Does your reader need to know one thing before another? Do you need to provide background information before making a claim or suggestion?

Later chapters will focus on various writing situations and on the requirements of specific types of letters. In general, logical development ensures that each part of your message is clearly understood because you have put the facts in the right order. Techniques such as spacing and enumerating can be used to emphasize main ideas.

Keep in mind that in business letters and memos, short paragraphs—even one-sentence paragraphs—are often desirable. Begin a new paragraph for each new idea.

Notice the effective use of short paragraphs in the following letter:

```
Your inquiry about the changes you should make
in your investment program came at just the
right time.

We are pleased to tell you that beginning next
month--November 1, to be exact--we can offer you
a way of making flexible investments to achieve
your investment goals sooner than with the plan
you are now following.

All you need to do to find out about this new
program is to read the enclosed brochure and
make an appointment with our customer adviser,
Emily Vorelli, when she calls next week.

Thank you for your inquiry. We can offer you
the kind of service you are looking for, as
Ms. Vorelli will explain when you meet with her.
```

The first paragraph contains a dynamic entrance that welcomes the reader with three *you* pronouns and the polite phrase, *at just the right time*. In the second paragraph the writer tells what is offered. In the third paragraph the writer tells how to obtain the specific information about the services available. Finally the writer uses a closing paragraph that returns to the idea introduced at the beginning of the letter.

Always keep in mind the importance of writing in such a way that the reader will want to read your message. Short paragraphs are more readily understood and are less overwhelming than long paragraphs.

GRACEFUL EXIT

A graceful exit allows you to end a letter or memo without sounding abrupt. Too often an otherwise well-written letter falls flat at the end. Sometimes a writer tries to avoid the abrupt ending by going too far in the other direction with excessive *thank you* sentences or apologies. As usual, simplicity is the key.

The last sentences of your letter should pull your reader toward you with gracious remarks and suggestions of future business. Remember to keep *you* and *we* in the message at the end as well as at the beginning:

> *Not:* **Your cooperation in this matter will be greatly appreciated.**
>
> *Write:* **We'll be grateful for your help.**

Be specific about what you expect your reader to do next:

> *Not:* **Please refer any questions you may have to this office.**
>
> *Write:* **If you need more information, just call me at 555-0923.**

If you use the last paragraph to repeat a thank you or an apology, try to avoid boring repetition:

> *Not:* **We regret that you had to be inconvenienced. We apologize for the mistake. We are sorry it happened.**
>
> *Write:* **Please accept our apologies and let us show how good our service can be.**

> *Not:* **Again let me say "thank you" for all your help. We really appreciate what you did. Thank you again.**
>
> *Write:* **Your assistance helped us finish on time, and we are grateful.**

There is nothing wrong in expressing appreciation or offering apologies, but repeating the thanks or apologies can be awkward. Just as it is important to learn when and how to leave an interview, a discussion with a colleague, or a party, so it is important to learn when and how to end a letter or a memo.

When to end what you are writing is the first thing to determine. If you have organized your ideas and developed them logically, your message should have a natural stopping place. When you have conveyed your message, you are ready to come to a close.

How you end your letter or memo can make the difference between a strong finish and a weak one. Just as you would not simply stop talking and walk away from a face-to-face encounter, so you would not just stop writing. Use your exit to suggest that you expect to offer additional service or merchandise:

> *Not:* **You should receive our bill in about six days.**
>
> *Write:* **You should receive our bill in about six days. You may find our summer rates a pleasant surprise. We look forward to serving you again soon.**

A graceful exit gives a finishing touch to your writing and leaves a favorable impression. In most cases it is a good idea to close with a suggestion of a future communication.

A. Determine the smoothest paragraphing for these letters.

1. Thank you for your invitation to speak at the March 15 meeting of the Stock Buyers' Club. Your organization is well known for its exciting programs, and I am pleased that you want me to participate. On March 15 I am planning to be in Dallas to help celebrate my parents' fiftieth wedding anniversary, and this engagement will prevent my attending your meeting. I'm sure you know how important this occasion will be to my family. I hope you will ask me again when you need a speaker. I would truly enjoy being with you.

2. On June 20 our department had its annual dinner at your restaurant in the Crown Room. I wish I could tell you that all went well, but I cannot. From the beginning of the evening, there were problems that could have been prevented by some concern on the part of your staff. Royalty House has a good reputation, and we are disappointed to have had such an unsatisfactory experience there. In the first place, there were no valets to park our cars. Your system of having all parking far away from the building enhances the attractiveness of the property, but on that night, when your promised valet service broke down, the inconvenience was annoying. Then we discovered that the Crown Room was set up for 45 persons, not the 54 of our confirmed reservations. There was a wait while the staff tried to find out if it was all right for them to supply the additional places. Next we found that the bartender assigned to our group was late, and no one had tried to find a substitute. Another annoying problem was that the music from the orchestra in the Princess Room was so loud that we could barely converse. When we had placed our orders, we thought all was going well at last. We were mistaken. Salad was served to half the group, and then there was a 30-minute wait before the rest of us were served. The entrees that should have been hot were barely warm, and the cold foods were too warm. One woman didn't get her main course until almost everyone else had finished. I am sure you understand that we shall think about finding another location for our annual dinner next year, as well as for our smaller celebrations during the year. I don't believe the committee will ever choose Royalty House again, but I thought perhaps you could look into improving service so that other customers would not get the kind of service given to the decorating department of Gillis Furniture.

3. This morning I was pleased to receive your order for 500 reams of paper, Stock No. 48. Our shipping department is prepared to handle such orders quickly. Your paper is already on its way, and you should receive it this week. We have charged your account for the cost of the paper and for the shipping charges. You will receive our statement at the end of the month. I am enclosing a folder that shows a new line of paper that will be available in April. Stock No. 48 has long been one of our best-selling papers, but we know our customers like a variety of new items from time to time. Look over these samples and send us your order by April 10 to take advantage of our introductory discount. Just use the enclosed envelope and order form.

4. We were pleased to learn from your latest catalog that you are now offering office furniture in the modules we have been wanting to buy. We want to reorganize our clerical offices so that each member of the staff will have a mini-office, providing privacy and work space but still giving access to other workers. Your catalog lists exactly what we are looking for except for one thing—the color. Your Unit 433, which includes a desk, three-drawer file, computer terminal space, and flexible partitions, comes only in the basic colors of brown and gray. We are convinced that we save money on lighting and also have a more cheerful office if we keep to lighter colors. We would prefer a light beige or sand color. Can you supply the modules in this color? We shall need 18 sets of equipment. So far no other office furniture has come as close to what we are looking for. We would be grateful if you'd check on the additional cost for custom-colored units. Please let us know, either by telephone (201-555-9098) or by letter. We have waited several years to do our remodeling, and we are determined to find furniture that is exactly what we want.

5. Did you know there is an expert adviser for your college-bound son and daughter right here in Green City? I have just set up my new college counseling service on Spelman Road, near the Highland Department Store. Both your son Eric and your daughter Erin will soon be making decisions about what colleges to attend. High school counselors may not have the time to give the personal attention I can give. For an initial fee of only $50, I shall give a preliminary interest test. Then I'll profile the colleges that are best suited to your children's needs. I can also make arrangements for campus visits and for the interviews that are so important. Choosing the right college is more important now than ever. A little extra care at the beginning can make the difference between a happy freshman year that leads to a successful four years and an unhappy experience that may result in a transfer and lost credits. Use the enclosed card to tell me that you are interested. I shall call you and arrange for a meeting with Eric and Erin very soon.

B. Here are some middle portions of short letters. For each, compose a suitable first paragraph and last paragraph. Keep in mind the principles of dynamic entrance and graceful exit.

1. We can provide plants that will enhance the attractiveness of your lobby. Grant Products is the largest employer in this city, and we at Greenfriends, Inc., would be pleased to have our plants on exhibit there. Our employees can advise you about the best choices, do the planting and arranging, and return on a weekly basis to take care of the plants.

2. Mr. Kenneth Young joins our staff after having been a member of the Realtors International Workshop for twelve years. He brings vast knowledge of the housing market around the world and can advise you and your employees about the best ways to relocate anywhere in the world. Adding Mr. Young to the staff of Bluehouse Realtors is another step in our effort to serve all the people of Chicago.

3. Our new office will open on Monday, April 18. The new building offers convenient parking, and bus lines from all parts of the city run right to our door. We are better equipped than ever to provide the kind of service our customers expect.

4. I know that you cannot control everything that happens in your repair shop, but as manager of Vinings Auto Repair you should be aware that your service people are not always helpful.

   Last Tuesday when I left my car for a minor tune-up, it was not ready at 5 p.m. Furthermore there were cigar ashes on the floor on the driver's side and a half-eaten banana behind the passenger's seat. I do not smoke cigars, and no one has been using the rear seats of this car. The radio was changed from the station I usually play.

5. Your local automobile dealer has not been able to obtain the part needed to repair the air conditioner on my car. I am enclosing full information about make, model, and year, as well as the dealer's name and address. This part was ordered in August, and here it is December. I don't need air conditioning now, of course, but summer will come.

6. There will be six of us, and we shall need three double rooms. We shall arrive before six o'clock on July 19 and plan to stay until July 26. Please provide rooms for all of us on the same floor if possible. Adjoining or connecting rooms would be even better. We understand that your rates range from $50 to $80 per night for a double room. We would prefer the lowest price, but we do want to be comfortable.

7. Security was not a problem when Kilo Oil occupied space in the Fellows Building, because the Fellows staff allowed only authorized personnel to have access to the building, even during the daytime.

   Now we must work out a system to account for all our staff members. I need your ideas and recommendations for ways of protecting our personnel.

8. During the past ten years the Charles V. Reynolds Scholarship Foundation has provided college money for many worthy young people. All the money collected goes directly to the fund. The expenses of operating the campaign are paid by the Charles V. Reynolds family, in gratitude for this memorial. This year the need for money is even greater than before, and we are hoping to show an increase in the amount raised in this campaign.

9. We are especially interested in obtaining several smaller word processors to supplement the equipment you sold us last year. Many of our executives do extensive composing of reports and other written matter. If we had four smaller units suitable for use by vice presidents, they could do their own rough drafting and their final output with less strain on our clerical staff.

10. You will see on the attached page the names of those who are requesting that Hamby and Notchley consider setting up a day-care center here at the plant. Many other companies have established similar programs to help their workers provide competent care for preschool children. The facility would surely cut absenteeism. It would also be a morale builder for all our workers.

Part Three
Types of Letters, Memos, and Reports

The kinds of letters written frequently in business fall into certain categories—orders, acknowledgments of orders, inquiries, responses to inquiries, credit letters, collection letters, adjustment requests and responses, employment letters, sales letters, and good manners letters. In many instances, memos in these same categories are required when the communication is within an organization.

In the following units, we shall examine each of these categories of written business communications. The assignments for each unit provide realistic business situations for which you will prepare correspondence.

As you complete the assignments for these simulated situations, you will be able to develop your own style. You will see how you can devise a form for writing many kinds of letters and memos. As you work, try to imagine the people involved, their motives, and their problems.

With practice, your imagination and insight will help you find the right words to express your message. Your reader will have a positive response to what you are saying.

10
Orders and Acknowledgments

Placing orders for products or services is an important business activity. Every business depends on other companies for supplies, equipment, and services. When you place an order as an employee, you help to ensure that the daily business of the company can continue smoothly. As a consumer, you will find that an accurate, complete order letter saves you money and time.

A company sometimes sends customers an acknowledgment notice or letter telling them that an order has been received. The acknowledgment letter usually tells when the order will be filled. If the order can be filled immediately, an acknowledgment letter is not needed. If the company expects a delay before the order can be filled, an acknowledgment letter assures the customer that the order has been received.

This unit will help you prepare both order letters and acknowledgment letters.

PLACING ORDERS

Placing orders for goods—materials, parts, or finished products—is an essential activity in any business. Besides ordering products, businesses order services such as cleaning, equipment maintenance, and mailing. Consumers also place orders for a great variety of goods and services.

An order may not always require a letter. Many companies find it convenient to place orders by phone. Even if you place telephone orders, you need to develop the skills needed for writing order letters. Every telephone order requires the same information provided in an order letter. In addition, most telephone orders must be confirmed in writing and mailed to the supplier or filed. Even if you place all orders over the telephone, you will need order writing skills.

Order forms are often used for placing orders by mail. A company may place orders on its own purchase order form. The seller might provide order forms as part of a catalog or separately with an order or invoice. An order form provides space for you to write all necessary order information. An order form also shows the kind of information you will need to supply in an order letter.

An order form must provide complete, accurate information (see Example 1). Be sure to include the following:

- Your company's complete address
- The address to which the shipment will be sent, if different from the company address
- The date
- Order details, including quantity, stock or item number, item name or service description, size, unit price, extension or item total, tax, and total cost
- Shipping method and date needed
- Payment information

An order letter should focus on the details of the order. Avoid adding unnecessary explanations that might confuse the reader (see poor order letter in Example 2).

As with all letters, determine your purpose before you begin writing. Be certain that everything you include in the letter fits that purpose (see Example 3).

FROST AND DICKINSON
OFFICE FURNITURE

1361 Old Salem Highway
Hartford, CT 60298

Date   April 19, 19--

Ship to   Northeastern Glassware Company

Address   777 Industrial Plaza

City <u>Wilmington</u>   State <u>DE</u>   Zip <u>19705</u>   Telephone<u>(302) 561-0712</u>

QUANTITY	STOCK NO.	DESCRIPTION	UNIT PRICE	EXTENSION
8	FC9981	4-drawer metal file cabinets, slate blue	$92.00	$736.00
3	BC641	5-foot bookcases, walnut, with glass doors	178.00	534.00
5	WB 67521	Metal wastebaskets slate blue	20.00	100.00

Check Enclosed _____   Plus shipping <u>52.00</u>
                                           (See chart on page 2)

C.O.D. _____

Charge our Account # <u>76740</u>   Plus Tax _____
                                           where applicable

Charge Super Charge _____
         Americard _____
Card No. _____   **TOTAL CHARGES** $1,422.00
Expiration Date _____

Example 1
Completed Sample Order Form

Dynamic Entrance. Since most order letters are short, you will not need an extensive beginning. You could begin with a sentence that focuses on the product or service you are ordering:

> **In your fall sales catalog, you list wooden dowels on page 42.**
>
> **I just read your advertisement in the** *Construction Newsletter.*
>
> **The mailing service you provided last year was extremely useful to us.**

Even in a short letter, take the time to write one or two sentences as an entrance.

Logical Development. An order letter should contain all the information you would give on an order form, plus any additional information you want to include. If you are ordering several items, you can set up a table very much like an order form.

Look at the poor order letter in Example 2. What important information is missing? What information is included that should be taken out?

Now look at the good order letter in Example 3. This letter is balanced with an entrance and a graceful exit, but it focuses on the items ordered. The letter supplies complete information about the order, including information on shipment and payment. The letter includes the information that is required on an order form.

```
                    Diamond Cardigans
                  1223 Bridgewater Creek Road
                   Denver, Colorado 80233

August 16, 19—


Linsholm Woolens, Inc.
Grigley Plaza
Dallas, TX 75234-9842

Gentlemen:

Please send us around 5,000 yards of the wool we ordered
last May. We need about 400 yards of blue, 450 yards of
green, 1,500 yards of dark brown, 1,000 yards of red, and
the rest white.

When we first began buying from you in 1983, our business
was located in a small factory. Now we have a much nicer
place. We'd send a check for this order, but we don't know
how much the charges will be. Can you please ship it to us
on open account and bill us?

We have a large order for sweaters from a Chicago department
store, and we hope you can send this yarn to us quickly so
we can fill the order. We hope to hear from you soon.

Sincerely,

Monte Whiteside

Monte Whiteside
Purchasing Agent

rc
```

Example 2
Poor Order Letter

Graceful Exit. Many writers are tempted to use the weak ending "Please let us hear from you soon" in an order letter. This ending is not a successful way to conclude any letter. Your exit will be only a sentence or two. You should try to make the most of these sentences. Make a specific reference to the order and leave your reader with a sense of friendliness on your part:

We rely on these disks in the office and will be glad to have them as soon as possible.

When you send our order, please include a copy of your latest catalog.

We hope to receive the letterheads within two weeks, in time to begin a large mailing.

Special Terms. A price may be quoted this way:

$450 f.o.b. Los Angeles

The term *f.o.b.* stands for *free on board* or *freight on board*. The term means that the price given is the cost of the item at the place named. If the item is to be shipped to a city other than the one named, the buyer must pay the shipping charges.

If the quotation reads

$450 f.o.b. destination

the cost of shipping is included in the $450.

The term *c.o.d.* or *COD* refers to a shipment for which the buyer pays all charges at the time of delivery—the cost of the item along with shipping charges.

Collect shipment means that shipping charges will be paid upon delivery. *Express* usually means shipment by motor freight.

```
                    Anderson's Department Store
                      Grove Street at Tenth Avenue
                        Atlanta, GA 30376-8510

          August 22, 19--



          Fillmore Box & Carton Company
          457 Prince Street
          Philadelphia, PA 19182-5312

          Gentlemen:

          We want to get an early start on ordering the boxes for our
          Christmas trade. Many of our customers commented favorably
          on the quality and style of the boxes we ordered from you
          last year.

          Here are the details of our order:

          42 dozen boxes    size 4 R, stock 566    $2.00         $84.00
          18 dozen boxes    size 2 R, stock 552     1.50          27.00
          600 boxes         size 9 P, stock 531      .40 ea.     240.00
          500 boxes         size 9 J, stock 850      .32 ea.     160.00
          800 boxes         size X J, stock 574      .75 ea.     600.00
                                                               $1,111.00

          Please charge the total of $1,111 to our open account and
          add the shipping charges by motor express.

          Boxes from Fillmore add to the special quality of Anderson's
          holiday service to our customers. We'll expect to receive
          this order by October 15 so that we can provide gift boxes
          to our very earliest shoppers.

          Sincerely yours,

          George Spruce
          George Spruce
          Purchasing Manager
```

Example 3
Good Order Letter

Parcel post is a type of package delivery through the United States Postal Service. There are restrictions on size, weight, and packaging. *Special handling* service is available for third-class and fourth-class mail. This service provides preferential treatment in mail dispatch and transportation.

Payment Methods. Except for orders sent c.o.d. or charged to an open account, all orders must be accompanied with payment.

A company check is the usual method for sending payment from one business to another. The company check is drawn on the company's bank and signed by an authorized person. If you are including a company check with your order, mention the check in your letter. Some writers also mention the amount of the check in the letter.

If you are including a personal check with an order, you do not normally need to use the word *personal* when you refer to the check in the order letter. You might use the term *personal check* if you were placing an order through your company for an item for your own use. Normally you will simply mention that you have included a check as payment for the order.

Sometimes a certified check or a cashier's check is needed. You can get a certified check from any bank where you have an account. You write the check on your own account. A bank officer then certifies it, guaranteeing that the money is available in your account. You can get a cashier's check from most banks. You pay the bank the amount of the check, and the bank issues you a check. A fee is charged for both certified checks and cashier's checks.

```
                    Shamrock Press
                      1212 Erin Road
                   Kansas City, MO 64150
                      (816) 555-5402

                          July 10, 19--


        Ms. Sara Cassell
        Conway Academy
        50 Bethune Road
        Des Moines, IA 50344

        Dear Ms. Cassell:

        We appreciate your letter of June 27, in which you placed
        your order for Shamrock books.

        We are shipping the following items by parcel post today:

        10 Shamrock Student Dictionaries @ $4.50        $45.00
        12 Spanish/English Dictionaries @ $6.00          72.00
        30 French/English Dictionaries @ $7.00          210.00
        50 Workbooks for Botany Today @ $2.00           100.00
                                                       $427.00

        Today we are charging your account $438.50, which includes
        the shipping charge of $11.50.

        Your order also includes 150 German/English dictionaries and
        our cassette program, Video Language Review. The dictionaries
        and the cassette programs should arrive at our warehouse
        later this month. These items will be shipped separately in
        August.

        I am enclosing our list of teaching aids. As you will note,
        some items are complimentary and will be sent at your
        request. Shamrock is ready to supply whatever you need in
        dictionaries, language programs, and science texts.

                          Sincerely,

                          Sean Doyle
                          Sean Doyle
                          Order Manager


        ref

        Enclosure
```

Example 4
Acknowledgment Letter

A money order can also be used for payment. Money orders are issued by the United States Postal Service, by banks, and by Western Union. When you buy a money order, you pay the face value of the order plus a fee. With the Postal Service and with banks, you must request the money order in person. Credit cards may be used for Western Union money orders, and therefore the money order can be arranged by telephone. A Western Union money order is transmitted immediately in most cases.

Never send cash through the mail. Besides the hazard of possible theft, mail can be damaged or misplaced. If you send cash, you have no record to serve as proof of payment. You also have no way to replace the money if it is lost.

ACKNOWLEDGING ORDERS

A seller sends an acknowledgment of an order to increase the customer's goodwill, especially if an order cannot be filled immediately. When an order can be filled at once and will reach the customer in a few days, an acknowledgment may not be needed.

If an order will not be shipped immediately, the seller sends the customer an acknowledgment letter to tell the customer that the order has been received and to provide information about shipment (see Example 4).

A company that does a high volume of mail order business may use a message printed on a postcard to let the customer know that the order has been received.

An acknowledgment is an opportunity to build goodwill. A business that takes advantage of this opportunity will gain a good reputation, especially if the company's service is good. Orders from new customers, large orders, and orders that require special handling offer excellent opportunities to build goodwill.

Sometimes an acknowledgment is necessary to request certain information that may be missing in an order. An ordered item may be out of stock, causing a shipping delay. Courtesy to the customer requires an acknowledgment letter in these situations.

Dynamic Entrance. The circumstances will affect the way you begin an acknowledgment letter. Usually the first paragraph expresses appreciation to your customer. Even a short sentence can stand alone as the beginning of an acknowledgment letter:

> **We were pleased to receive your letter of September 18, in which you ordered your supply of stationery for the holiday season.**
>
> **When we received your order of September 18, we were glad to learn you will be using our Grantiles in your new store.**
>
> **Thank you for your order of September 18.**

Even if you must tell your customer that you need more information, that there will be a delay, or that you cannot fill the order, a pleasant beginning is important. In fact, the less pleasant the message, the more you need to begin on a note that gives your reader positive feelings about you and your company.

Logical Development. Use the main part of an acknowledgment letter to repeat the details of the order just as the customer gave them—quantity, stock number, name and description of the item, color, size, and price. If the number of items is long, make a list preceded by an introduction like this:

> **We are pleased to send you the following items:**

If the list is very long, provide a photocopy of the customer's order list and include a sentence like this:

> **We are sending you the items listed on the attached page.**

If a problem exists because the order is not clear, explain exactly what you need to fill the order accurately:

> **The following items can be shipped at once: (name the items). Before we ship the eight electronic typewriters, we need a stock number. We offer four models, and we want to be sure that we're sending the model you want.**

If there is a delay in filling an order because a certain item is out of stock, mention the delay in a separate paragraph:

> **We are temporarily out of stock on our T-20 personal answering machine. We expect to ship your order of two T-20 machines on December 12.**

If appropriate, offer a substitute for items that are unavailable. Above all, give your customer a feeling of confidence in your company and a sense that you care about the customer's needs.

Keep in mind that you should acknowledge every part of a customer's order, including the method of payment indicated. You should also be sure to give specific information about how and when the order will be shipped.

Graceful Exit. The ending of an acknowledgment letter should always leave an open door between you and your customer. Avoid meaningless phrases, just as you would in conversation:

> *Not:* **We hope to hear from you again soon.**

Your ending should encourage the customer to do business with your company again:

> **I'm enclosing an envelope for your next order.**
>
> **I'm enclosing our new catalog. You can send your next order on the handy order form on page 76.**

10
Worksheets

General Instructions for All Letter-Writing Assignments

- Use one of the standard letter styles described in Unit 6. Include an envelope only if your instructor specifies that you should.

- Use the current date except when a date or time period is given in the assignment.

- Use your own initials wherever reference initials are needed unless the assignment specifies the name of the secretary or typist.

- If the assignment specifies that you are the writer, use your own name in the signature line.

- In any letter, you may add details and names to give greater depth to your message. For example, you may provide color and size information, dates, and other facts.

1. Veronica Fudge, one of the partners in Jones & Fudge, Attorneys-at-Law, asks you to write for her signature an order for the following items:

   - 8 dozen boxes paper clips, size H, costing $1.80 a dozen

   - 2 electric pencil sharpeners, Model 387 K, priced at $22 each

   - 14 printer cartridges for the Masterkey processor, $8.50 each

   - 3 electric staplers called Electrastapes, priced at $9.50 each

   The order is to be placed with Potter and Spruce Office Supplies, Spruce Building, 887 Walker Highway, Salt Lake City, Utah 84118.

   Have the order sent parcel post, special handling, and charged to the company's account: Jones & Fudge, Attorneys-at-Law, 321 Case Circle, Seattle, Washington 98175. Ask for delivery by August 31.

2. In a magazine, newspaper, or catalog, find an item you would like to order by mail. Write the letter, using your own address and name. Attach the advertisement or catalog page to the letter.

3. Monte Whiteside is the purchasing agent for a sweater manufacturer, Diamond Cardigans, 1223 Bridgewater Creek Road, Denver, Colorado 80233.

   Diamond has received an order for sweaters from a Chicago department store that wants delivery by August 1. In January, Mr. Whiteside asks you to write a letter for his signature, ordering the following amounts of synthetic yarn from Linsholm Woolens, Inc., Grigley Plaza, Dallas, TX 75234-9842: 4,000 ounces Sky Blue @ $.08 an ounce; 4,500 ounces New Green @ $.08 an ounce; 6,000 ounces Clay Brown @ $.08 an ounce; 6,000 ounces Cherry Red @ $.08 an ounce; and 9,000 ounces Pure White @ $.11 an ounce. All the yarn is Stock #4458.

   Ask to have the total, including shipping costs, charged to Diamond Cardigans, shipment by Priority Mail, to be received by February 1.

4. Franklin Publishers, 1985 Third Avenue, New York, NY 10098, has advertised leather-bound appointment books that can be imprinted with the owner's name. You are the customer relations manager for Dabney, Stuart, and Plimsoll, a stockbroker firm with offices at 26 Trinity Street, New York, NY 10042. Order three of the diaries, to be imprinted with the names of June Abrams, Anthony Day, and Marcia Woods. Each appointment book costs $24.95, including tax. You are sending a check to pay for the books. Ask to have the books delivered collect by a messenger service.

RING BINDERS
#328 9 × 12 inches (black or gray) $3.00 each
#329 5 × 8 inches (blue or black) $2.00 each

SCISSORS
#230 6-inch blades $5.75 each
#240 6-inch blades (left-handed) $8.00 each
#610 10-inch shears $10.50 each

BALLPOINT PENS
#468 fine point (black or blue) $9.50 dozen
#470 medium point (red, blue, or black)
    $3.60 dozen

MANILA FILE FOLDERS
#162 letter size $2.12 dozen
#180 legal size $3.00 dozen

**McEachern
Wholesale Office Supplies**
489 Neely Road
Los Angeles, California 90076
(213) 555-0333

5. As an employee of Harris Books and Papers, Inc., 1264 Park Street, San Francisco, CA 94167, you have been asked by Gerald Bragg, manager, to place an order based on the advertisement McEachern ran in the September 19 issue of *Business Herald*.

Place the following order, to be signed by Mr. Bragg:

100 #328, black; 102 #468, blue; 108 #470, red; 1 dozen #230; 1 dozen #240; 2 dozen #610; 102 #162; 198 #180

Say that you are paying by check, and ask for shipment express collect.

6. Write a letter acknowledging the order received on the following order form. Explain that AHMED biscuits are no longer available in this country. The other items will be shipped by November 24 as requested.

ALLEGRO FOOD SHOPS

34 St. Cecelia Avenue
Minneapolis, Minnesota 55467

** Shops in Five States **   (612) 444-4000

PURCHASE ORDER NO. _____62111_____   DATE _November 13, 19--_

TO   SHIP TO

Follensbay Gourmet Foods   Allegro Food Shops
1988 Hillsdale Road   at address given above
Chicago, Illinois 60677   Please ship items
                                             listed below.

QUANTITY	DESCRIPTION	STOCK NO.	UNIT PRICE	EXTENSION
24 boxes	AHMED biscuits	778	1.22	29.28
4 cases	American caviar	990	120.00	480.00
18 tins	smoked oysters	88	1.20	21.60
100 boxes	wild rice (1 pound)	111	3.50	350.00
1 case	chestnut puree	12	18.00	18.00
			TOTAL	$898.88

Ship by   Express   _____   Payment
             Parcel Post _____   C.O.D. _____
             Other   _____   Check enclosed _____
                                           Charge to
Ship by   (date) _November 24_   Account # ___1167___

                          SIGNATURE ___Bill Burnet___

7. Write a letter acknowledging the order to Potter and Spruce (Exercise 1).

8. Here is an order letter your company has received. Write an acknowledgment, asking for the additional information needed and explaining that the customer has misunderstood the meaning of f.o.b.

GORDON AND GRANTLEY
Riverside Plaza
Camden, Ohio 44321

November 10, 19—

Gillis Chair Company
344 Industrial Park Road
Denmark, NC 27777

Gentlemen:

In your catalog of last summer, you list an office chair that is available in brown or red. Please enter our order for six of them and ship them to us by motor express.

The price given in the catalog is $49.95 f.o.b. factory. We understand that this means that your factory will pay the freight charges. We are therefore enclosing our check for $299.70.

Please send these chairs as soon as possible. We are planning a sales meeting for December 3, and we'd like to have the chairs by then.

Sincerely,

Don Sheridan Lee

Don Sheridan Lee
Office Manager

9. Here is a poor acknowledgment of the letter assigned in Exercise 4. Rewrite it, keeping in mind the idea of using an acknowledgment to reinforce your company's good reputation and to promote further sales of your product.

Franklin Publishers
1985 Third Avenue
New York, NY 10098

July 10, 19—

Dabney, Stuart, and Plimsoll
26 Trinity Street
New York, NY 10042

Gentlemen:

This will acknowledge our receipt of your order of July 7. We will send it by messenger as you requested as soon as the books come from the printer.

Your interest in our product is greatly appreciated.

Sincerely,

Benita Ruiz

Miss Benita Ruiz

ct

10. Write a letter acknowledging the order from Anderson's Department Store to Fillmore Box & Carton Company (Example 3).

11
Inquiries

In many business situations, a person must request additional facts or explanations. Consumers have questions about products or services. Business firms need additional information from each other, and departments within an organization communicate to ask for facts.

Often the most efficient way to obtain information is through a letter or memo. Written communications have the advantage of giving the reader time to think and to locate material needed for a response.

Letters and memos designed to elicit information should be written with the greatest possible clarity. How can a reader respond to an inquiry if the question is not clear? This unit will help you prepare inquiry letters. A later unit will provide a guide to writing responses to inquiries.

CONSUMER INQUIRIES

Whatever a person's job may be, he or she is also a consumer—a person who uses products and services for noncommercial purposes. Consumers write inquiry letters for many purposes. You might want to ask where you can buy a certain product, or you might write to learn more about a service. You might want to request free materials. As a consumer, you need to know how to prepare an effective inquiry letter.

Be Specific and Clear. Make it easy for the reader to understand what you want. Specify how you first learned about a particular item or service. If your inquiry is the result of an advertisement, name the publication or television or radio program that first brought the item to your attention. Let the reader know what kind of information you need (see Example 1). Use an enumerated list if necessary (see Example 2).

Provide Information for Response. Make it easy for your reader to respond to your inquiry. It may seem obvious to say that you should be sure to include your name and address, but many inquiries cannot be answered because mailing information is incomplete.

You may want to enclose a stamped, addressed envelope for the reader's response, especially if you are writing to a nonprofit group, such as a charity. Most companies prefer to use their own envelopes and may have prepackaged responses ready to mail.

Provide Background. Let your reader know why you are asking for the material or the answers to your questions. If you are a potential customer, be sure to say so. If you want information for a report or other project, tell the reader some of the background.

```
                    115 Trilby Street
                    Philadelphia, PA 19144
                    December 28, 19---



                    Dakin Travel Service
                    61 Bay Road
                    Miami, FL 33111-9834

                    Gentlemen:

                    In the December 12 issue of Travel Magazine, I noticed your
                    advertisement about cruises to the Caribbean that are to
                    begin the second Saturday in February.

                    Please send me any information you have available regarding
                    rates, accommodations, and schedules. I am interested in
                    taking a cruise in March, and I'll need accommodations for
                    two people.

                    Thank you for helping me make my plans.

                    Sincerely,

                    Norman Willoughby
                    Norman Willoughby
```

Example 1
Good Inquiry Letter

Be Courteous. Even if you are writing in response to an advertisement, a polite request usually gets better results than does a curt demand.

INQUIRIES BETWEEN ORGANIZATIONS

Often a business needs information from another firm. A business may also need to make inquiries to government agencies and to professionals such as attorneys and accountants.

Letters between one organization and another should be written with the same clarity and politeness you would use in a consumer inquiry. Too often business writers mistakenly believe that a letter to a business should be formal and impersonal. No letter needs to sound like a form letter. Your reader will respond well to a letter that reflects warmth and humanity.

A business might write to another company to inquire about a product or service. Perhaps this product or service might be useful for improving some aspect of a company's operation. Inquiries between businesses or other organizations often focus on price, function, and time schedules (see Example 3).

Governmental groups and government agencies have a great effect on the operation of business today. Permits are needed, fees must be calculated, and regulations must be met. Businesses have many reasons for making inquiries of local, state, and federal organizations (see Examples 4 and 5).

```
          Apartment 44 A
          1836 Vermont Street, N.W.
          Washington, DC 20046

                         July 19, 19---


          Ms. Kate Johnson, Reservations
          Hillside Community Theater
          Parkside Place and Newton Road
          Hillside, Virginia 22768

          Dear Ms. Johnson:

          I was glad to see your advertisement in the Washington Press
          on Sunday, July 17, for the world premiere of Douglas Ash's
          Highland Azaleas.

          I want to arrange a party to attend the play in September,
          on either the 14th or the 21st. Would you please answer
          these questions for me:

          1. Could I obtain a block of 30 seats in the orchestra for
          either of those nights?

          2. Would there be any discount from the usual price of $15
          per ticket?

          3. What facilities do you have for handicapped persons? My
          aunt will be in the party, and she is in a wheelchair.

          4. What is the approximate driving time to Hillside from
          Washington?

          I am enclosing a stamped, addressed envelope for your reply.
          I'm eager to make these arrangements as soon as possible so
          that I can invite my guests.

                         Sincerely,

                         Cynthia MacGregor

                         Mrs. Cynthia MacGregor


          Enclosure
```

Example 2
Inquiry Letter
with Enumerated List

INQUIRIES WITHIN AN ORGANIZATION

The form of communication used most commonly within a business is the memorandum or memo. Memos between departments or individuals are used for many purposes, and inquiry memos are written frequently. Discussions may take place over the telephone or in person, but a written memo provides a useful record of what took place.

Companies sometimes use preprinted forms for memos. The heading provides a format for the names, date, and the subject of the memo (see Example 6).

Memo sheets may be half sheets or even quarter sheets. As mentioned earlier, memos that will be kept in permanent files should be written on full sheets for convenience in filing.

A memo is usually shorter than a letter and should be concise. Do not write a separate opening or ending paragraph. Your memo will most likely focus on service, location, or scheduling.

In any inquiry letter or memo you write, keep in mind the need for clarity, the importance of being specific about where the reply should go, and the advantage of being warm and courteous in your inquiry. Consider your letter from the point of view of the reader. If you received the inquiry,

- would you understand the request?

- would you be able to reply?

- would you want to reply?

Hector & Sebastian, Inc.
835 Willow Street
Baltimore, MD 21278-6543

November 3, 19--

Ms. Isabel M. Martinez
Grant Advertising Agency
441 Madison Avenue
New York, NY 10065-7782

Dear Ms. Martinez

When you called us in June, we were not thinking of making
any changes in our advertising plans. Since then, we have
had some problems with our current firm. We'd like to
review some of the ideas you mentioned in June.

You presented some suggestions for an advertising program
that would include television, magazine, and direct mail
advertising. Could you please provide some information
about this plan? I'd like to take these ideas to the Board
of Directors in early January.

Please provide the following information:

--cost estimates for the various parts of the program
--time schedule for starting the new plan
--a date for your formal presentation to our Board

Let me know as soon as you can if you are able to provide
this information.

Sincerely yours

Juan Kim

Juan Kim

jj

Example 3
Letter of Inquiry about Service

100

Patton & Bradley
Public Accountants
441 West Elm Lane
Thorntonville, TN 37866

April 9, 19—

City of Thorntonville
Zoning Office
Room 77, City Hall
Thorntonville, TN 37866

Gentlemen:

When we bought this building three years ago, we planned to use it only for our own offices. Since that time, however, several other firms have expressed an interest in leasing space at 441 West Elm Lane.

Our occupancy here is based on a variance granted by the City Council in April 1988. Please provide information on any additional permission needed if the building is used by these potential tenants:

1. A caterer
2. A music shop
3. A telephone message service
4. A dressmaker

We'd like to have an idea of the work required for a change like this. We want to notify our prospective tenants of our decision before the end of the summer.

Sincerely,

Mercedes Bradley

Ms. Mercedes Bradley

ss

Example 4
Inquiry Letter to Municipal Office

E. J. Goleb Pharmaceuticals Inc.
94 Madison Avenue
Boston, MA 02145-1243

May 6, 19—

Mr. Miles Alden, Director
U.S. Food and Drug Administration
Federal Plaza
Boston, MA 02116-9274

Dear Mr. Alden:

At last we are ready to market and advertise our new line of
analgesics, for which we have chosen the brand name Akegone.

I am enclosing the proposed labels for the full line of
tablets and capsules—from children's strength through the
strongest over-the-counter line.

Please let me have your comments about the labels as soon as
you can. We can proceed with our marketing and promotional
activities as soon as the labels are ready for use.

Thank you for your help.

Sincerely,

Epworth J. Goleb

Epworth J. Goleb
Vice President

gp

Enclosures—10 labels

Example 5
Inquiry Letter to Federal Agency

TO: Department Supervisors
FROM: Gilda Ramirez, Security Chief *G.R.*
DATE: November 5, 19—
SUBJECT: New Locks

To help increase the security of our equipment and records,
the Budget Bureau has approved the purchase of new locks for
all areas that are not now secure.

Please survey your department and let me know these facts:

1. Number and size of file cabinets without locks
2. Number of doors that need replacement locks
3. Day and time you'd prefer to have work done

As soon as I have an estimate of the equipment needed, Tom
Kyong, Bill Adams, and I will make a physical survey of the
area to confirm your exact request.

I know you're as eager as we are to complete this project as
soon as possible.

Example 6
Inquiry Memo

11
Worksheets

1. Thelma Ortiz is the office manager for Amara Data, Inc., 1962 Peachtree Street, Atlanta, Georgia 30399-7753. She has been asked to locate a suitable place for the first convention of the Association of Data Managers. In February she begins to make inquiries of hotels that might be able to accommodate the group. The convention will be for four days in October, exact dates not set pending choice of site. There will be between 75 and 100 people, and the group would like a package plan that includes meals. She also expects the hotel to be able to give basic information about transportation from the nearest airport and about other transportation from New York, where about one-fourth of the members live.

   Write the letter she might send to Knoll Haven Inn, 9 Queen Street, Brooksley, Vermont 05666. She visited Knoll Haven several years ago.

2. Joseph Gridley, 435 West Emerson Road, Alingham, New Jersey 07933, is writing a report on the history of boxes for a course he is taking in college. Write the letter he could send to Fillmore Box & Carton Company, 457 Prince Street, Philadelphia, Pennsylvania 19182-5312. He would like information about the growth of small manufacturers into the large corporations of today. He has already obtained material about the use of boxes in other countries and about their manufacture in colonial America.

3. The law firm of Quimby, Jagel, and Callao has offices in the Intervale Building, 117 Green Street, Newark, New Jersey 07101. On September 15 the office will move to its new building at 45 Winthrop Road, also in Newark. Mrs. Bella Darthwood, Office Manager, asks you to write a letter for her signature to Nomad Van Lines, 889 Kennedy Highway, Piketon, New Jersey 07000, requesting information about charges and plans for the move. She would like to have a representative come to discuss the plans, and she is especially concerned about the security of files during the move. The telephone number for Quimby, Jagel, and Callao is (201) 555-9120.

4. Mrs. Abigail Endicott, 889 West Tremont Trail, Lincoln, Massachusetts 02155, has inherited some antique silver from various relatives. She would like to sell the silver and has found an advertisement in November's *Country Estates* for a company that buys old silver—Creasely and Lee Silversmiths, 933 Hancock Road, Boston, Massachusetts 02187. Her collection consists of these items:

   - Service for 12, plus 10 serving pieces, Romantic Lace pattern, made by Hinton & Wilcox in Boston in 1689

   - 16 sterling teaspoons, Duchess pattern, made by Grogan Inc. in the eighteenth century

   - 6 soup spoons, Alice pattern, also by Grogan

   Write her initial inquiry letter to Creasely and Lee. She knows she would need to show them the actual silver to obtain a firm estimate.

5. Your office, Amsterdam Office Systems, received the announcement shown below. Your supervisor, Ms. Leila Chung, asks you to write Pandora and ask for printed material about how to make a building more secure. The address of your company is 558 Sixteenth Street, Des Moines, Iowa 50322.

PANDORA SECURITY, INC.

established in St. Louis in 1948

is pleased to announce

the opening of our Des Moines office

at 1356 Grand Avenue

September 5, 19--

6. Your town of Spencer, Illinois, is in an area that has frequent tornadoes. The Civil Defense Chairman, George Unger, is preparing a survey of local citizens to determine the location of handicapped persons, elderly persons, and other residents who might need special help in an emergency. Write the letter that he will send with his questionnaire. The address of the Civil Defense Corps is 2 Town Square, Spencer, Illinois 60781.

7. Prepare the questionnaire needed for the Civil Defense information, using about ten questions that can be answered with single words or very short phrases.

8. The Alumni Association of MacRae College is considering the publication of a monthly newsletter in addition to its present quarterly magazine. Prepare a letter that could be sent to all alumni, exploring the interest in such a project. The address of the alumni association is Douglas Student Center, MacRae College, Inverness, Ohio 44389. The letter will be signed by Andrew Evans, Executive Secretary.

9. Write a memo to the members of the Research and Development Department of your company, Springfield Products, Inc., Room 94, Massey Building, Cleveland, Ohio 44133-4141. You want to know what they think of the new hospitalization plan the company is proposing. Information about the plan has already been distributed to employees. You would like to have the responses by April 14, in time for a meeting you will attend on April 17.

10. Write a memo to your boss asking if you can have two days off to attend your sister's graduation in June. Supply details of company, date, and department, and use your name.

11. In early April, Meredith Ambrose attended the Heart of the Mountains Crafts Fair in Marlboro, a town in eastern Tennessee. She was impressed by the exhibits and the number of people in attendance. She would like to return for the fall fair, October 14–15, to exhibit her own paper sculpture. From a brochure, she has learned that the director of the fair is Ms. Lee Stuart. The address is Heart of the Mountains Crafts Fair, P. O. Box 333, Marlboro, Tennessee 37666.

Ms. Ambrose has previously displayed her work only at local exhibitions. Her small business is known as Castles of Paper, and the address is 446 Million Pines Road, Douglas, New Jersey 07982.

Write the letter Ms. Ambrose could send to Ms. Stuart, requesting information about fees, requirements for exhibitors, and accommodations in the Marlboro area. She will include some photos of her work so that Ms. Stuart will understand what kind of paper sculpture is involved.

12. Paul Whitfield Saffell is a student at Gallatin Community College. For a course in sociology, he is conducting research on his family history. In the *Gallatin Gazette* of September 28, he read an article about Mrs. Elizabeth Saffell Drake and her recent trip to Scotland to search for information about Saffell ancestors.

Paul believes that Mrs. Drake can give him some information about William Saffell. Paul knows that in 1810, William Saffell moved to Gallatin in McRae County with his wife, Eleanor Meredith.

Write the letter Paul could send to Mrs. Drake asking for information about the dates and places of birth of William Argonne Saffell, Eleanor Meredith Saffell, and their twin daughters, Polly and Esther. Paul is also interested in identifying a person named Anna Cleary, whose name recurs in letters and diaries as a member of the Saffell household. Mrs. Drake's address is 5608 North Bermuda Parkway, Columbus, Ohio 43200. Paul's address is 303 College Street, Gallatin, Illinois 60788.

12
Responses to Inquiries

Businesses and other organizations receive many requests for information. Inquiries frequently come from customers or prospective customers. Sometimes the writer is a student or other person who is writing a report or planning a presentation for a group.

Some organizations prepare special information packages to send as a response to general inquiries. You may be asked to write a form letter to be included with the package, providing details on how to get more information.

A personal letter of response can supply information and promote the goodwill of the reader. This unit will show how to write responses to inquiries from consumers, from other businesses, and from others within a company.

Writing a response to any kind of message costs money—for paper, for postage, and for the time of the writer. Sometimes it might seem a waste of time, money, and effort for a business to reply to the many requests for information it might receive. When you consider, however, that any response could bring new business if the response is handled well, you will see that it is worthwhile for a business to respond to most requests.

If the request is clearly written and the material or information needed is available, you should be able to write a response with little trouble. The response will take longer if you have to search for information before writing.

When you write a response letter, give as much information as you can. Write in a courteous tone, showing that your company is glad to be of service. Finally, send your response as soon as possible after receiving an inquiry.

FORM LETTERS

Responses to inquiries are often form letters, but form letters do not have to sound impersonal.

If you compose a form letter, imagine a real person as your reader. Use the name of the person you are addressing, never "Dear Customer." You can also make the letter more personal by referring to a specific person your reader has spoken with in the past or should speak with in the future:

Not: **You were told about our speakers' bureau.**

Write: **Ms. Lanier told you about our speakers' bureau.**

RESPONSES TO CONSUMERS

Sometimes it may seem like a nuisance to respond to an inquiry letter from a consumer. The reader of an inquiry might ask, "What's in it for us? Why should we bother?" Most companies do find it worthwhile to bother because they want a consumer to have a good impression of the company and because they want to build goodwill whenever they can (see Example 1).

An inquiry from a consumer could result in an order sometime in the future. If it is worth taking time to answer the letter at all, it is worth answering in a considerate, courteous tone:

Not: **You will find enclosed the material you requested.**

Write: **We are glad to send you this information about the use of kerosene heaters in the metropolitan area. Good luck on your report to the volunteer firefighters.**

Silver & Bell Garden Center
Warren Pike Road
Burnside, Maine 04155
Telephone: (207) 555-6492
FAX: (207) 555-6532

September 12, 19--

Mr. Merlin Boaz
122 Quimby Highway
Springfield, ME 04176

Dear Mr. Boaz:

I apologize for our delay in responding to your letter of
August 30, in which you asked about the possibility of
obtaining free plants for the botanical display at the
science fair.

I have set aside some plants for you--rhododendrons and
acacia in several varieties. If you could stop by at the
Garden Center, you can take a look and see if these
plants are what you have in mind.

If you are looking for more unusual flowers, you might try
Ezra's Exotic Plants in Lincoln. I haven't seen their
display, but I've heard it is very interesting.

I'll look forward to seeing you any afternoon next week.

Cordially,

Bob Silver

Bob Silver

Example 1
Response to Inquiry from Consumer

Pandora Security, Inc.
14 Woodridge Avenue
Scotia, Missouri 64551

April 20, 19—

Mr. Lee Kyang
Wiggins Electronics
12 Wakefield Road
Kansas City, MO 64102-9321

Dear Mr. Kyang

We appreciated your letter of April 9, in which you praised the plantings of tulips and dogwood at our new building. We are pleased with our quarters here in Scotia, although the decision to move to the suburbs was not easy after all our years in downtown Kansas City.

The landscaping of our grounds was done by Gerald and Grace Garwood, who have just opened their new gardening business. I am enclosing a copy of their brochure. They will be glad to get your call and to discuss the possibilities for your outdoor improvement project.

Let me know how the project turns out. Please call me if I can help you in any other way.

Sincerely yours

Diane Caldwell

Diane Caldwell

dda

Enclosure

Example 2
Response to Inquiry from Another Business

Princeton Caterers, Inc.
445 Dallmine Avenue
Cincinnati, OH 45233-8954

September 24, 19—

Mr. David Spruell
6689 Goodpark Road
Cincinnati, OH 45290-1762

Dear Mr. Spruell:

We appreciate your letter of September 12, in which you praised the menu, food, and service at the recent benefit dinner for the Cincinnati Zoo. Princeton Caterers is proud of its reputation for such excellence.

We wish we could supply our recipes for Shrimp Safari and Chocolate Lemon Chantilly. We agree with you that both dishes are unique. That uniqueness is the very reason we cannot give you the recipes! Our chef, Lee Charlroi, has developed these recipes and several others that make up our special menus. If we published the recipes, we would no longer have their exclusive use.

You can enjoy these two specialties and many others whenever you visit our new restaurant, Princeton Pavilion, next door to our catering office.

Thank you again for your comments on the benefit dinner. We look forward to serving you at the restaurant.

Sincerely yours,

PRINCETON CATERERS, INC.

Geneva Knightsbridge

Ms. Geneva Knightsbridge
Vice President

Example 3
Response Explaining Inability to Provide Information

RESPONSES BETWEEN BUSINESSES

The tendency to sound formal and impersonal is somehow very strong in replies to inquiries from other businesses. Always read the response letter you have written to determine how you would react if it were addressed to you. You can use warm and friendly language without increasing the cost, time, or effort of writing your response (see Example 2). Your letter will make a better impression on your reader, and it could bring more direct results.

RESPONSES DENYING INFORMATION

Sometimes you will be unable to provide the material or the information a writer has requested. The writer may not understand your company's line of business. Consumers may make such a mistake if they base their thinking on the name of the company alone. A courteous answer can still be effective. If it is easily possible for you to suggest an alternate source, you can include that helpful advice.

A writer may ask for information that your company does not give out. If you receive a request like this, do not hide behind "company policy." Even if company policy is the reason for refusing, you will sound more sympathetic toward your reader and less critical of your company if you give your reasons in some other words (see Example 3).

RESPONSES WITHIN A COMPANY

Often you can respond orally to an inquiry memo, or you can carry out the action requested in the memo. Whenever you think there is any reason to put your reply in writing, be sure to do so. Too often a person must say, "I thought you understood what I told you at lunch last Tuesday." Taking the few minutes necessary to write the response to a memo can be well worth the effort.

When you respond to an inquiry memo, you will normally be able to supply the information

```
                            M E M O

        TO:      Jeremy Valdengo, Sales Department Manager

        FROM:    Lola Grimes, Assistant Credit Manager

        DATE:    June 20, 19—

        SUBJECT: Establishing New Accounts

        I've just read your memo of June 17, in which you asked for
        an explanation of the procedures for establishing new
        accounts.

        Look in your files for the bulletin that came from George
        Prism just before he retired last March. He was the one who
        set up the new program, and you will find a complete outline
        of procedures in that bulletin.

        After you read the bulletin from George, please call me if
        you need further information.
```

Example 4
Response to In-House Inquiry

requested. If you do not have the facts needed, your response can include your promise to get the information and an estimate of when you can supply the facts requested.

If you've been asked for information normally not shared outside your department, you can refer the reader to the person authorized to release the information. If you've been asked for something that you think the writer can find without your help, be courteous in your response (also see Example 4):

> **The manual sent out last week is so detailed that none of us has had time to read all of it. The information you're looking for is on page 45.**

Remember these important guidelines for writing response letters or memos:

1. A courteous response is worth the slight extra effort.

2. The information you supply should be as complete and thorough as you can make it.

3. Your letter or memo should be one you yourself would like to receive, even if you must provide a negative response.

4. Even with in-house messages, a written response is a good idea because it serves as a record.

12
Worksheets

1. Reply to this letter, supplying information about the colors and sizes you have in stock and suggesting how the order can be placed.

Winston High School
4499 High View Road
Philadelphia, PA 19187-9922

Larry Dorman, Head Coach   Athletic Department

April 4, 19—

Mr. Everett Chance, Jr.
Vice President
T. E. Chance
Sports Uniforms and Equipment
889 Arkansas Pike
Memphis, TN 38160

Dear Mr. Chance:

At the recent coaches' convention in Dallas, I met Sam Oldwig. Sam told me about the new football helmets your company is now selling, and I liked what he showed me at the exhibit hall.

Winston is planning to change its colors for helmets and jerseys. We've decided on white and blue for the jerseys, and we are still considering the color for the helmets. We definitely will change to the safety helmets your company displayed in Dallas.

Please send me additional information about the helmets and jerseys—especially colors and sizes—before we place our order.

Sincerely,

Larry Dorman

Larry Dorman

2. Exercise 2, Unit 11, was a letter written by Joseph Gridley to the Fillmore Box & Carton Company. Reply to the letter in the name of George Endicott, Director of Public Information. Send Mr. Gridley a copy of a short history of your company, compiled and edited by your retired comptroller, Abigail Fillmore. Also send a copy of an old pamphlet, *The Importance of Containers*.

3. Write a response to Mrs. MacGregor's inquiry to the Hillside Community Theater (Unit 11, Example 2). The letter should answer all Mrs. MacGregor's questions:

- September 21 is available; September 14 is booked for a field trip from Lincoln Country Day School.
- The purchase of thirty orchestra tickets will bring a discount of 20 percent from the usual $15 ticket price.
- Handicapped facilities are available.
- Driving time is about one hour, via Interstate 95.
- There is a restaurant called Silverhill Room on the premises. (Enclose sample menu.)

Your letter will be signed by the box office manager, Kenneth Padonia.

4. Here is an inadequate response to the inquiry letter written by Ms. Mercedes Bradley to the Zoning Office in Thorntonville (Unit 11, Example 5). Rewrite the letter, making it a good response to the inquirer.

City of Thorntonville

ZONING OFFICE
CITY HALL, ROOM 77
THORNTONVILLE, TN 37866

April 30, 19—

Ms. Mercedes Bradley
Patton & Bradley
Public Accountants
441 West Elm Lane
Thorntonville, TN 37866

Dear Ms. Bradley:

This is in response to your recent inquiry. We are looking into the points you raised in your letter, and we'll get back to you as soon as we have anything to report.

Your continued support of the programs of the city is greatly appreciated.

Very truly yours,

Halyard K. Bruce

Halyard K. Bruce
Zoning Officer

5. Your office has received the following letter. Miguel Ramirez, your supervisor, asks you to reply. Explain to the writer that you cannot give him the information he is requesting. Mr. Ramirez will sign the letter as the Director of Information.

MacRae College
Economics Department
Inverness, Ohio 44389

January 10, 19—

United Systems and Circuits
International Headquarters
779 Wheaton Road
Minneapolis, MN 55466

Gentlemen:

I need your help in a research project I have undertaken as part of my graduate studies.

United Systems and Circuits is recognized as the largest company of its kind in the world. I am doing a study on the relationship of salaries to titles in large corporations, and I would like to have the following information from you:

1. How many employees do you have?

2. How many employees have job classifications in the middle management category?

3. What are the titles of your middle management positions?

4. What is the salary range of each title?

5. Do you have any nonmanagement personnel whose salaries are equal to or greater than those of middle management?

So that you can answer me as soon as possible, I am enclosing a stamped envelope. I hope you can help me.

Sincerely,

Roland Quimby

Roland Quimby

6. Nomad Van Lines, a national company that specializes in household moves, has advertised in several magazines a new booklet available free to anyone who writes for it. The name of the booklet is *Home Is Where the Heart Is*. Write a form letter that could be personalized to use as a cover letter for the booklet. Nomad's headquarters address is 6081 Washington Pike, Baltimore, MD 21219.

7. Write a paragraph that could be used to personalize Nomad's letter (Exercise 6) for a request from a large corporation that is about to relocate 30 employees and wants copies of the booklet for each family.

8. Ms. Rita Sterling is a teacher of consumer education at Winston High School, 4499 High View Road, Philadelphia, PA 19187-9922. She has written to Nomad Van Lines requesting 100 copies of the booklet to be used in her classes. Nomad Van Lines never intended to distribute the booklet in such quantities. Mr. Trent Roberts, Customer Advisor, has asked you to write a letter for his signature, explaining that you can send Ms. Sterling two copies of the booklet.

9. The personnel manager of your company has asked you to supply him with information about the driving and parking situation for the 20 employees in your department. Write a memo in which you explain that for the 20 employees, including you, 13 parking spaces are needed. Four of the employees come in car pools with employees from other departments, two ride the bus, and one walks to work except in bad weather. You want to know if the personnel manager needs the name of each employee and if he wants to know which other departments are affected by the car pooling.

10. You have received this memo:

TO: Staff

FROM: Activities Director

DATE: August 13, 19—

SUBJECT: Evening Classes for Fall

We are now planning the schedule of classes to be offered here at Clamwood Distributors this fall. We plan to offer one foreign language (Russian, Italian, or Portuguese), Advanced Computer Mathematics, an art course (art appreciation or study of architecture), and a continuation of the Great Books Series. Please let me know by August 17 what courses you would like to take.

Write your reply, saying that you had expected Greek to be among the languages, you would like the Great Books course, and you'd like to know when some sports activities will be added.

11. The head of the research department of E. J. Goleb Pharmaceuticals Inc. in Boston has received the following memo from the Director of Human Resources:

TO: Michael Ortega, Director of Research

FROM: Kiri Soong, Director of Human Resources

DATE: April 2, 19—

SUBJECT: Summer Employees

Human Resources is planning for the annual summer employment of high school and college students. Within the next few weeks, we'll be receiving applications and resumes from the many students who want to work for us during the summer.

You can help us meet the needs of your department by giving us information about the qualifications you expect in your summer staff and by estimating the number of summer employees you need. Keep in mind that we often recruit valuable permanent employees through our summer employment program, since some top-quality students choose to work for us when they finish school. In addition, Goleb is committed to providing summer employment for at least 12 high school students through the Boston Area Summer Help Association.

I'd like to have your information by April 7.

                KS

Reply to the memo, using the same form Ms. Soong used. Tell her that you will need three research assistants who have had at least three years of college with emphasis on biology and chemistry. You would also like to have someone who can use a word processor and take dictation to fill in for the clerical staff members who will take vacations during the summer.

One of your staff, Dr. Rachel Brack, will be on a leave of absence for study in Europe from June 15 to September 30. To fill in for Dr. Brack, you would like to have a summer hire who would be interested in and qualified for a permanent position next summer when the company plans to expand its research.

Because research deals with controlled substances, all employees in the department must be at least 21 years old.

12. The Yardley Landscape Service is located at 456 West River Road, Paducah, Kentucky 42233. When Turner Yardley, the owner, started the business ten years ago, he was able to provide landscaping and yard service to both residential and commercial customers. Last year the business had grown so much that Mr. Yardley decided to discontinue work for residential customers. He arranged to transfer his residential accounts to one of three newer landscape services.

Often the Yardley office receives calls from private homeowners asking about the possibility of obtaining lawn service. Write a form letter Mr. Yardley could send to these callers, explaining that his company no longer handles residential contracts. Refer the callers to three newer services, all of whom Mr. Yardley recommends:

> Centipede Landscapes, 115 Forest Road, Sandtown, Kentucky 42233; phone number: 555-4985

> Yards by Zoysia, 10 Millington Highway, Millington, Ohio 41906; phone number: (412) 555-1777

> Bermuda Lawn Service, 785 Sandtown Parkway, Paducah, Kentucky 42233; phone number: 555-7654

Millington and Sandtown are both suburbs of Paducah.

13. In Unit 11, Exercise 12, Paul Whitfield Saffell wrote a letter requesting family history information from Elizabeth Saffell Drake.

Write Mrs. Drake's reply, giving the following information: William Argonne Saffell was born in Sheffield, England, in 1780. His wife, Charlotte Eleanor Meredith, was born in London, England, in 1792. They were married in London in 1810 and immediately emigrated to the United States. They lived in Gallatin, Illinois, until they died. William died of pneumonia on March 12, 1860, and Eleanor died of typhoid fever that same year on August 12. They are buried in the Community Church Cemetery Park in Gallatin. The daughters, Polly and Esther, were not twins. Polly was born January 11, 1812; Esther was born January 11, 1813. Polly died in 1817. Esther married Dr. James Whitfield on June 20, 1835. They had no children. They went to California, where Dr. Whitfield provided care for miners during the Gold Rush. Mrs. Drake has never heard of Anna Cleary.

14. The *Greenville Daily Herald* receives many requests from school groups for tours of the newspaper. Compose a form letter that could be signed by the editor, Leila Kahlil, to respond to such requests. The letter should explain that students may tour in groups of not more than fifteen, each group accompanied by a teacher or adult sponsor. The tour takes about an hour, and tours begin every fifteen minutes from 10 a.m. to 3 p.m. There are no tours on Mondays. Children under 10 are not permitted. Arrange tours by calling Melissa Kim at 555-3908.

The address of the *Greenville Daily Herald* is 2020 Courthouse Square, Greenville, CA 91876.

13
Credit Letters

Letters related to credit require especially careful treatment. Credit letters deal with the financial status of a firm or an individual. We tend to believe that credit correspondence reflects the honesty and reliability of customers. Credit correspondence is important because a company's reputation may be greatly affected by its credit rating. The same is true for an individual consumer. Furthermore, federal and state laws determine what we can and cannot say in correspondence about credit.

This unit will help you write the various types of letters involved in the credit process.

Our society has been called "cashless" because of the frequent use of credit buying. We take credit for granted to such an extent that it comes as a shock when someone is denied credit. We tend to consider credit as our right, but in fact it is a privilege given to those who are judged by businesses or other organizations to be worthy of it.

Most businesses expect their customers to have open accounts for credit buying. Manufacturers and suppliers offer discount systems for prompt payment. One typical system is represented as **2/10, n/30,** meaning that a 2 percent discount will be offered for payments made within 10 days and that the net balance is due within 30 days. Other discount plans are also used.

Consumer-oriented industries such as retail stores issue their own credit cards, as do oil companies and some hotel and restaurant chains. Major credit cards, issued by credit card companies, can be used for many different kinds of purchases. Businesses and consumers use these kinds of credit arrangements. Businesses also deal with each other on a credit basis.

WHAT IS CREDIT?

Credit is a way of delaying payment for something we are able to have and use in the present. The idea of "Buy now, pay later" has many variations. When we buy something on credit, we are able to use the item or service before we have to pay for it. Since the merchant from whom we buy has probably already paid for the product, we are in a sense using

the merchant's money until we pay for the merchandise. The merchant is our creditor.

We get the merchandise, and the creditor gets our promise to pay. Usually a service charge is added if the bill is not paid within a stated period. Consumers are often willing to pay the extra charge for the convenience of credit.

WHO IS CREDITWORTHY?

When individuals or companies apply for credit, they are asked to supply the creditor with certain information. Before credit is granted, an evaluation is made to determine how much risk is associated with the potential credit customer. The evaluation involves checking in the following areas.

Ability to Pay. A person or company that is a good credit risk has a steady and sure source of income. Type of employment, length of employment, and amount of income are all considered in this phase of credit evaluation. Another consideration is the amount of debt already incurred.

Emergency Resources. A good credit risk has some money available for an emergency if normal income is cut off or reduced. Savings accounts, property owned, and other resources are considered in this phase of the evaluation.

Evidence of Stability. A good credit risk has a history of being responsible and of meeting obligations. Ability to pay is not worth much if the individual or company has a reputation for being careless about paying bills or meeting other obligations.

Anderson's Department Store

Willow and Spruce Streets
Springfield, NC 32448

CREDIT APPLICATION

DATE _____

NAME _____ SOCIAL SECURITY NUMBER _____

PRESENT ADDRESS _____
　　　　　　　　　STREET　　　　　　　　CITY　　　STATE　　　ZIP

SPOUSE'S NAME AND ADDRESS. ONLY IF SPOUSE IS TO USE THE ACCOUNT _____

PREVIOUS ADDRESS (IF AT PRESENT ADDRESS LESS THAN TWO YEARS) _____

_____
　TELEPHONE　　　　　　　OCCUPATION　　　　　　　ANNUAL SALARY

BUSINESS ADDRESS _____
　　　　　　　　NAME OF COMPANY　　　　　　　　　TELEPHONE

_____
　STREET　　　　　　　　　CITY　　　STATE　　ZIP

PREVIOUS EMPLOYER IF PRESENT EMPLOYER IS LESS THAN TWO YEARS _____

_____

NAME OF BANK　　　　　ADDRESS　　　　　　　　TYPE OF ACCOUNT

OTHER RETAIL ACCOUNTS

_____　　_____

_____　　_____

_____　　_____

OTHER CREDIT CARDS _____
　　　　　COMPANY　　　　　　　NUMBER　　　　　　EXPIRATION DATE

_____
　COMPANY　　　　　　　　NUMBER　　　　　　EXPIRATION DATE

I AFFIRM THAT THE INFORMATION GIVEN ON THIS APPLICATION IS TRUE AND ACCURATE.

SIGNATURE _____

Example 1
Sample Credit Application Form

For a new company or an individual just beginning a career, proving stability is sometimes the most difficult aspect of establishing credit. A record of having paid even the smallest loan or charge account is a step toward building a credit history.

Everyone knows someone who proudly says, "I never use credit. I always pay cash, and I don't owe anything to anyone." Such statements sound admirable, but reality may demand that we be able to obtain credit when an emergency or an unexpected opportunity arises. A person or a business firm should consider establishing a credit history when credit is not needed. Then credit should be easier to get when it is needed.

Advice on how to build a good credit background and on how to use credit wisely is available from various federal and state government agencies and from nonprofit consumer groups across the country. Information about the rights included in the Equal Credit Opportunity Act may be obtained from the Federal Deposit Insurance Corporation and from several other federal agencies.

CREDIT APPLICATION LETTERS

Most credit applications are handled through application forms provided by the organization offering credit (see Example 1). At other times, a letter of application is required.

Under some circumstances a person might write to a store and request credit. The letter would offer references and other information normally included on an application form (see Example 2).

11 Kenilworth Road
Chicago, IL 60673
September 15, 19--

Follensbay Gourmet Foods
1988 Hillsdale Road
Chicago, IL 60677

Gentlemen:

In the August issue of <u>Eating Well</u>, I saw your advertisement
for gift packages. These packages would make ideal gifts
for many people I know.

I'd like to place an order for the holidays, and then I plan
to order early next year. Could I open an account with you
and then place my orders by telephone? You may use these
references to check my credit history:

   Billings and Dollar Stationers
   99 West Furger Street
   Chicago, IL 60689

   Dingley & Alwich
   445 West Trinity Road
   Chicago, IL 60698-9941

   Barton & Fish
   1999 State Street
   Chicago, IL 60698-9388

I am employed as a computer programmer at Pandora Security,
Inc., 443 Waskeston Road, Evanston, IL 60789. Ken Soong,
my supervisor, will confirm that my annual salary is
$29,900.

Please send me an order form and a copy of your latest
catalog. I hope you can open an account for me in time for
me to place my holiday orders.

Sincerely yours,

Ilsa Cornwall

Ms. Ilsa Cornwall

Example 2
Credit Application Letter

Springfield Products, Inc.
Room 94, Massey Building
Cleveland, Ohio 44133-4141

April 23, 19—

Amsterdam Office Systems
558 Sixteenth Street
Des Moines, IA 50322

Gentlemen:

We recently received our first order from a company that
gave your name as a reference—Bixby Publishers, 13322 North
Stetson Street, Minneapolis, MN 55467. Mr. Kenneth David
wrote that Bixby has been a customer of yours since he
became purchasing agent six years ago. He wants a 30-day
credit arrangement, with a credit limit of $3,000.

We'd appreciate knowing your answers to these questions,
based on your credit experience with Bixby Publishers:

1. Are their bills paid on time?

2. Have you ever notified them of an unpaid bill?

3. Is the amount of their credit with you fairly constant,
or is it an occasional large amount paid off in small
installments?

4. Would you accept this company as a new account?

You can be sure that any information you are able to give us
will be kept confidential. Please use the enclosed envelope
to reply. Thank you for your help.

Sincerely,

Hilda Menninger

Mrs. Hilda Menninger
Credit Manager

lb

Enclosure

Example 3
Reference Request

REQUESTS FOR CREDIT INFORMATION

Business credit applications can be handled like consumer applications. Another method of establishing business credit occurs before an order is submitted or when an order is placed. If no previous credit relations exist, the firm placing the order gives credit history information and requests that an account be opened before the order is filled. Since a new account is likely to bring much business, the crediting firm is pleased to make the credit investigation promptly.

REQUESTS FOR CREDIT INFORMATION

Modern methods of maintaining credit histories have minimized the number of letters written to obtain credit information about a potential customer. Today credit bureaus usually provide this information for creditors.

If you need to write a letter asking for credit information, include these facts (also see Example 3):

Norton, Archer & Swiggert
Certified Public Accountants
500 Pike Street, Suite 800
San Francisco, CA 94133-2288
(415) 555-2020

February 20, 19—

Ms. Karen Delmar
Delmar Richardson, Inc.
River Road at State Street
Los Angeles, CA 90088-6612

Dear Ms. Delmar:

Thank you for your letter of February 12, in which you
inquired about our knowledge of Withrow and Wiggins Media
Consultants. We have checked our records, but we are unable
to provide credit information on this company.

We have no record of any business with Withrow and Wiggins
Media Consultants, 4498 San Giorgio Boulevard, Los Angeles.
In fact, we can find no record of any connection we have
ever had with a company with a similar name.

I wish we could help you, but I think your customer has made
a mistake. I checked our telephone book to see if there
might be a similar name among the CPA firms. The closest I
could find is Borden, Bowman, Frenez, and Smith!

Please let us know if we can be of any further help.

Sincerely,

Anne Williams

Miss Anne Williams

Example 4
Response Denying Credit Information

- Name and address of applicant
- Type of credit requested (amount, terms of payment)
- Specific information you hope to get from the reader
- Assurance that information will be confidential

CREDIT INFORMATION RESPONSES

When you write a letter responding to a request for credit information, give the information requested in a straightforward manner without being judgmental. Recent laws require that a consumer have access to the facts in his or her credit history that have caused denial of credit. Be sure that what you say in such references is fair and truthful (see Examples 4–6).

LETTERS GRANTING CREDIT

When a potential credit customer is given credit, the letter that grants credit provides an excellent way to

Bridges Electronics
552 Ninth Avenue
Detroit, Michigan 48218-6711
(313) 555-4000

September 15, 19—

Mrs. Linda Alvarez
Amara Data Inc.
1962 Peachtree Street
Atlanta, GA 30399-7753

Dear Mrs. Alvarez:

We are pleased to respond to your request for credit
information about Underwood and Diamond Publishers of
Dallas, Texas.

Underwood and Diamond Publishers has been one of our best
customers for electronic word processing equipment since the
days of our first pioneering machines. They use our entire
line of equipment in their offices.

In the six years we've done business with Underwood and
Diamond, all payments have been made on time. When Allan
Underwood retired two years ago, I was concerned that the
company might be less careful about meeting its obligations.
Such was not the case. Evelyn Fillmore, who succeeded Allan
as treasurer, has been equally conscientious about making
payments on time.

With no reservations I recommend Underwood and Diamond to
you as a credit customer. Please call on us again whenever
we can be of help.

Sincerely,

Paul Lee

Paul Lee

Example 5
Response to Credit Information Request

Amsterdam Office Systems
558 Sixteenth Street
Des Moines, Iowa 50322

April 28, 19—

Mrs. Hilda Menninger
Springfield Products, Inc.
Room 94, Massey Building
Cleveland, OH 44133-4141

Dear Mrs. Menninger:

In your letter of April 23, 19—, you inquired about our
credit experience with Bixby Publishers. You mentioned Mr.
Kenneth David, the purchasing agent for Bixby. Before he
joined Bixby six years ago, their record of payment was
different from what it is at present.

To answer your questions:

1. Yes, their bills have been paid on time during the six
years Mr. David has been at Bixby.

2. Yes, we had to write to them about overdue bills before
the change of personnel six years ago.

3. Their usual credit with us is used for the purchase of
computer software. The amount of their indebtedness to us
varies from $500 to $1,800, always paid within 60 days.

4. Yes, we would accept this company as a new account under
its present management.

Please let us know if we can be of further help to you.

Sincerely,

James Foxcroft

James Foxcroft
Director of Credit Services

Example 6
Response to Credit Information Request

---

reinforce the customer's good opinion of your company. The letter should sound friendly and spontaneous, even if it is a form letter adapted for each new credit customer.

Some companies have a credit limit for new accounts. Credit limit information should be expressed in a positive way:

> *Not:* **We have to limit your credit to $500.**
>
> *Write:* **We are pleased to offer you credit up to $500.**

A letter welcoming a new credit customer should clearly state the terms of the credit agreement or should explain that the terms are included on the contract or in the material you are enclosing (see Example 7).

LETTERS REFUSING CREDIT

Sometimes an applicant does not qualify for the credit desired. A letter refusing credit is one of the most difficult letters to write. Keep the following important points in mind (also see Example 8).

Confidentiality. You must not violate your promise of confidentiality to those who gave you references.

Goodwill. Try to encourage the applicant to do business with your company. The applicant might later become an excellent charge customer. Meanwhile, you want to receive that business on a cash basis.

Good Attitude. Always try to write with a positive attitude.

GUIDE FOR WRITING

Each type of credit letter requires a different kind of dynamic entrance, logical development, and graceful exit. Study the sample letters given in this unit for good beginnings and endings.

Anderson's Department Store
Grove Street at Tenth Avenue
Atlanta, GA 30376-8510
(404) 555-0999

August 14, 19—

Ms. Beth Cameron
7790 Library Lane
New Orleans, LA 70122

Dear Ms. Cameron:

We are delighted to welcome you as one of the Anderson
family of charge customers!

Now that you have completed college and have your first job,
Anderson's is pleased to be a part of so many important
FIRSTS in your life.

Your credit card is enclosed. Please be sure to sign it
right away. It is also a good idea to record your charge
number in a safe place so that you can report the number
easily if the card is lost or stolen.

The enclosed brochure explains the details of your account.
You will notice that your credit extends to $500.

We are enclosing a special invitation to our fall fashion
show for career women, Saturday, August 29.

Cordially yours,

Maribeth Stanhope

Maribeth Stanhope
Vice President

dm

3 Enclosures

Example 7
Letter Granting Credit

Fillmore Box & Carton Company
457 Prince Street
Philadelphia, PA 19182-5312

April 2, 19—

Mr. Drew Woods, Purchasing Manager
Cross and Chase Games Programming
11456 Livingstone Boulevard
Philadelphia, PA 19185-0192

Dear Mr. Woods:

We appreciated your letter of March 1, in which you gave us
your credit references and asked us to establish an account
for you. We are glad to know of your interest in our
products.

There seems to be a point in any business at which taking on
additional credit obligations is likely to cause problems.
Right now, we believe that Cross and Chase is at that point.
Adding to your obligations now might endanger your ability
to meet them.

We are eager to be of service to you on a cash-with-order or
a c.o.d. basis. You then gain the advantage of a discount,
as you can see from the brochure enclosed.

We are sending you a price list and order form. Please
place your c.o.d. or cash order with us for all your
packaging needs.

Sincerely,

Louis Scarpia

Louis Scarpia
Credit Manager

ft

3 Enclosures

Example 8
Letter Refusing Credit

13
Worksheets

1. Fortunato Winery, Santa Domingo, California 94907, has decided to stop making its own labels and to order them from Davina Special Labels, Inc., 113 French Street, San Francisco, California 94133. In May, Ms. Sherry Lawrence must write to the Credit Department at Davina to explain the situation and offer references so that an open account can be established by July, when the present supply of labels will run out. References include Golden Gate Trust Company, 44 Market Street, San Francisco, CA 94186; Dalton & Peterson Glassware, 99 West Gregory Boulevard, Kansas City, Missouri 64139; B & G Computers, Temple Building, 314 Collins Road, Suite 314, Denver, Colorado 80285; Pottleby Spices, Inc., 776 Front Road, San Francisco, California 94132; and Grant & Withers Oil Company, Highland Road at St. Cloud Street, San Francisco, CA 94155.

   Write the letter Ms. Lawrence could send. She is the purchasing agent for Fortunato.

2. Davina Special Labels has a credit manager named David Plimsoll. Mr. Plimsoll asks you to devise a form letter that could be used in obtaining information about the credit reliability of a firm asking for credit. Write the letter, keeping in mind that a form letter doesn't have to sound like a form. Also remember the kind of information for which you need to ask. Write the letter for Mr. Plimsoll's signature.

3. All the references Fortunato gave have had good things to say about the company. Davina was ready to offer the credit requested. On May 29 an article appeared in the *Valley Journal* announcing the plans of Fortunato to merge with another winery, Montresor Vineyards. The management of Davina decided not to go ahead with opening an account for Fortunato—at least until the merger plans are completed. Write the letter to Ms. Lawrence, explaining your company's position.

4. James Woodrow, a recent college graduate who has just started his first job, has applied for credit to Traveler's Oil Company, Lancaster Building, 198 Fulton Way, Suite 99, Houston, TX 77077. He gave as a reference Anderson's Department Store, 554 Elm Street, Houston, TX 77054, where he was employed part-time while he was a student. Traveler's has written to Anderson's, assuming that Woodrow was a credit customer. Write the letter Anderson's credit manager, Walter Thomas, would send to Traveler's, explaining that James Woodrow had been a part-time employee, not a credit customer.

5. Traveler's Credit Manager, Charles Knox, is a kind and understanding person, but Traveler's cannot offer credit to James Woodrow because he has been on his present job for only three weeks. Write the letter to Mr. Woodrow to be signed by Mr. Knox. Woodrow's address is 557 Hillary Heights, Apt. 33, Houston, TX 77033.

Exercises 6–10 are all related to the efforts of E. J. Goleb Pharmaceuticals Inc. to obtain an account with Northeastern Glassware Company. Goleb's address is 94 Madison Avenue, Boston, MA 02145-1243. Northeastern's address is 777 Industrial Plaza, Wilmington, DE 19705.

6. E. J. Goleb must find a new supplier of glass and plastic containers because their previous supplier is going out of business at the end of June. On March 31 you are asked by Ms. Cynthia Marlowe, Purchasing Manager, to write a letter to Northeastern Glassware to apply for an account, giving these references: Hancock National Bank, 77 Bunker Hill Road, Boston, MA 02145-1288; Hecate Chemicals, 809 Beech Street, Baltimore, MD 21278-0211; and Fillmore Box & Carton Company, 457 Prince Street, Philadelphia, PA 19182-5312. Ms. Marlowe will sign the letter.

7. Mr. Edwin Craftwood, Credit Manager of Northeastern Glassware, asks you to write a reply to Goleb's letter of March 31, explaining that the references are being checked and mentioning a new catalog that will be out on April 15, Northeastern's discount plan, and a special inventory system. The letter will be signed by Mr. Craftwood.

8. Write the letter Mr. Edwin Craftwood would send to Fillmore Box & Carton Company, requesting credit information about E. J. Goleb.

9. Write a favorable reply from Fillmore, to be sent over the signature of Mrs. Kenya Delotta, Credit Manager. Goleb always pays within the 30-day period and occasionally is able to take advantage of the 2/10 feature of Fillmore's credit terms.

10. Northeastern has decided to grant credit to Goleb. Write the letter to Ms. Marlowe from Mr. Craftwood, mentioning the booklet you are enclosing that explains the credit terms. Tell her that Mr. John Kim, your Boston representative, will be calling on Goleb in a few days.

Exercises 11–13 are related to the credit application of Ms. Ashley Clarke to Anderson's Department Store. Although Ms. Clarke lives in New Orleans, where Anderson's has several branches, all credit matters are handled through the main office in Atlanta. The address is Grove Street at Tenth Avenue, Atlanta, GA 30376-8510.

11. Ms. Ashley Clarke has been employed for 10 months by Beauregard Securities, 10 Bay Street, New Orleans, LA 70128. She has decided to apply for a credit card with Anderson's Department Store and has submitted as references her landlord, Crescent Properties, 198 Devereaux Road, New Orleans, LA 70198; her bank, First Bank of the Bayou, 56 Broad Street, New Orleans, LA 70155; and Cardinal Furniture, Inc., LaMonde Plaza, New Orleans, LA 70111.

The credit manager of Anderson's is Kassim Doremus. Write the letter Mr. Doremus could send to Ms. Clarke's employer.

12. Mr. Doremus has written to Crescent Properties asking for a reference for Ms. Clarke. Write the letter that Crescent might send, stating that Ms. Clarke is a good tenant who pays her rent on time and holds a three-year lease. She was recommended to Crescent by Dr. George Plummer, one of Ms. Clarke's teachers at a nearby university.

13. The credit check has shown Ms. Clarke to be an acceptable credit risk. Since she has not had a retail account before, Anderson's limits her credit line to $1000. Write the letter Mr. Doremus would send to welcome Ms. Clarke. Refer to an enclosed folder that explains credit terms and to an enclosed description of Anderson's New Orleans stores.

14
Collection Letters

As we have seen, much buying and selling is based on credit. Business firms expect their consumer and commercial customers to use various forms of credit for most purchases.

Businesses that grant credit are sometimes faced with accounts that are not paid when they are due. No one likes having to remind customers to pay, yet few businesses can afford to let bills run without payment. Most customers would prefer to pay bills on time and not receive overdue notices, but sometimes circumstances make on-time payment impossible.

This unit will help you prepare letters used in the collection process. It will also consider the point of view of the customer who cannot pay on time.

The process of collecting money owed begins when a company sends each customer a monthly statement. The statement lists activity on the account for the past month and gives the amount due on the account. Customers normally do not make any payment until they receive a statement. The statement tells the due date for payment and may offer certain discounts for early payment. If the bill is not paid by the due date, a copy of the statement or some other billing notice is sent. A courteous line like this is often included on this second billing notice:

If you have already sent your payment, thank you.

If a bill is still not paid after the second notice is sent, the company begins the collection letter process to persuade the customer to pay as soon as possible.

PURPOSE OF COLLECTION LETTERS

The main purpose of a collection letter is *to get the money owed*. Some methods that might persuade the customer to pay, however, would cause him or her to avoid your company in the future. Keep your second purpose in mind—*to keep the goodwill of the customer*.

After making an attempt to collect the money owed, your company may decide that collecting the money is more important than keeping the customer. Until that point, try to write in such a way that you don't sacrifice future orders for quick payment of a present bill.

THE CUSTOMER'S POSITION

No matter what business position you may hold, you are also a consumer. One of the best ways to write a letter that keeps the goodwill of the customer is to put yourself in the place of the person who owes money. Why does a bill go unpaid?

- A customer may not understand the statement or the terms of the account.
- The customer may be dissatisfied with your product or service.
- A customer may have forgotten that the bill was due, even after receiving a second notice.
- An unexpected lack of money may prevent a customer from paying current bills.
- The customer may have no intention of paying for the product or service purchased on credit.

If the customer doesn't plan to pay, the company will have trouble collecting the debt. In most cases, however, a payment problem can be resolved through effort and understanding on the part of both buyer and seller.

THE WRITER'S ATTITUDE

Write your collection letter with a courteous attitude, just as you would write any business letter. The following guidelines are especially important in collection letters.

Be Positive. Tell your customer about the benefits he or she will receive when payment is sent. Don't focus on what will happen if the bill is *not* paid:

> *Not:* **If we do not receive your check by April 5, we cannot continue providing our fine service.**
>
> *Write:* **If you send your check by April 5, we can continue to give you the fine service you deserve.**

Show Your Willingness to Cooperate. It is better to get part of an amount owed than to get nothing at all. Offer to help your customer plan payment of the bill in small amounts on a specific schedule. Don't insist that your customer find a way to pay on his or her own:

> *Not:* **Please make every effort to pay this bill in full. If this is not possible, send partial payment.**
>
> *Write:* **If you can't send the full amount, why not send your check for $100 today? Then call our billing office and let us help you set up a payment schedule for the remaining amount.**

Sometimes a bill is not paid because the customer has a complaint regarding one or more charges included in the total amount due. Let your customer know you're willing to be reasonable:

> **While we review the charges you consider unfair, won't you send us payment for the remaining items on your statement?**

Be Firm and Direct. Being willing to cooperate doesn't mean letting the customer take advantage of you. Remember that the bill is past due and your customer knows it is past due. The customer also knows the bill should be paid.

Your letter should provide the details of the situation without any vagueness. Your reader can then see clearly why the bill should be paid:

> *Not:* **We filled an order for you earlier this year, and so far we haven't received any payments. Do you know if there is any problem?**
>
> *Write:* **In April you purchased 30 typewriters from us, and we charged your account $9,000. We have not received the payments due in May and June.**

THE COLLECTION LETTER SERIES

The number of letters depends on the amount of money owed, the creditor's need for the money, and the previous dealings between the creditor and debtor.

Letter-writing costs have risen with the increased costs of labor and postage. For most situations, a series of three collection letters will suffice.

The First Letter. In your first letter, try to get the customer to *want* to pay. You might mention something you have to offer and let your reader draw the conclusion that no more charges can be made until the present balance is paid or greatly reduced:

> **We know you want to clear up this bill before the spring sale begins.**
>
> **You can use the enclosed envelope to send us your new order along with your check for the April balance.**

Your first letter should be friendly. Try to convince the customer that your company deserves payment (see Example 1). Give your reader a positive reason for making the payment.

The Second Letter. In the second letter, you want to make the customer aware of the consequences of not paying the bill:

> **You still have time to pay this bill before the lack of payment has an undesirable effect on your credit rating.**

At this stage you still hope you can save the account, and you want the customer to have some hope of saving face (see Example 2).

In some cases, a customer responds to the first letter but does not send payment. The customer may have offered an explanation or a promise to pay soon. If so, mention the customer's response at the beginning of your second collection letter:

> **In your letter of October 9, you said we'd receive your check within a week.**

The Third Letter. When you write the third or final letter, never threaten to do anything your company would not carry out (see Example 3).

Your company might not go to court over every unpaid bill. However, you can tell the customer that an attorney is being consulted without saying the customer will necessarily be sued:

> **Unless we have your check by June 15, we will turn over the matter to our attorney.**

Your third or final letter should set forth clearly the action you are prepared to take if the customer does not fulfill the obligation to pay the money owed.

Example 1
First Collection Letter

WRITING THE LETTER

Dynamic Entrance. The dynamic entrance for a collection letter should summarize the background of the situation. In a first or second letter, the entrance can also show your consideration for the customer and emphasize the quality of your company:

> **We were pleased to receive your first order in May and to welcome you to the family of Frost's satisfied customers.**

> **By now you've had time to see how well our tweed sweaters sell in your store.**

> **We know you've been busy with construction at your plant.**

Even in the final letter of the collection series, remember that you have much to gain by establishing a pleasant attitude at the beginning:

> **We really don't want to lose you as a customer. That's why we're writing one more time to ask for payment of our bill.**

Logical Development. A collection letter should provide all information needed by the customer to send payment promptly. Provide the following information:

- The specific amount due (total and minimum amount due)

- Important dates (date balance was due, date of earlier payments, date items charged)

- Description of products or service

- Envelope for sending payment (mention enclosure in letter)

Whitepage & Blankley Stationers
777 Allanby Road
Denmark, NC 27890

September 12, 19--

Mr. Willard Post, President
Post & Graham Furnace Company
44 Hightower Road
Chicago, IL 60698-9451

Dear Mr. Post

As I mentioned in my letter of August 10, we were delighted
to be able to supply personalized notepads and pencils for
your sales meeting back in July. The Post & Graham meeting
was a great success.

In my letter of August 10, I also explained that we hadn't
received your check for the $760 remaining on your bill.
Your deposit of $1,200 was made on June 30. When I spoke
with you on the telephone the day of the meeting, July 7,
you told me we could expect to receive the balance of your
payment by the first of August. We still have not received
your final payment.

There is still time to send your check before this overdue
account affects your credit standing. Won't you please use
the enclosed postage-paid envelope and send us your check
for $760 today.

Very truly yours

Basil Bass

Basil Bass, Assistant Director

qj

Enclosure

Example 2
Second Collection Letter

Pandora Security, Inc.
14 Woodridge Avenue
Scotia, Missouri 64551

August 12, 19--

Mr. Owen Lee
Calico Arms Apartments
444 West Thrailkill Road
Scotia, MO 64553

Dear Mr. Lee:

We have been trying to reach your office by telephone, but
there has been no answer. We are concerned that we've had no
replies to any of our messages about the work we did for you
at your Calico Arms building last March.

You will recall that you were required by City Ordinance
3345A to install secure deadbolt locks on all the apartments
in your building. We agreed to sell and install the 45 locks
for $40 each. You were concerned about having the work
completed before the ordinance went into effect on March 31,
and we completed the work on time.

We sent you a statement on April 10, showing the balance of
$1,800. A second statement on May 10 contained a reminder
that the bill was overdue. Since then, we have written you
on June 1 and on July 8. Our messages have brought no
response from you.

Unless we have your check by August 23, we'll turn the matter over to our attorney. That step is one we'd prefer not to
take. All you need to do to avoid this embarrassment is to
use the enclosed envelope to send us your check for $1,800.

Sincerely yours,

MacGregor M. Grimes

MacGregor M. Grimes
Credit Manager

mbb

Enclosure

Example 3
Last Collection Letter in Series

This information makes it easier for the customer to
pay, and the customer also has an envelope for
sending the check.

Graceful Exit. In a collection letter, your final words
should be brief and direct. You have already told the
reader what you want, and you have made your attitude clear—friendly, firm, or final. In your closing
sentence, you can make clear what you expect from
the reader:

> **Won't you use the enclosed envelope to send
> us your check today.**

> **Only your prompt action can prevent the
> involvement of our legal staff in this matter.**

Be sure your closing sentence is consistent in fact
and tone with the rest of your letter. Don't introduce
a new fact or suggestion in the last paragraph.

THE ONE WHO OWES MONEY

For customers with debts they cannot pay, a collection letter is an embarrassment that tells them what
they already know. Any consumer or company can
have temporary cash flow problems.

If you cannot pay a bill on time, tell your creditor
why you cannot pay the bill and let the creditor
know when you expect to be able to pay (also see
Example 4):

The bad weather this spring has
seriously limited our earnings. I know
the situation will improve by summer.
In the meantime, we are unable to pay
the $3,200 due on our account on May 1.
We are enclosing our check for $1,000.
If you can be patient with us for the
next few weeks, we think we can pay the
balance on our account by June 15.

```
1515 Murray Lane
Chicago, IL 60651
July 15, 19--


Ms. Nicole Ortiz
Consumer Credit Manager
Topline Credit Company
1800 Penn Road
Philadelphia, PA 19182-0180

Dear Ms. Ortiz

I just received your letter of July 10, in which you reminded
me that my credit account with your company is three months
overdue and has a balance of $2,900.

In March I used my account to pay for a trip to Puerto Rico.
I was employed by the J & B Coffee Company in the auditing
department, and I thought my employment would continue
indefinitely.

Since that time, however, the J & B Coffee Company has gone
bankrupt. When I returned from Puerto Rico on April 12, I was
given two weeks' notice and promised two weeks' pay. I have
not received the promised pay. During the past three months
I have been unemployed.

I have recently obtained a position with the Chicago branch
of Fillmore Box and Carton Company, and I can begin to pay
the balance on my account with you.

If you can be patient with me a little longer, I'll send a
check for $400 on August 1, and I'll make monthly payments of
at least that amount until I have paid my debt.

I appreciate your help as I recover from this financial
setback.

Sincerely

Raoul Fremont

Raoul Fremont
```

Example 4
Response to Collection Letter

LANGUAGE AND TONE

A few guidelines will help you keep a courteous, natural tone in collection letters.

Don't Be Sarcastic. Never insult a customer with sarcasm, especially in a collection letter. Always show a positive attitude:

> *Not:* **We know you have some good excuse for not paying, but you haven't let us in on it yet.**
>
> *Write:* **We hope you will do your best to pay this bill before May 3.**

Don't Be Harsh. Even in a final collection letter, simply state the circumstances without being judgmental:

> *Not:* **Surely you have been in business long enough to know the consequences of unpaid bills.**
>
> *Write:* **We regret that we must refer the matter to our attorney if you do not send payment for this bill.**

Don't Use Worn-Out or Wordy Expressions. Certain expressions have been used so often they have lost their meaning. Expressions that can be used in other situations may sound insincere in a collection letter:

> *Not:* **We must receive the check on or before June 1.**
>
> *Write:* **We must receive the check by June 1.**

> *Not:* **Please send your check now if at all possible.**
>
> *Write:* **Please send your check now if possible.**

Never write "This is a friendly reminder." No matter what the writer may think, this expression does not sound friendly and is likely to provoke an unfriendly response from the reader.

Don't Be Too Formal. You can encourage cooperation from the customer by using wording that sounds natural and relaxed. Avoid formal expressions:

> *Not:* **No payment has yet been received.**
>
> *Write:* **We have not received your payment.**

> *Not:* **Your cooperation in this matter will be greatly appreciated.**
>
> *Write:* **We'll be grateful for your cooperation.**

A well-written collection letter will save time, money, and effort. When your customer pays before there are hard feelings, harsh words, or threats of unpleasantness, the smooth flow of business transactions can continue.

14
Worksheets

1. You are employed in the credit department of the Yardley Landscape Service, 456 West River Road, Paducah, KY 42233. Your company provided the initial landscaping for a new building belonging to Girardeau Dairy Products, 444 Lincoln Street, Sandtown, KY 43111. The contract included these services:

Initial landscaping **$26,500**

One year's service—lawn and shrubbery . . **23,400**
   (payable monthly, $1,950 per month)

Seasonal plantings
   (billed when provided)

You received the initial payment of $26,500 on April 23, shortly after the work was completed. One monthly payment was made on May 14. It is now August 2, and no other payments have been made.

A. Write a series of three letters suitable for trying to collect this bill. Date them one month apart, beginning with August 2. Mrs. Mary Fleetfoot is the building and grounds superintendent at Girardeau.

B. Write a memo to your Operations Manager, George Davidson, telling him to suspend service to Girardeau on October 10.

2. You are a credit trainee for Whitepage & Blankley Stationers, 777 Allanby Road, Denmark, NC 27790. The credit manager, Ms. Arden Domingo, has asked you to begin a review of the accounts of all customers from whom orders are received in the current month of your training, with the idea of writing letters to those whose accounts are overdue.

The Gillis Chair Company, 344 Industrial Park Road, Denmark, NC 27777, has sent an order for 20 reams of letterheads. You find that the last order from that company, for billheads and memo sheets, was dated three months ago. It totaled $356.50, and it has not been paid.

A. Write the first letter you would send to Gillis.

B. Write the memo you would send to Ms. Domingo. Tell her what action you have taken, tell her you are enclosing a copy of the letter, and ask for suggestions.

3. Kimberley & Farini Photographers specializes in wedding and portrait photography. A deposit of $150 is required, to be applied toward the cost of the finished photographs. Kimberley & Farini offers a selection of proofs within a week of the photography and finished photos ten days later. Payment in full is expected when the photos are picked up.

A. Write a series of three letters that could be used as guidelines or forms for collecting consumer accounts when the customer has not picked up or paid for the finished work.

The letters will be signed by Bob Greystone, Credit Manager. The address of Kimberley & Farini Photographers is 9942 West Silver Road, Denver, CO 80213.

B. Using the form you created in Part A, prepare the letter you would send on May 27 to Mr. and Mrs. Glenn Wolff, whose wedding Kimberley & Farini photographed on April 12. The selections were made from proofs on April 20, and you called the Wolffs on April 27 to tell them their pictures were ready. They promised to pick them up before May 1, but they have not done so.

C. Mrs. Lee Wardell has brought her daughter Susan to Kimberley & Farini to be photographed every three months during Susan's first year. The photographs have been well received, and Mrs. Wardell has always paid for the work promptly, a total so far of $1,300.

The most recent photographs were taken on October 1, Susan's second birthday. Selections were made from proofs on October 6, and on October 14 you notified Mrs. Wardell that the pictures were ready. Mrs. Wardell has not picked up her pictures. Using the form you created in Part A, write the letter you would write to Mrs. Wardell on November 15.

4. The Hillside Community Theater, Parkside Place and Newton Road, Hillside, Virginia 22768, had a fund-raising campaign in June. Pledges were made, and statements of the pledges were sent to all those who didn't pay at once. Now, in September, Donald Lee of the theater's staff is trying to collect the unpaid pledges. Write the letter he would send to Miss Audrey Soong, 558 North Devlin Road, Willington, Virginia 22478. Her pledge was for $40.

5. Your company is Aaron Calculators, 987 McGee Street, Kansas City, Missouri 64198-2218. Shortly after you made a purchase of furnishings for your new office, totaling $4,380, a patent dispute held up the manufacture of the calculators you sell and caused a serious financial problem. You have not been able to pay the $4,380 you owe. The dispute has been settled, and manufacturing has resumed.

Write a letter to Frost & Dickinson Office Furniture, 988 Wornall Road, Kansas City, Missouri 64551, explaining that you are aware that your bill is a month overdue and that it will be another month before you can make any payment.

15
Adjustment Requests

Whenever we transact any kind of business, we hope everyone involved will be satisfied with the outcome. We all know, however, that many things can go wrong in business transactions.

When customers are not pleased with a product or service, they should let the seller know. A customer may sometimes request an adjustment even when a product or service is exactly what it was described to be. A seller wants to know if customers are dissatisfied. Commercial customers and consumers use similar methods to get a satisfactory response to their adjustment requests.

This unit will help you write effective adjustment requests. Examining the reasons for dissatisfaction and planning how to explain those reasons carefully will lead to letters that get the response desired.

REASONS FOR ADJUSTMENT REQUESTS

Situations that require an adjustment request occur frequently.

Unreasonable Delay in Delivery. Delay in delivery is one of the most frequent reasons for dissatisfaction, especially among consumers. Many sellers specify that delivery will take six to eight weeks. After more than eight weeks have passed, a customer should request an explanation (see Example 1).

Mistake in an Order. The buyer or the seller may have made a mistake in an order. The customer may be dissatisfied with the seller because of the seller's mistake, or the customer may be dissatisfied because he or she made a mistake in ordering. With computerized ordering procedures, both buyers and sellers can sometimes cause problems by noting numbers incorrectly (see Example 2).

Item Different from What Was Expected. The order may be filled correctly, but the customer may then realize that he or she expected something different. A customer cannot always determine exact size, color, or style from a description in a catalog. An item might be what you ordered but might be different from what you expected (see Example 3).

Damaged or Nonfunctioning Merchandise. Products may be damaged in shipment, or they may not operate properly (see Example 4).

Unsatisfactory Service. A service such as equipment repair may not be satisfactory. A problem may recur too soon after the seller was supposed to have corrected it (see Example 5).

Undesirable Performance of an Employee. Customers have a right to be treated with courtesy and consideration. Carelessness, rudeness, and incompetence can lead to an adjustment request (see Example 6).

MAKING ADJUSTMENT REQUESTS

Few people find it useful to write or speak in anger, yet almost all of us have a tendency to do both. We want the temporary satisfaction of saying "I guess I told *them*." For getting good results in the long run, however, anger is not usually effective. The following techniques will help you get the results you want.

1. Make the request in writing whenever possible. If you have an emergency situation, such as a leaking roof one day after the roof has been repaired, you should make your adjustment request over the telephone. Under other circumstances, however, a written request is more effective than a request made by telephone. Your letter gives the seller an opportunity to check the facts. A letter also gives the customer an opportunity to put the problem and complaint on record.

3214 Albany Road
Boston, MA 02189
August 29, 19—

Executive Tips
379 West Fordham Avenue
Des Moines, Iowa 50388

Gentlemen:

I sent my subscription for Executive Tips in May, and I
included my check for $18.50.

I understand that there is often a delay in beginning subscriptions, and I was prepared to wait the six to eight
weeks specified in your advertisement. My check was dated
May 16, and it cleared in my June statement. As I am sure
you realize, more than eight weeks have passed. If I had
followed my usual procedure of paying for a subscription
only after I receive the first copy, I could simply forget
about Executive Tips until I hear from you.

Please look into the problem and find out why the magazines
are not reaching me. If there is a reason why you cannot
send the magazine, please use the enclosed envelope to let
me know and to refund the money I have sent you——$18.50.

Sincerely,

Lucille Dobey

Mrs. Lucille Dobey

Enclosure

Example 1
Adjustment Request After Unreasonable Delay

2. Know your rights. Buyers have certain important rights. Read the guarantee or warranty on a product. Find out if you have paid in full for the product or service. Check to see whether the credit card company has recorded the charge, or verify that your check has cleared the bank.

3. Be clear when you explain. If you have to tell a long story, organize the facts to help the reader follow the connections.

4. Be truthful. If you made a mistake, admit it. Admitting that you made a mistake in ordering an item may get better results than a suggestion that the seller made a mistake.

5. Give complete details. Give all the facts the seller needs to make the adjustment you want. Provide an order number, stock numbers, date ordered and received, and all addresses needed.

6. Write with a positive attitude. You can show your cooperative attitude by having a sense of humor about the situation. Your letter doesn't have to begin with a joke, but it should show that you can see the lighter side of your problem. An informal style is likely to have a good effect on your reader.

7. If you are asking a favor, say so. Recognize the difference between an adjustment the seller should feel obligated to make and one that would be a favor to you. If you are asking a favor, tell the reader you realize it is a favor.

8. Give a reason for granting your request. Whenever you can, give your reader a reason for wanting to grant your request. Your future business is a good incentive for the company to try to accommodate you.

9. Suggest a reasonable adjustment, if possible. Sometimes a customer can explain the adjustment that should be made. At other times a customer does not know every solution possible and should let the seller suggest an adjustment.

10. Focus on resolving the problem. Keep in mind that your purpose is to obtain a satisfactory resolution of the difficulty. There is much to be gained by an attitude of patience and willingness to cooperate, even when you really do not feel patient or cooperative.

Whitepage & Blankley Stationers
777 Allanby Road
Denmark, NC 27890

April 14, 19—

Mr. Raymond Morin
Richmond Computers and Calculators
4498 Jonesboro Road
Atlanta, GA 30365-3211

Dear Mr. Morin:

Some problems have arisen with the order we received from you on April 10. I hope you can help us.

We ordered 16 disks, Stock No. 199. I am attaching a copy of the original order. We received 19 disks, Stock No. 66, which are also listed on the invoice that came with the order. We cannot use these disks with our equipment.

Please send the correct order as soon as possible and credit our account for the 19 units of Stock No. 66, which we are returning to you by insured mail. We need the correct disks by April 23.

Please call me at (206) 555-0912 if there are any problems with this order. I'll have to make some other arrangements if your company cannot fill the order as sent.

Very truly yours,

Calvin Branch

Calvin Branch
Purchasing Agent

Enclosure

Example 2
Adjustment Request After Mistake in Order

Dynamic Entrance. In the first sentence of your adjustment request, you want to persuade your reader to take an interest in your situation. If you can obtain the name of the appropriate person in the company, address your letter to that person. Make your appeal directly to him or her:

> **I think you can help resolve the problem that arose when we ordered filters last month.**

> **I can hardly believe the number of problems we've had with the equipment we bought from you last month. I hope you can help straighten things out.**

Save the details for a later paragraph, but make clear the kind of situation that has led to your adjustment request.

```
1962 Broadway
New York, NY 10074
June 14, 19--


Bagley's Shop
167 Water Street
Brooklyn, NY 11208

Gentlemen:

It's never easy to admit you've made a mistake, but I have
no choice! The color of the towels I received on my last
order from you simply will not do--but they are the color I
ordered.

I was ordering from your catalog of Spring 19--, and the
description of "angel blue" sounded just right for the new
bath just added to my apartment. I didn't realize there
would be so much green in this shade.

I know you sent me just what I ordered, but I cannot use
these towels. May I please return them in exchange for
"angel white," which shouldn't cause any difficulties?

As soon as I hear from you, I'll send these towels back and
look for the shipment of six sets of "angel white" in the
Grecian pattern.

Sincerely,

Gera Lopez

Ms. Gera Lopez
```

Example 3
Adjustment Request for a Favor

Logical Development. To organize your explanation, make an outline of the items you intend to include in an adjustment request. Be consistent. Avoid going back and forth between one idea and another.

A good plan for development of an adjustment letter would be this:

- Background

- Problem

- Suggested solution

Graceful Exit. Don't come to an abrupt halt after you explain what has happened and what you suggest as a remedy. Use your final paragraph to emphasize your request for a solution:

> **May I hear from you by January 8 to determine a date for your roofers to return to fix our roof.**
>
> **I'm sure you'll do your best to resolve this problem as soon as possible.**

Sometimes you can conclude by suggesting that future business with the company depends on the successful resolution of the present problem:

> **We'll be making plans for our June banquet next week. I hope you can resolve this billing problem before we make our decisions about the banquet location.**

PROBLEMS WITHIN A COMPANY

Problems that arise within a business may require a kind of adjustment request. Usually a company has a formal procedure for handling serious difficulties that arise among employees. Once in a while, however, a problem can be solved before it has to be handled "officially." In these cases, a memo can point out unsatisfactory or unacceptable conditions or performance:

```
TO:       Chris Norris

FROM:     Paul Davenport

DATE:     May 16, 19--

SUBJECT:  Late Arrival


I don't want to be unreasonable about punc-
tuality during the current transportation
strike, but I am asking your cooperation in
regard to the time of your arrival from now on.
The staff in this department has an excellent
record within the company, and I believe you'll
want to do your part to keep it that way. Please
understand that lateness of more than ten
minutes could result in the loss of pay at the
end of the week.
```

GETTING HELP

A seller may not respond in a reasonable way when a customer requests an adjustment. If the seller does not respond, you can seek help from consumer organizations.

Some consumers routinely send copies of adjustment requests to consumer rights organizations or agencies. You will probably want to postpone this step until you give the seller a chance to solve the problem.

Fillmore Box & Carton Company
457 Prince Street
Philadelphia, PA 19182-5312
(215) 555-4111

October 14, 19—

Mr. Paul Lee, Customer Service Agent
B & G Computers
998 Spruce Street
Baltimore, MD 21290-5417

Dear Mr. Lee:

When we bought our new Model 007 computer from you in June, your sales representative, Ms. Lola Ahmed, assured us that we would always get prompt service. I hope we can count on that assurance.

As I told you on the telephone this morning, our computer is not working. Our orders are accumulating because we can't fill them without the aid of computer information. We are losing money because of delays in sending our orders.

In our telephone conversation today, you said you could not send anyone to make repairs until October 28. During the two-week interval, I estimate that we will lose $12,900 in orders that cannot be filled.

I believe you have an obligation either to send someone to make the repairs immediately or to absorb the loss that Fillmore will suffer as a result of the delay.

Please call to let me know how soon you can send someone to do the work needed.

Very truly yours,

John Quimby
Vice President

dh

Example 4
Adjustment Request for Repair

Fillmore Box & Carton Company
457 Prince Street
Philadelphia, PA 19182-5312
(215) 555-4111

November 1, 19—

Mr. Paul Lee, Customer Service Agent
B & G Computers
998 Spruce Street
Baltimore, MD 21290-5417

Dear Mr. Lee:

Once more I have to ask your help in getting service for our Model 007. I appreciated your arranging for Mr. Richard Trilby to come October 16, and I was glad he could make the repairs necessary.

That was only two weeks ago. Yesterday the machine stopped working again. I was unable to reach you by telephone and we haven't been able to find the problem.

Please see that Mr. Trilby or some member of his staff gets to us by November 5. Once more I remind you that Fillmore loses money when our orders are delayed, and I assure you that I consider B & G obligated to absorb the loss.

Unless I have spoken with you by the time this reaches you, please call me immediately. I need to know when we can expect Mr. Trilby.

Sincerely yours,

John Quimby
Vice President

dh

Example 5
Adjustment Request After Inadequate Repair

If you do ask for outside advice or intervention, be sure that you give the details fairly. Show that you want to resolve a problem, not get revenge or punish a particular seller.

Your local telephone book provides information on consumer organizations in your area. Organizations such as the Better Business Bureau and your local chamber of commerce do not have the authority to force a company to cooperate, but they can offer suggestions about how to proceed.

Most states, cities, and counties have government offices that focus on consumer problems or complaints. Many communities also have active volunteer consumer groups.

On the national level, various agencies help consumers and other buyers. Check an almanac (see Unit 5) for addresses and exact names of organizations like the Department of Transportation, the Federal Trade Commission, the Department of Agriculture, the Food and Drug Administration, and the Consumer Products Safety Commission.

In any request for an adjustment, remember that reliable businesses want to keep their customers. Don't create a situation in which no one wants to cooperate. Resist the temptation to be angry or sarcastic. Always write as though you take the seller's good faith for granted, unless you have a clear reason to believe otherwise.

Wiggins Electronics
12 Wakefield Road
Kansas City, Missouri 64102-9321

January 14, 19--

Mr. Gerard DeValle
Chimney Corner Inn
11 Sherwood Lane
Brookfield, MO 64211

Dear Mr. DeValle:

Ever since you opened Chimney Corner, all of us at Wiggins
have thought it the ideal spot for a quiet dinner not too
far from town. We've been impressed with the food and the
service, and we have often had company dinners there. I
considered not mentioning the poor service we received
recently, but I believe you would want to know about it.

On December 15 I brought three clients to the Chimney Corner
for dinner. The evening was a disaster from the beginning.

We waited almost an hour before a waiter took our orders.
After the salad was finished, I noticed that one of my
guests lacked a fork for the next course. When I asked the
waiter for another fork, he brought back the one from the
salad course.

That same waiter (Walter) objected when I told him we needed
a clean fork. When he brought the clean one, he spilled a
glass of wine on me. He then disappeared for the rest of
the evening.

I know you will understand my reluctance to bring other
guests to your restaurant. I hope you can restore your
former reliable service; we need good restaurants.

Sincerely,

Jordan Wiggins

Jordan Wiggins, Manager

Example 6
Adjustment Request Describing
Undesirable Performance

136

15
Worksheets

1. Melissa Durgan, of the Grant Advertising Agency, 441 Madison Avenue, New York, NY 10065-7782, has just received an order shipped to her by Bixby Publishers, 13322 North Stetson Street, Minneapolis, Minnesota 55467. She had ordered 16 diaries at $4.50 each, 16 calendars at $3.00 each, and 8 copies of *Bixby Standard Dictionary* at $14.00 each. The order was filled correctly except that the diaries were for the current year instead of the coming year, as Ms. Durgan had specified. She placed the order on October 15 and received the shipment on November 8. She wants the calendars and the diaries as holiday gifts for clients. Write the letter she would send to Bixby.

2. Ned Carnaby is your supervisor at Dakin Travel Agency, 61 Bay Road, Miami, Florida 33111-9834. When he was trying to reach a customer, Jed Wilkes, he got an answering service. When Mr. Carnaby asked when Mr. Wilkes would be available, the operator said, "How should I know?" The answering service is the same one used by Dakin—Callamighty, 75 Lincoln Highway, Miami, Florida 33223. Write a letter to the answering service for Mr. Carnaby's signature.

3. A toy store, Games and Play, is located at 45 South Mall, Tulsa, Oklahoma 74044. On December 4 the store received a shipment of stuffed animals called Woodland Critters from Hansel's Toys, 778 Gresham Road, Denver, Colorado 80203. The shipment was delivered by Marks & Blotz Express Company, whose local address is 5678 Highway 44, Tulsa, Oklahoma 74099. The shipment consisted of six dozen toys, packed one dozen to a carton. Three of the cartons showed water damage. Mr. Luis Valdez refused to accept those three from the express company. The driver said that he would take them to the Marks & Blotz warehouse but that Mr. Valdez would have to write to the shipper to explain what had happened.

Write the letter, supplying any additional information needed. Send a copy to the express company.

4. Donald Cortez of Cortez Industries is responsible for arranging the moving procedures when people in his company are transferred. Nomad Van Lines, the company he most often uses, has branches all around the country. Recently he tried to make arrangements with the Washington, D.C., branch to handle the move of his brother George from Washington to Roanoke, Virginia. His brother has a small number of possessions, has just finished college, and is about to begin his first job. When Mr. Cortez receives the following letter, he asks you to write to Nomad's regional office at 445 Vincent Street, Atlanta, GA 30399. Address the letter to Mrs. Jean Caruso, Customer Service Representative, with whom Mr. Cortez has had much correspondence in the past. Enclose a copy of this letter. Tell Mrs. Caruso you are enclosing a copy of the letter from Mr. Carry.

NOMAD VAN LINES
457 Ninth Street, N.W.
Washington, DC 20005

January 23, 19--

Mr. Donald Cortez
1988 West River Road, N.W.
Washington, DC 20098

Dear Mr. Cortez:

We have received you're request for information about the move you are going to make in March. You have'nt given us enough information about it, and we dont know what you expect us to do.

It sounds like you dont have much furniture to be moved and we're not sure we want to be bothered. We handle the pristigeous moves of people like senators and congressmen and other important people who move in and out of Washington.

Give us some more information and we'll see about helping you if it looks important for us to take it on. We have to reserve our facilities for important people, I know you understand.

Yours truly

G. C. Carry

G. C. Carry, Agent

5. Rewrite this poor adjustment letter.

```
115 King's Road
Hartley, Minnesota 55321
February 20, 19--
```

```
Corona Air Lines
8 University Plaza
Minneapolis, MN 55467
```

```
Gentlemen?
```

```
I don't know whether the people in your
office are gentlemen or not, but the
employees I ran into on my latest flight
were not. I don't know how you people can
stay in business if you run an airline like
that.
```

```
I demand a refund of the $430 I paid for
first-class service because there certainly
wasn't any service, first-class or
otherwise. After we boarded the plane, we
had to sit for ONE HOUR AND THIRTY-FIVE
MINUTES before takeoff. No one would tell
us why we were waiting, and no one would
let us get off to wait in a more
comfortable place. When I tried to get them
to notify my Chicago office of the delay,
they just said they couldn't do anything
about it. I missed an important meeting and
lost money.
```

```
When we finally took off, the girls said
the coffee machine wasn't working and we
never got any coffee during the whole
flight. The passengers were all just as mad
as I am about the way everything was
handled and we were three hours late
getting to Chicago.
```

```
Let me hear from you about this. Your
company is really not much good and I'm not
going to take such treatment.
```

```
Very truly yours

Frank Bellamy
Frank Bellamy
```

6. In June, Hector & Sebastian, Inc., 835 Willow Street, Baltimore, MD 21278-6543, ordered 10,000 letterheads from Whitepage & Blankley Stationers, 777 Allanby Road, Denmark, NC 27890. To be sure that the new letterheads were accurately printed, Beth Chamberlain of Hector & Sebastian sent a copy of the old letterhead, which was printed by a company no longer in business. Here is how the old letterhead looked:

HECTOR & SEBASTIAN, INC.
835 Willow Street
Baltimore, MD 21278-6543
(301) 555-4985

When the new letterheads arrived, this is what Miss Chamberlain saw:

HECTOR AND SEBASTIAN INCORPORATED
835 Willow Street
Baltimore, MD 21278-6543
(310) 55504895

Write the letter Miss Chamberlain would send to Whitepage & Blankley. Date the letter July 18.

7. Edgar Ashton, Treasurer of Scottish Products, with offices at 900 Lexington Avenue, New York, NY 10076-0543, has noticed that the coatroom reserved for guests and visitors is usually full of coats, although the company doesn't always have visitors. He checked and learned that the employees of the Packing Department are using that coatroom, rather than the one designated for them, because it is closer to the Packing Department. Write a memo from Mr. Ashton to the members of the Packing Department, asking that they use the appropriate coatroom.

8. Select some situation in your own life about which you would like to write a letter of complaint. Follow the principles of a good adjustment letter and write a letter that you think would get results.

9. For many years Dingley & Alwich, Fine Caterers, has been ordering smoked oysters from Chosan Importers, 702 Front Street, New York, NY 10089. The most recent order, for ten cases, was placed on October 2. On November 2, Joan MacPherson realizes that the order has not been received and that there has also been no acknowledgment of it. Write the letter she would send. This product is an important part of Dingley & Alwich's line. The address of Dingley & Alwich is 445 West Trinity Road, Chicago, IL 60698-9941.

10. Almost a year ago, Mr. Abner Collini of the Fillmore Box & Carton Company ordered a chair for his office from Frost and Dickinson Office Furniture, 1361 Old Salem Highway, Hartford, CT 06298. The chair was delivered promptly and was just what Mr. Collini had ordered—an easy chair upholstered in rust leather. A few weeks ago a visitor to Mr. Collini's office said that the chair was the only item in the office that was out of style. Mr. Collini has decided that he wants to return the chair, for which the company paid $298. Write the letter he would send. Fillmore's address is 457 Prince Street, Philadelphia, PA 19182-5312.

11. The Childcare Center at Inverness Mills has been in operation for almost a year. In general, the employees who have been bringing their children to the center have been pleased with the service. Recently, however, employees have arrived as usual at 7:45 a.m. to leave their children and found that the childcare center staff is not arriving until after 8:00. The parents are not able to leave their children until the center is open, and therefore they are late arriving at their own work areas in the company.

Employees in the Accounting Department begin their work day at 8:00 a.m., the earliest of any workers at Inverness. Accountants Eva Gonzales, Bob Russo, Andy Kim, and Hilary Perry have spoken to the childcare staff members to no avail and have decided to bring the matter to the attention of company management.

Andy Kim has agreed to serve as the correspondent to express the group's dissatisfaction about the situation. The head of the Accounting Department, Mrs. Laura Putnam, is trying to be patient, but these four workers are a major part of her staff.

Write the memo Mr. Kim would send to Ruth Pollone, Vice President of Human Resources.

12. Adrian Beecham is vice president of sales for the Cendrix Insurance Company. In October he ordered 30 leather attache cases from Baumgartner Leather Goods, 887 Grafton Parkway, Simonsville, NJ 07818. The cases cost $115 each. Twenty-six of the cases were used as Christmas gifts for the sales representatives in the Winchester, Virginia, sales district.

Two weeks after Christmas, Mr. Beecham learned that the lock didn't work on one of the cases. He also discovered that the handles broke on four cases after only two days' use.

Mr. Beecham followed up on the other 21 cases and learned that only 12 of them were totally without flaws.

Write the letter Mr. Beecham would send to Esteban Fiori, sales manager for Baumgartner. Mr. Beecham would like to return all 30 of the cases for a refund. The address of Cendrix is 99 Lakeview Road, Winchester, Virginia 22601.

13. On March 2, while Linda Travers was visiting Chicago, she bought four silver trays from Silver Outlets Incorporated, 2000 State Street, Chicago, IL 60699.

The trays were priced at $111 each, including tax. Ms. Travers asked that the trays be charged to her SOFO credit card and shipped to her home, 55 Buckingham Drive, Kansas City, MO 64101. Ms. Iris Neyto of Silver Outlets promised to take care of the matter personally and told Ms. Travers that the trays should reach her within two weeks.

The credit card statement arrived on March 15, and Ms. Travers paid the charge of $444 on March 20. On April 2 Ms. Travers had not received the trays. She telephoned Silver Outlets and spoke with Ms. Neyto, who assured her that the trays had been shipped and would reach Kansas City in a few days.

The trays did not arrive. Write the letter Ms. Travers would send on April 24 to Max Millina, president of Silver Outlets. She would also send a copy of her letter to the Illinois Consumer Service Department, State Office Building, Springfield, IL 62706. She would like to receive the trays before May 3. If not, she expects a refund of the money she has paid.

16
Adjustment Responses

"The customer is always right." In the past that idea has expressed the official attitude of most businesses. Today businesses have grown more cautious, customers have grown more critical of services and products, and the "rightness" of the customer is not always taken for granted. Still, most businesses find that building goodwill is worth the time and effort involved. The customer may not always be right, but the customer is vital to the success of any business.

Adjustment responses will vary with circumstances. No company can follow a single policy of "no adjustments" or allow a policy of "all adjustments." Once a company decides *what* to do, the writer must decide *how* to communicate the information.

This unit will help you write responses to the requests for adjustments that a company is likely to receive.

Whenever a company receives a letter asking for an adjustment, making a claim, or expressing dissatisfaction with a product or service, someone must decide how to reply. In larger companies, a customer service department makes the decision. In smaller companies, certain people are authorized to make adjustment decisions.

Adjustment requests fall into three categories, no matter what the size of the company. Before you prepare an adjustment letter, identify the category of the request to help you respond properly.

Reasonable Requests. Some adjustment requests are reasonable. The customer may not have received the items ordered. There may have been a long delay in filling the order. The customer may have been inconvenienced by an employee.

Unreasonable Requests. The customer may be asking you to allow something that is unfair to your company and to other customers. The customer is then making a claim for something to which he or she is clearly not entitled.

Favors to the Customer. The customer wants something that you could either grant or refuse with good reason.

REASONABLE REQUESTS

When a customer writes or calls to explain that something has not measured up to expectations, the seller normally wants to resolve the problem. An article may be the wrong color, the wrong size, or in some way not what the customer ordered. The best thing the seller can do is be sure the right article is on its way as quickly as possible.

Since an adjustment to a reasonable request is definitely going to be made, the response letter should be cordial and gracious (see Example 1). The customer was right, and you, as the seller, are making amends for a mistake. You have much to gain by sending a pleasant response:

Not: **We sent you the wrong disks, as you said. Please return them and we'll send you what you ordered.**

Write: **We are glad you noticed the error in time enough for us to take care of it. We're sending the right disks in today's mail. We'll appreciate your returning the other ones by express collect.**

Diamond Cardigans
1223 Bridgewater Creek Road
Denver, Colorado 80233

March 1, 19——

Mr. Gregory Pounds
Sportswear Buyer
Anderson's Department Store
Grove Street at Tenth Avenue
Atlanta, GA 30376-8510

Dear Mr. Pounds:

You are absolutely right! The shipment you received from us
on February 9 was short two dozen men's golf sweaters.

I'm glad to know that the rest of the order was shipped
correctly. The carton containing the golf sweaters had been
set aside for special labeling, and we shipped the larger
package without adding the smaller one.

We shipped the sweaters today by Priority Mail. You should
have them within a day or two. We are sorry about the mix-
up. Thank you for letting us know about it so promptly.

We are planning to bring out a new line of children's
sweaters in time for the fall trade. I'm enclosing a
brochure so that you can begin planning your order.

Sincerely yours,

Karen Valdez

Ms. Karen Valdez

tk

Enclosure

Example 1
Adjustment Response to Correct a Seller Error

When there is a long delay in filling an order, an acknowledgment letter from the seller explaining the delay can often ease the situation (see Example 2). Once the customer has written to ask about an order, your response should give an idea of when to expect the order:

> *Not:* **There has been a delay in shipment. We'll get to your order as soon as we can.**
>
> *Write:* **We apologize for the delay in shipping your order. You should receive it by March 15.**

Sometimes employees behave in a way that is embarrassing to the company. At other times, customers have an unrealistic idea of what to expect from company employees. A customer who writes to complain about the language or behavior of an employee usually does not expect anything to be done to the employee. Your response should normally be just an apology for what happened:

> **We know how frustrating it must have been for you to receive such casual treatment. We are sorry you were inconvenienced.**

Within your company, a supervisor would probably investigate the situation and take steps to see that discourteous or negligent behavior did not continue. It is not necessary to tell your customer what procedures your company follows (see Example 3).

UNREASONABLE REQUESTS

Sometimes a customer wants special treatment or asks for a privilege that your company cannot allow. You want to maintain good relations with this customer, even though you cannot grant the customer's request (see Examples 4 and 5). How do you say "no" without offending the customer?

No matter how tempting it may be, don't mention *company policy*. Even if company policy *is* the reason for your refusal, you will make a better impression by avoiding these words completely:

> *Not:* **It is against our company policy to make such refunds.**
>
> *Write:* **We are not able to make such refunds.**

Whenever possible, say what you *can* do even when you must say what you *can't* do:

> *Not:* **We make these decisions early in the year, and your request came in too late.**
>
> *Write:* **Even though our list is already complete for this year, we have put your name on our list for next year.**

Don't tell your customer that the problem has never happened before. No one is ever comforted by the idea that a problem is unique. This idea makes most people feel especially mistreated: "Why did this happen only to me and to my order?"

Don't tell your customer that no one else has complained. The customer does not want to feel as if he or she is being singled out as a complainer.

Try to give your customer the impression of your company's fairness, but don't be patronizing. You embarrass Mr. Jones if you tell him that no good businessperson would make a request like the one he has made.

Keep in mind that you want to keep the customer's business even when you cannot grant the customer's request. You should do everything you can to be sure the customer gets fair treatment.

FAVORS TO THE CUSTOMER

Customers may ask to return something or to be allowed an extension of time, or they may protest about something they consider unfair. Often your company has some flexibility in deciding how to handle the request. If you can easily do a favor for a customer, you will usually do the favor. You'll also want to make clear that you know you're doing a favor, but don't emphasize the point too much:

> *Not:* **We don't usually allow returns, but as a favor to you we can let you return the 60 notebooks you bought last month. It's a favor we cannot do for everyone.**
>
> *Write:* **We are pleased to be able to allow you to return for credit the 60 notebooks you bought last month. We like to help our customers whenever we can.**

WRITING ADJUSTMENT RESPONSES

As soon as you receive an adjustment request letter, find out what other information is available. Look for an original order form, records of telephone conversations, and a copy of any other correspondence your firm has had with the customer.

When you have collected your information, you will need to look into what can be done about the problem. Often the adjustment decision is made by people in two or more departments of the company, such as the order department and the accounting department.

Be sure that you have all the information you need, and be sure that your company will back up the response you give the customer. Write the letter with the idea of service to your customer, even when you cannot do what he or she has asked.

Example 2
Adjustment Response to
Explain Delay

Dynamic Entrance. Begin an adjustment response with a reference to the letter that brought the matter to your attention. Use strong, active words:

> *Not:* **This is in response to your letter of June 4.**
>
> *Write:* **I've just read your letter of June 4 describing the problems with our dial loop.**

Be informal and natural. Sometimes contractions can give a natural, relaxed tone to your writing.

Logical Development. Give a summary of the main idea of the problem, but do not repeat too many details of the situation. Your customer already knows you have read the original letter, since you are responding to it. You might want to give a brief description of what has happened:

> **As I understand it, the buttons on all the raincoats are attached so loosely that they fall off right there in the store. You have had several returns because of the lost buttons.**

After your summary of the problem, you can provide a brief explanation of why or how the problem occurred. Resist the temptation to place blame on specific people within or outside your company. If you criticize your company employees, you are only giving a bad impression of those who hired them and of the company in general.

```
                    Melton & Sharpless Realtors
                          452 Eighth Avenue
                        New York, NY 10055-9518

September 30, 19—


Dr. Katherine Potter
E. J. Goleb Pharmaceuticals Inc.
94 Madison Avenue
Boston, MA 02145-1243

Dear Dr. Potter:

I was dismayed to read in your letter of September 23 that
you were subjected to discourteous treatment when you
telephoned me last week.

We take pride in the fact that our staff is friendly and
helpful to all who call our offices. Please accept our
apologies for the lack of courtesy you encountered.

I have located several apartments that might suit you for
the three months you will be lecturing at Franklin Medical
Center. I'm enclosing information about three of them, and
I will be calling you in a day or two to make plans for
showing them to you whenever you can arrange to come down.

Sincerely yours,

B. F. Sharpless

B. F. Sharpless, Realtor
```

Example 3
Apology for Undesirable
Employee Performance

Most people have grown tired of hearing that a computer error caused a problem. They also do not like to hear that a shipping delay was caused by the post office or other delivery company. If you expect the mail service to be slow, the customer is justified in expecting you to ship sooner. If you are looking for someone to blame, it is usually better just to offer *your* apologies:

We aren't sure what caused the delay in your shipment. We are very sorry you did not get the order on time.

Graceful Exit. A response to an adjustment letter is an excellent opportunity to emphasize the quality of your company's product or service.

As you bring your letter to a close, be sure you have left the door open for future communications with this customer. You might refer specifically to an event in the future:

I'm glad I was able to help straighten out this difficulty for you. Be sure to look for our exhibit when you attend the computer show in May.

Carpenter & Adam Furniture
456 University Place
Dallas, Texas 75233-9831

November 8, 19—

Mr. James Howard Williams
987 Fourteenth Street
Dallas, TX 75209-1827

Dear Mr. Williams:

We are always pleased to hear from our customers. Your letter of October 28 was welcome, but it has caused us some concern.

We are sorry to hear that you are not happy with the two desk lamps you purchased in our store on August 16. You explained that they work properly, but you did not know that you could not use three-way bulbs in them.

When we checked the sales slip, we found that you bought the lamps during a highly advertised sale featuring a 50-percent reduction with all sales final. Our ability to offer such savings once a year is based on sales with "no return, no refund." We wish we could accept the lamps for credit, but we must say no this time.

You might be able to have the lamps rewired for three-way bulbs. We can recommend Anderson Electric Repairs, 1822 Walnut Street, in Dallas.

On November 22 we are having a sale on lamps suitable for office use. We promise great savings on quality products.

Very truly yours,

Peter Schubert
Customer Service Manager

jg

Example 4
Response Refusing Adjustment

The business world is competitive. A dissatisfied customer can almost always take business to another company and have no further dealings with your company. No company can afford to lose too many of its customers.

Duval Office Cleaning Service Inc.
4410 Thibodaux Road
New Orleans, Louisiana 70155-5498

June 25, 19—

Mr. Pierre Metairie
Gulfport Insurance Company
99 River Street
New Orleans, LA 70153-4444

Dear Mr. Metairie:

We appreciate your letter of June 14, in which you explained the problems you have had with our cleaning service.

I can certainly see that it would be much easier for your office if we could change the hours we work at Gulfport. Now that some employees work from 5 p.m. to 11 p.m., I know you'd prefer that we do the cleaning after 11 p.m.

I wish we could change the hours to accommodate your new schedule, but we cannot do so—at least not within the next three months. We'll be making some changes in our staff when the school year begins. If you can be patient that long, we should be able to change the hours in September.

Thank you for explaining your new hours to us. Please let us try to work out a new schedule in the future.

Sincerely,

Bernard Michaelson
Manager

kw

Example 5
Response Offering Later Adjustment

Customers or clients who write to tell you what is wrong probably want to continue to do business with your company. A cordial reply to dissatisfied customers does much to restore the customers' patience and their faith in your company.

16
Worksheets

1. Radio station WMIX is located at 186 East 48th Street, New York, NY 10018-7612. WMIX recently conducted a fund-raising drive in which it offered a premium of a two-volume edition of *Music and You*, by Jean Faveau, to all those who contributed at least $30. The response was great, and within three days all copies were gone. No more are available. Write the letter that can be sent to contributors whose letters came too late, offering instead a recording of their choice from an enclosed brochure. The letter will be signed by the director of promotion, Ms. Zoe Crown.

2. Reply to the adjustment request sent to *Executive Tips* magazine by Mrs. Lucille Dobey (Unit 15, Example 1). Explain that the first copy of the magazine should have arrived in early August (the September issue). Mr. Luis Martinez, Subscription Manager, does not know the reason for the delay, but he has arranged to send the October issue with this letter. Mr. Martinez believes the problem will not happen again. Mrs. Dobey's subscription will begin with this issue and will run through October of the following year, even if she eventually receives the issues that should have been sent before September.

3. You are the secretary to John Victor Edwards, Mayor of Hawthorne, New Hampshire 03211. At the center of Hawthorne's business district, State Highway 42 intersects with Rosewood Avenue, a local street. The city has been receiving complaints that the traffic light at the intersection gives a much shorter green light to Rosewood traffic than is usual for green lights elsewhere in town. Mr. Edwards knows that the complaints are justified, but the duration of the traffic light is set by the state, not the town. Write the letter that could be sent to the citizens who write or call to complain. Mr. Edwards will sign the letter.

4. Reply to the adjustment request letter sent to Bagley's Shop (Unit 15, Example 3), telling Ms. Lopez that she can return the towels. Explain that Bagley's wants its customers to be satisfied. Enclose a brochure about the August sale of kitchen gadgets. Use your own name as the manager of the company.

5. Read this request for an adjustment that is a favor to the customer.

CHESTERFIELD TOWERS
Apartment 2012
1882 Lake Shore Drive
Chicago, IL 60611-9922

September 14, 19--

Thoren Fine Pianos
Attention: Mr. George Grommetz
344 La Salle Street
Chicago, IL 60619-7755

Gentlemen:

On September 8 my new Thoren piano was delivered. There was quite a problem when we discovered that it could be placed in my apartment only by hoisting it through a window from a tenth floor terrace, since the doors of my apartment are not wide enough to accommodate it. I'm certainly glad that your delivery people thought to do some measuring before they tried to bring it in that way.

The rosewood molding on the piano is detaching in several places. The lovely tone is not affected, but the beauty of the instrument is lost when the molding is not in place.

I would not look forward to having to send this piano back to you. The logistics of moving it in caused enough concern last week. Furthermore, I will begin my fall classes and my concerts in just one more month. That is why I ask that you send someone with knowledge of furniture finishes to take care of the problem.

Please call or write to let me know when someone will be here to make the needed repairs. Under the circumstances, you can see why I say the repairs must be done here.

Sincerely yours,

Boris Lehmann

Boris Lehmann

Reply to Mr. Lehmann, assuring him that Mr. David Rudolph will be at his apartment whenever Mr. Lehmann is ready. Give a telephone number so that Mr. Lehmann can call to make an appointment.

6. Nomad Van Lines has received the following letter. The writer, Mr. Kingsley, is employed by Amara Data, Inc., a company with many employees and offices all over the country. Nomad wants to maintain good relations with Amara and its employees. Reply to the letter.

4433 Silver Oaks Road
Atlanta, GA 30319

August 22, 19--

Nomad Van Lines
1788 Bankhead Highway
Atlanta, GA 30388-1112

Gentlemen:

I have just moved to Atlanta to begin a new job with Amara Data, Inc., in the Peachtree Street office. My family of five and I previously lived in Terre Haute. We chose Nomad to handle our move to Atlanta.

The departure from Terre Haute was smooth enough, but we are certainly not pleased with the way things were handled as we moved into our house here.

1. The frame on an antique mirror was broken. The employees did not even apologize.

2. On several occasions when a large piece of furniture was to go upstairs, the men on the truck tried to persuade my wife to leave it on the first floor. One table was left; I moved it later.

3. At lunchtime we found the driver and his helper eating hamburgers inside the van, placing their food on one of our chairs.

I don't know how you can explain such service. I am inclined to think that I would allow Nomad to handle our next move only if it were the last moving company in the country.

Sincerely,

John Willoughby Kingsley

John Willoughby Kingsley

cc Human Resources Department, Amara Data, Inc.

7. Refer to Unit 15, Exercise 9. Write a reply to Miss MacPherson from John Walters, Customer Service, explaining that your most recent shipment of smoked oysters has been detained by the Food and Drug Administration at the port in New York. The shipment will not be admitted because the product does not meet FDA standards. Chosan Importers has found another source and will be receiving a new shipment within ten days. Dingley & Alwich's order will be filled within two weeks.

8. Refer to Exercise 10, Unit 15. On May 10 Mr. Abner Collini, Assistant Controller of Fillmore Box & Carton Company, wrote to Frost and Dickinson Office Furniture to ask if he could return a chair he bought for his office the previous June. The chair was upholstered in rust leather, and the only reason for the return is that Mr. Collini has decided that he doesn't like the chair. The price of the chair was $298 plus tax, charged to the company.

Mrs. Kathy Lee of Frost and Dickinson has decided that the company will not accept the chair as a return, since Mr. Collini has been using it for almost a year. Write the letter that Mrs. Lee would send. She is the Manager of Sales. The address of Frost and Dickinson Office Furniture is 1361 Old Salem Highway, Hartford, CT 06298. Fillmore's address is 457 Prince Street, Philadelphia, PA 19182-5312.

9. Rewrite this unsatisfactory reply to Exercise 1 in Unit 15.

Bixby Publishers
13322 North Stetson Street
Minneapolis, Minnesota 55467

November 12, 19--

Ms. Melissa Durgan
Grant Advertising Agency
441 Madison Avenue
New York, NY 10065-7782

Dear Ms. Durgan:

This letter is in reference to your letter of November 8, in which you claimed that we sent you the wrong diaries on your order of October 15. Our order department did not think anyone would be ordering for next year so soon and so they naturally sent the diaries for this year.

Upon receipt of the 16 diaries that you want to return, we will ship you the ones you think you ordered in the first place.

If you want the new diaries in a few weeks, you'll have to return the others right away.

Cordially,

Benjamin Bennett

Benjamin Bennett
Order Manager

it

Exercises 10–12 are all based on the following letter, which Mr. Paul Stanlov received from one of his company's clients.

First Bank of College Park

667 COLLEGE PARK ROAD
SAN FRANCISCO, CA 94178

May 5, 19--

Mr. Paul Stanlov
Supervisor of Personnel
Camelot Courier Service
1412 Robinson Street
San Francisco, CA 94152

Dear Mr. Stanlov:

Ever since First Bank of College Park began
to use your service five years ago, we have
been pleased by the outstanding job you do
and by the professional appearance of all
your couriers.

Yesterday I saw something that made me fear
that your standards are slipping. One of
your couriers, D. G. Macall, was waiting in
our main office while some documents were
being prepared. I happened to walk through
the waiting area, and I noticed that he was
wearing a wrinkled, stained uniform. He was
chewing gum, and furthermore it was obvious
that he was not wearing socks.

Please do something to ensure that such a
situation will not arise again. We will
have to make other arrangements for courier
service if we can't count on professional
standards of appearance from Camelot.

Yours very truly,

FIRST BANK OF COLLEGE PARK

Christina Lee

Ms. Christina Lee
Consumer Loan Officer

10. Mr. Stanlov verified the facts with Ms. Lee and then spoke with Mr. Macall, who agreed that his appearance had been careless on the day in question. An official reprimand was noted in Mr. Macall's personnel file.

Write a memo from Mr. Stanlov to Mr. Macall, confirming the conversation between the two, in which Mr. Macall agreed to improve. Date the memo May 10, for Mr. Macall's personnel records, and point out that he will be dismissed if such behavior occurs again. Emphasize the importance of the company's image.

11. Write a memo from Mr. Stanlov to all couriers, dated May 12 and summarizing the following points of the company's dress code: uniforms must be clean and pressed; men must wear socks and women wear hose; and no smoking, eating, drinking, or gum chewing is to take place while couriers are on duty. This memo is to be a reminder, based on the College Park incident, but it should not sound like a rebuke to the employees in general.

12. Write the letter Mr. Stanlov would send to Ms. Lee, expressing appreciation for her having called the situation to his attention and briefly explaining that he has taken steps to correct the situation. (He should not promise that the problem will not recur, since he cannot be sure. He should be optimistic about improvement.)

17
Employment Communications

Some people go to work for one business and remain there throughout their working years. Other workers make frequent job changes for the sake of increased opportunities. It can be demanding to apply for a new job, but the applicant is willing to make the effort it takes to get a more rewarding position.

Job-seeking circumstances may vary, but certain written materials are required in any effort to obtain employment—application forms, cover letters, resumes, reference letters, and letters of appreciation. Business firms also write employment letters—letters asking for references, offering employment, or refusing employment.

This unit will help you prepare the various letters and other materials needed in the employment process.

How do you obtain the job you want? First you prepare yourself with the skills and knowledge needed in your area of interest. Then you present yourself to your best advantage in writing and in person. Your writing skills are very important in your effort to get a job.

Your current employment status determines how you apply for a job. These categories include most people seeking employment:

- Young people seeking a first full-time job after they finish school or college
- Women or men returning to work after time at home with their children
- Any employee looking for better opportunities within or outside the company
- Laid-off or unemployed workers looking for new employment

No matter what your current employment status might be, communications skills play a vital role in helping you get the job you want.

APPLICATION FORMS

Many businesses use application forms to get the information they need from prospective employees. Sometimes an applicant can fill out the form at home. Often the form is filled out in the Employment Office (also called *Personnel* or *Human Resources Department*).

Complete the form carefully and neatly. Too often an applicant treats the application form casually. As a result, the applicant makes a bad impression on the potential employer in the very first step of the application process.

Gather Your Information. Before you fill out the form, gather all information you will have to supply.

HECTOR & SEBASTIAN, INC.
835 Willow Street
Baltimore, MD 21278-6543

EMPLOYMENT APPLICATION

NAME		DATE	SOCIAL SECURITY NUMBER

STREET		CITY	STATE	ZIP CODE

TELEPHONE NUMBER

POSITION DESIRED

EDUCATION

INSTITUTION	DATES	DEGREE OR DIPLOMA

EXPERIENCE *(LIST MOST RECENT FIRST)*

EMPLOYER	TYPE OF WORK	DATES	REASON FOR LEAVING

REFERENCES *(DO NOT INCLUDE PREVIOUS EMPLOYERS)*

NAME	ADDRESS	TELEPHONE

I affirm that this information is true and accurate

SIGNATURE

Example 1
Sample Application Form

Know all the pertinent facts, including dates. Have your Social Security number handy. Be sure to spell the names of people and companies correctly, and write legibly.

Follow Instructions. Read and follow all instructions on the form. Give complete information and place the items where they belong on the page (see Example 1).

COVER LETTERS

If you send your application form by mail, write a cover letter to go with it. A cover letter is also sent with a resume, a summary of your background and qualifications. The cover letter gives the reader a good idea of how you express yourself in writing and how carefully you check your work. Your cover letter should give the reader a sense of your strengths as an employee.

Your cover letter should be brief. A brief letter accompanied by a complete application form or resume helps the reader see your various strengths and judge your suitability for a position.

Write a cover letter when you apply for positions like these:

- A job advertised with the name and address of a company
- A job advertised in a *blind advertisement*, in which the identity of the company is not given
- A job you hear about through word of mouth
- A job that might be available (an unsolicited application)

Examples 2–5 provide sample letters for these different application situations.

Remember the following guidelines when you write your cover letter.

Dynamic Entrance. Always begin your cover letter with a clear statement telling why you are applying for the job. The first sentence of your letter should make a favorable impression on your reader. Don't waste the first sentence by stating something obvious:

> *Not:* **I am writing this letter to apply . . .**

Your reader already knows that you wrote the letter. Be specific and direct:

> **The position of secretary you advertised in _____ sounds very interesting.**

If the application is in response to an advertisement, be specific about the publication, the date the ad appeared, and the exact position advertised:

> **I have just read your advertisement in *The New York Times* of September 15, and I would like to apply for the secretarial position.**

If there is some reason why you cannot mention the source, then you should write your letter as an unsolicited application. If you are applying to fill a vacancy you have learned about through a friend or acquaintance, specify the source of your information:

> **My friend Catherine Dubois has told me she has resigned from her job with Fillmore Box & Carton to return to school. I am interested in applying for the job she will be leaving as associate administrator of claims.**

825 Penrose Drive
Boston, MA 02189
March 15, 19--

Grant Advertising Agency
441 Madison Avenue
New York, NY 10065-7782

Gentlemen:

Your advertisement in this morning's <u>Boston Globe</u> described just the job I am looking for--advertising copy assistant.

I am enclosing my resume for your review. I am especially interested in the position advertised because I have enjoyed writing advertising copy for my uncle's inn in Vermont. I began this work in high school and have continued to write for him during my years at college.

I graduate from Thornwood College in May, and I would like to begin working this summer.

Thank you for considering my application. Please let me know when I may come for an interview. I can come to your office any day that is convenient for you. My telephone number is (617) 555-4985.

Sincerely yours,

Olivia Rolandi

Ms. Olivia Rolandi

Enclosure

Example 2
Cover Letter to Accompany Application Form or Resume in Response to Advertisement

---

When you are applying for a job without knowing whether there is an opening, begin with some suggestion of why you are writing:

> **As soon as I complete my secretarial training, I hope to begin working for a firm that is progressive and innovative in the field of computers. B & G Computers has a strong reputation in this area.**

> **For many years I have admired the work of Pandora Security in industrial security systems. I would like to help develop the effective products for which Pandora Security is so well known.**

Logical Development. In the main part of your cover letter, refer to the application form or the resume you are enclosing. Do not repeat the information given in the form or resume, but focus on a fact in the form or resume that you think is important:

> **You will see from my application that I have had 12 years of experience as a credit manager.**

153

Room 456, Benton Hall
Marcus University
Kansas City, MO 64119-9156
February 14, 19—

Mr. Leonidas Paranones
Wiggins Electronics
12 Wakefield Road
Kansas City, MO 64102-9321

Dear Mr. Paranones:

Almost everyone who was present at the recruitment session
with you on February 6 is planning to send an application.
We were all impressed with the scope of activities of
Wiggins.

Wiggins sounds like an exciting place to work. As you can
see from my application form, my family is from Springfield.
It has always been my intention to work in Kansas City after
my graduation.

I am enclosing the completed application form, as you
suggested. Please consider it favorably and let me know
when I may come for an interview.

When you have decided about the interview, you may call me
at (816) 555-9152. I can come to your office any afternoon.

Sincerely yours,

Michael Fanwood

Michael Fanwood

Enclosure

922 West Green Mountain Road
Denver, Colorado 80277
September 18, 19—

Ms. Edith Bando, Personnel
Springfield Products, Inc.
Room 94, Massey Building
Cleveland, OH 44133-4141

Dear Ms. Bando:

For the past few months, I have been enjoying the television
series On to the Future sponsored by Springfield Products.
The commercial messages have given interesting facts about
your company.

In January I am planning to leave my present job to move to
Cleveland, where I will be married in February. My future
husband is an attorney there. I want to obtain a job with a
company that has the kind of outlook reflected by your
recent television messages.

I am sending my resume with this letter. For the past three
years, I have been working as an administrative secretary
for a civil engineering firm. I have the kind of skills and
background that would enable me to do a good job for
Springfield Products.

I shall be in Cleveland from November 20 to November 28.
Please let me know if I may come to your office for an
interview then. I can be reached at (303) 555-0133, my
office number.

Sincerely yours,

Beth Poindexter

Ms. Beth Poindexter

Enclosure

Example 3
Letter to Accompany Application During Recruitment

Example 4
Letter to Accompany Unsolicited Application

You do not want to sound too impressed with yourself, but you should write about yourself in a way that sounds confident:

> *Not:* **You can be sure I will bring some life into your accounting department.**
>
> *Write:* **I believe I could contribute to the efficiency of the accounting department at Wiggins Electronics.**

When you write a reply to a blind advertisement, you do not know the company name. You may be sending your letter to the company address or to a box number assigned by the publication in which the advertisement appeared.

It can be difficult to avoid sounding formal or awkward when you do not know the company name. Try to imagine a real person working at the company and reading your letter. Your letter will then sound more natural.

Certain phrases and expressions are tempting to use in cover letters. Try to avoid all expressions that weaken your position or sound insecure:

> **I was wondering if . . .**
> **I don't have much experience, but . . .**

Sometimes there is a weakness in your qualifications that must be considered. If the weakness is a lack of experience, your resume or application will make that clear. Do not refer to your lack of experience in a cover letter unless you can add something positive:

> **I have not yet handled a large volume of correspondence, but I believe my interest in learning new procedures will help me prepare effective materials.**

Graceful Exit. As you come to the end of the cover letter, specify what you hope for as a result of the letter. You probably want a chance for an interview. Make it easy for your reader to invite you. Sound as friendly in your letter as you will sound in person:

> **Thank you for considering my application. I look forward to the opportunity to visit your office for an interview.**

```
988 Fairmount Avenue
Dallas, TX 75201
August 24, 19--


Box 999
Houston Chronicle
Houston, TX 77021

Gentlemen:

The secretarial position described in your advertisement in
today's Chronicle sounds like the very job I would like to
have.

An engineering consulting firm offers the kind of variety I
want. You will see from my resume that I have worked for
three kinds of companies--an electronics firm, a contractor,
and an architect. I have gained much valuable experience
from each job.

My present employer, T. J. Mahal, Inc., knows that I am
planning to leave because I want to work for a larger firm
with more opportunities. I can arrange to come to Houston
for an interview.

Thank you for considering my application. Please call my
office, (214) 555-0011, if you need more information or
would like to discuss an interview.

Sincerely yours,

Darcy Abernathy
Ms. Darcy Abernathy

Enclosure
```

Example 5
Letter to Accompany Resume
in Response to Blind
Advertisement

RESUMES

Many employers require a resume from all job applicants. A well-written resume tells your employer more than an application form can tell.

A resume provides a summary of an applicant's goals, education, work experience, and outside interests. Your resume shows your organizational skills and your ability to communicate clearly. It also shows your willingness to check your work for errors before submitting it to your reader.

Gathering Education and Employment Information. To prepare your resume you should first collect the information you will need to describe your work experience and your educational background, including the dates of attendance. Make a list of your qualifications and skills.

Providing References. You should have available three or four personal or professional references. When you write your resume or go to an employment interview, be sure you have complete information about your references. Write the correct names, addresses, and telephone numbers of your references.

Some writers omit the names of references and substitute a statement such as "References supplied upon request." Unless you are told to do otherwise, you should name your references in the resume.

Most companies prefer that your references not be former employers, whose names are provided elsewhere on the resume or application form. Your references should be people who know you well enough to give reliable information about you. They should also be people whose recommendation of you will supply the company with useful, relevant information.

Always ask permission before you list a person as a reference. Write to your potential references to ask permission to include them on your resume (see Example 6). Your potential references want to know when their names are being used, and they also need time to think about what they want to say. Also, your potential reference might have to refuse to help you. A person who does not remember an applicant clearly or who might have certain reservations about the applicant's abilities will usually decline to be a reference.

In addition, tell your references when you are applying for a job. They can then anticipate a phone call or letter from an employer.

Give complete information in your resume, just as you would on an application form. If there are gaps in time, the reader may not see the complete range of your experience or education.

Once you have compiled your information, be sure that you have not omitted anything important. Include active memberships in organizations, honors and awards, and experiences such as travel. Verify dates and confirm the correct spelling of names.

Preparing the resume. The arrangement of information in your resume should emphasize your strongest qualities. This arrangement may change as you update the resume from time to time. Students applying for a first job should emphasize school courses and activities. After you have been employed for some time, you should focus on experience instead of educational background (see Examples 7 and 8).

Be sure your resume is neatly typed or printed. *Never send carbon copies of your resume.*

```
1361 Van Courtland Way
Philadelphia, PA 19166
January 31, 19—

Dr. Ricardo Xavier
Greenville Health Center
Greenville, PA 19876

Dear Dr. Xavier:

My four years at James Monroe College are almost over, and I
am now applying for employment to several companies that
interest me.

Would you allow me to name you as a reference on my resume
and application forms? I think you know me well through the
two years that I have worked with the Little Leagues here in
Greenville. I would be pleased to have a person of your
stature on my list of references.

I will telephone you before the end of next week to ask your
decision. I do hope you will say yes.

Sincerely yours,

Michael Sanchez

Michael Sanchez
```

Example 6
Letter Requesting Reference Permission

In the past, personal information such as marital status, age, sex, and race was included on resumes. Employers are now prevented from discriminating against prospective employees based on these personal details.

When you apply for a job, you should expect to be judged on the basis of your experience, skills, and attitude. Your race should never be mentioned in your resume.

Omit all personal details from your resume unless they would make you especially qualified to obtain a certain position. For example, a person who is single might be able to travel more often than a married person with several children.

156

Michael David Sanchez
1361 Van Courtland Way
Philadelphia, PA 19166
Telephone: (215) 555-8762

Education

B.S. in Business Administration   James Monroe College
(June of this year)   Greenville, PA 19876

Diploma 19--   Van Courtland High School
College Preparatory Course   Philadelphia, PA 19167-6512

College Courses

Accounting, Business Law, Small Business Management, Advertising,
Business Communications, Executive Planning

Experience

Frozen Sweetreats   Salesperson, Summer 19--
42 Ocean Street
Chatham, MA 02298
(617) 555-1111

Spencer Computers   Assistant, part-time
557 Commerce Road   19-- to 19--
Greenville, PA 19876
(215) 555-9150

Fillmore Box & Carton Company   Shipping Clerk, part-time
457 Prince Street   19-- to 19--
Philadelphia, PA 19182-5312
(215) 555-4111

Activities and Special Skills

Member of Space Inventions Club, James Monroe College, 19-- through 19--;
President, 19--

I speak fluent Spanish and have spent four summers in Colombia with my
grandparents, most recently 19-- and 19--.

References

Mr. Kenneth Digby, Mayor   Dr. Helena Durham
Greenville, PA 19876   Van Courtland High School
(215) 555-6652   Philadelphia, PA 19167-6512
                                         (215) 555-1923

Mrs. Laura Way   Dr. Ricardo Xavier
The Pines   Greenville Health Center
Chatham, MA 02298   Greenville, PA 19876
(617) 555-1212   (215) 555-6666

Example 7
Resume for Student Seeking First Full-Time Job

Ms. Denise E. Lambert
712 East 81st Street, Apartment 7A
New York, NY 10052
Telephone: (212) 555-4985

Career Goal: Recording Engineer-Producer

PROFESSIONAL EXPERIENCE

Audio Engineer

Soho Studio
455 Canal Street
New York, NY 10055-6445
Telephone: (212) 555-0111

In this small studio, I am the audio engineer for recording groups making demo records and videos to be used in seeking performance contracts. (1988 to present)

Assistant Sound Mixer

Sewanee Studio
147 River Street
Nashville, TN 37281

While attending the Astor Technical School, I worked as an assistant sound mixer for Swanee Studio, which makes videotapes for local television stations. (1987)

Related Experience

During the school year, I was keyboard artist for Delta Combo, performing for various parties and dances in and near Kansas City. The business manager is Mr. Les Traverso, 3099 Wornall Road, Kansas City, MO 64111. (1982-1986)

In the summers of 1985 and 1986, I was substitute church organist for several churches in suburban Atlanta.

In the summers of 1983 and 1984, I worked as a waitress at the Mountain Chalet in Asheville, North Carolina. It was not rebuilt after it was destroyed by fire, but my supervisor, Richie Pardo, can be reached at the Delgado Hotel, St. Simons Island, GA 31522.

Example 8
Resume for Experienced Applicant (Page 1)

EDUCATION

Certificate in Audio Technology   1987
Astor Technical Institute
1313 Vanderbilt Highway
Nashville, TN 37280

B.A. from Crown College   1986
666 Amsterdam Boulevard   Major: Music
Kansas City, MO 64112   Minor: Spanish

When I became interested in the production side of the music
industry, I enrolled at the Astor Technical Institute because it
is a pioneer in sound technology for videotaping.

VOLUNTEER SERVICE

I work six hours a week with the Teach Me To Read program offered
through the New York Public Library. Primarily the work is a
one-to-one situation with adults who are functionally illiterate.

OTHER INTERESTS

Hiking, performing chamber music

REFERENCES

Miss Grace Land
Director, Teach Me To Read
New York Public Library
443 Fifth Avenue
New York, NY 10018
Telephone: (212) 555-7771

Dr. Jessup Quinlan
Organist and Choir Director
Emory Methodist Church
113 Ansley Road
Atlanta, GA 30333
Telephone: (404) 555-8256

Mrs. Suzanna Ninco
Director, Soho Studio
455 Canal Street
New York, NY 10055-6445
Telephone: (212) 555-0111

Resume for Experienced Applicant (Page 2)

```
                              922 West Green Mountain Road
                              Denver, Colorado 80277
                              December 1, 19—



                              Mrs. Lila Johnson
                              Human Resources Director
                              Springfield Products, Inc.
                              Room 94, Massey Building
                              Cleveland, OH 44133-4141

                              Dear Mrs. Johnson:

                              Now that I have visited the executive offices of Springfield
                              Products, I am even more enthusiastic about the prospect of
                              working there.

                              I appreciate the time and attention you gave to me during
                              the interview. I am glad that Springfield does have some
                              openings for which I may be qualified. As I told you during
                              our interview on November 28, I am definitely interested in
                              the position of secretary to Mr. Frederick Kim in the
                              marketing survey department. I look forward to meeting him
                              on December 20 when I return to Cleveland.

                              Thank you for such an interesting and informative morning.
                              I enjoyed the lunch in the Calumet Room with you and Miss
                              Green.

                              Sincerely yours,

                              Beth Poindexter
                              Ms. Beth Poindexter
```

Example 9
Letter of Appreciation
for Interview

AFTER THE INTERVIEW

An interview requires good speaking skills and other abilities. Unit 22 offers guidelines for the interview itself.

After the interview, write a courteous, thoughtful letter of thanks to the interviewer. You can make this thank-you letter your own form letter and adjust it for similar situations in the future.

In your thank-you letter, be *absolutely*, *positively*, *100%* sure that you have the correct name and title of the person who interviewed you, including the correct spelling. Eileen Bryan will not be impressed if you call her Ellen Byron. This kind of carelessness can damage any good impression you made in the interview.

Write and mail your letter within a day or two of the interview. The idea is to keep your name in the mind of the interviewer.

Keep your thank-you letter short. A simple "thank you" can be followed by a sentence or two of specific remarks about the company. You can then conclude with one or two sentences reminding the interviewer of your availability (see Example 9).

114 Wilmington Road
Hightower, Missouri 64390
March 12, 19—

Mr. Robert Key
988 West Grover Street
Omaha, NE 68144

Dear Bob:

Yes, I do remember that you were one of my students four
years ago at Abbey College. I am interested to learn that
you have decided to apply for a job at the State Department,
and I am flattered that you wanted to use my name as a
reference.

Much as I should like to be among your references, I must
tell you that I cannot. I am working on the last few
chapters of a book that must go to press by June 1. I know
from experience that the State Department requires very
thorough investigations. I am afraid I cannot guarantee my
availability for this lengthy process.

I wish you success in your employment efforts and hope you
understand my unwillingness to serve as your reference right
now. Please keep in touch with me.

Sincerely yours,

Sarah Steinmetz

Dr. Sarah Steinmetz

Example 10
Letter Refusing Reference Permission

Grant Advertising Agency
441 Madison Avenue
New York, NY 10065-7782

March 22, 19—

Ms. Olivia Rolandi
825 Penrose Drive
Boston, MA 02189

Dear Ms. Rolandi:

I was pleased to receive your letter in response to our
advertisement in the Boston Globe on March 15. Your prompt
attention shows that you really are interested in the job
with Grant.

The position of copy assistant in an advertising firm can be
very exciting, but it can also be demanding. If you can
visit us on April 3, several members of the staff and I will
let you see what it's all about. Plan to arrive around ten
o'clock. After a full interview, we'll provide a tour of
the facilities and lunch.

I look forward to meeting you. I will call you on March 27
to make sure that the date is convenient.

Sincerely yours,

Melissa Durgan

Melissa Durgan
Account Manager

Example 11
Letter Offering Interview

OTHER EMPLOYMENT LETTERS

An individual or business writes employment letters
in these situations:

- Reference permission is given (or refused)
- An applicant is invited to come for an interview
- An applicant is told that he or she is hired (or is not hired)

Replies to application letters and to requests for reference permission should be brief. Favorable messages are easy to write. If you must refuse permission or deny employment, try to write a sincere message without sounding curt or indifferent. Most people want to know the truth, but they also want to preserve their pride and their hope (see Examples 10–12).

RESIGNATION LETTERS

If you are leaving your current job for a new position, write a letter of resignation to your employer. You should always prepare a resignation letter, even if you communicate your decision orally to your supervisor or employer. Write an official letter of resignation whether your company is formal or informal.

The resignation letter becomes a part of your personnel records at the company you are leaving. Later on you may need a reference from the employer, and those who knew you well may no longer be employed by the company. Your reason for leaving is recorded in your letter of resignation, which can be very helpful to the person trying to provide reference information (see Example 13).

Traveler's Oil Company
Suite 99, Lancaster Building
Houston, Texas 77077-9854

September 3, 19—

Ms. Darcy Abernathy
988 Fairmount Avenue
Dallas, TX 75201

Dear Ms. Abernathy

Thank you very much for your interesting letter in response to our advertisement in the Chronicle on August 24.

Your resume certainly shows a wide range of activities and types of jobs. I wish you had had all the qualities we want, because your diversified background would surely be a benefit to us.

Ms. Abernathy, you missed an important item in our advertisement—we must have a secretary who can speak and write in French. Your fluency in German is an asset to you, but we require the ability to communicate in French.

I wish you well in your search for the right job. Your qualifications are otherwise outstanding.

Sincerely

Truman Coolidge
Truman Coolidge
Director of Human Resources

Example 12
Letter Refusing Interview

8341 Bismarck Road
Minneapolis, Minnesota 55410
September 1, 19—

Mr. Eric Svanholm
Plobersk Industries
823 Marquette Street
St. Paul, MN 55122

Dear Mr. Svanholm:

As you know from our conversation yesterday, I have accepted a position with B & G Computers in Denver. I plan to leave Minnesota next month to begin my new job.

Please accept my resignation from Plobersk Industries effective September 28. During the two years I have worked here, I have appreciated the high morale and the innovative techniques that are evident in every department.

Thanks for all the help you have given me in the Marketing Department. It was a pleasure to work with you.

Sincerely yours,

Ian Fremstad
Ian Fremstad

Example 13
Resignation Letter

17
Worksheets

For Exercises 1–8, create your own package of employment correspondence to be used as guidelines for you as you seek employment now and in the future.

1. Write your resume. If you have already prepared one for another course, you may submit it for this assignment.

2. Write a cover letter to go with your resume to be sent to any company of your choice in another city, requesting the opportunity to come for an interview.

3. Write a cover letter to go with your application, using a real company that might recruit at your school. If you can obtain a "generic" application form, fill it out.

4. Write a letter to someone you'd like to use as a reference, requesting that person's permission.

5. Assume that the company to which you wrote in Exercise 3 has invited you to come for an interview. The interview has been completed, and you know you would like the job. Write a thank-you letter to the interviewer.

6. Assume that you have been interviewed by a company other than the company you used in Exercises 3 and 5. You know you would not like the job the company has available. Write a thank-you letter to the interviewer.

7. Several weeks have passed since you wrote the thank-you letter for Exercise 5. You have not heard from the company. Write the letter you would send.

8. Write a letter of resignation. Use the job you now have or one you have had in the past. If you have not worked, resign from a fictitious job.

9. Your supervisor, Annabel Grant, has received a letter from the son of a family that used to live next door to her. He is asking if he may use her name as a reference on his resume when he looks for employment after college graduation this year. Write the letter granting him permission. His name is Stephan Ariedes, and his address is 447 South Boulevard, St. Louis, Missouri 63166. Ms. Grant is Director of Human Resources at Athenia Insurance Company, 826 Trilby Road, Denver, Colorado 80285.

10. Refer to the application letter from Michael Fanwood (Unit 17, Example 3). Assume that Mr. Paranones has interviewed Mr. Fanwood and has decided to hire him. Write the letter Mr. Paranones would send to tell Mr. Fanwood that he should report for work on May 1.

11. Refer to Melissa Durgan's letter offering an interview to Olivia Rolandi (Example 11). After the interview, Ms. Durgan decides that Ms. Rolandi is not the best-qualified applicant. Write the letter Ms. Durgan would send to Ms. Rolandi.

12. Michael Fanwood (see Exercise 10) has been working part-time at the Sioux Trail Pharmacy, 8811 Marlowe Road, Kansas City, Missouri 64182. Write his letter of resignation to Dr. Kilmer Payne, the pharmacist and owner. Mr. Fanwood has worked at the pharmacy for three years and has had an excellent relationship with Dr. Payne and all the employees at the pharmacy.

18
Sales and Fund-Raising Letters

All letters your organization sends are potential sales letters, but sales and fund-raising letters focus on *selling*—selling a product, a service, or an idea. Sales and fund-raising letters are free of some of the restraints of style and form that apply to other kinds of letters. Sales and fund-raising letters also require the use of basic sales techniques.

Selling by mail can be extremely effective. Direct mail advertising, including sales letters, can reach potential customers on a more personal level than other advertising can. Although sales and fund-raising letters are sometimes written by advertising specialists, many are written by regular company employees.

This unit will help you write effective sales and fund-raising letters.

Sales and fund-raising letters fall into a few general categories.

Giving New Product Information. Some sales letters provide information about a new product or service. When you write an informational letter, keep your paragraphs short. Write in a tone and style suited to your reader. If you are writing to professionals, technical terms are acceptable. Avoid technical terms when you write to consumers who have only a casual interest in the topic (see Example 1).

Supporting Sales Representatives. Some sales letters are written to help set up a sales call. A letter may also be written to follow up a visit from a sales representative. This personal appeal is an important part of effective selling. Sales letters in support of sales efforts are written frequently in many businesses (see Example 2).

Inviting a Purchase or Contribution. Some sales and fund-raising letters make a direct appeal to the reader to buy products or services or to contribute to a cause. These letters are often written by professionals in advertising, but you may be asked to write a letter if the mailing is local or otherwise limited. A mailing like this often includes brochures, order forms, or reply cards (see Example 3).

Supporting Nonprofit Activities. Many businesses offer support to nonprofit organizations working in such areas as medical research and the arts. As an employee, you may be called upon to write a fund-raising letter in support of a nonprofit or political group outside your company (see Example 4).

STYLE AND FORMAT

When your main objective is to sell or raise funds, you can use certain style and format variations that would not be suitable in other types of letters. These devices can be useful to catch your reader's eye:

- Headings worded like a newspaper headline
- Color added for certain words or signature
- Sentence fragments to give casual, emphatic effect
- Dashes, series of periods, and exclamation points
- Enthusiastic style with strong adjectives

This example illustrates some of the devices available for sales letters:

> **Visit our elegant new condominiums this weekend ... tomorrow ... maybe even today! Enjoy the ocean view ... bask in the warm breezes on a private deck!**

165

Aaron Calculators
987 McGee Street
Kansas City, MO 64198-2218

August 1, 19--

Name
Purchasing Agent
_____ School System
Address
City, State, Zip

Dear _____:

Many schools are now encouraging their students to learn how
to use small calculators. Not all the calculators on the
market are durable; some are so poorly made that they last
only a week or two.

We have been able to obtain a large shipment of the kind of
small calculators most schools and most colleges want to
buy. For a short time we can offer you these calculators in
the quantity needed by the students in your system.

Please use the enclosed card to let us know of your interest
in buying these marvelously efficient instruments. We will
send you a free one so that you can see for yourself how
well it works.

Sincerely yours,

Benjamin Vinings
Sales Manager

ck

Enclosure

Example 1
Informational Sales Letter

Though sales and fund-raising letters have certain special qualities, remember to follow the general guidelines for writing effective letters. Focus on the interests of your reader. Tell the reader what the product or service will do for him or her:

> **Let us show you how to save money with our new Electrobroom.**

> **You'll sleep better at night knowing that your money has helped a stray dog or cat find a home.**

> **Your participation in our campaign will show the legislature that you care about good air and water for all.**

Write with an attitude of helpfulness, offering the reader complete information:

> **Here is a coupon redeemable for a free bottle of Neverdirt.**

> **Return the enclosed coupon for your free sample of Waxoff.**

FORM LETTERS

A mailing list is a list of names and addresses of *prospects*—individuals or organizations that might be interested in buying a product or service or in contributing to a worthy cause.

E.J. Goleb Pharmaceuticals Inc.
94 Madison Avenue
Boston, MA 02145-1243

September 12, 19--

Dr. _____
Address
City, State, Zip

Dear Dr. _____:

At last our laboratories have developed a new medication for
preventing dry skin in normal adults! Many physicians are
besieged with calls during the cold and dry months because
their patients have a problem with itching, scaling skin.

I am enclosing a sample packet of Crocogon, along with some
descriptive material. I'll be in _____ in the first
week of October, and I'll call on you during that week.

You can count on good results with Crocogon, just as you
have always been able to count on Goleb products.

I look forward to seeing you next month.

Cordially yours,

Mrs. Leila Sanchez
Product Representative

cw

Enclosures

Example 2
Sales Letter Preceding Call or Visit

Mailing lists are sometimes compiled within a company from information such as sales records of existing accounts. Sometimes mailing lists are purchased
from businesses that specialize in maintaining and
renting lists for sales purposes. All good mailing lists
have one valuable quality in common: they provide
the accurate names and addresses of people who are
considered good sales prospects.

Compiling and maintaining mailing lists has become
a sophisticated business in itself, since addresses
must be updated and list effectiveness must be studied. Much of the work of list maintenance is done
by computer.

The computer has also changed the way many sales
and fund-raising letters are prepared for a mailing.
Form letters have come a long way from the old
mimeographed forms that began "Dear Reader" or
"Dear Friend." Since it is easy to personalize form
letters, today's sales and fund-raising letters can have
a strong, personal impact on each reader.

Camps for the Handicapped
Post Office Box 22
Wilmington, DE 19877

March 16, 19--

Name
Corporation
Address
City, State, Zip

Dear _____:

Just outside Wilmington there is a big farm, complete with
ducks, sheep, horses, even a scarecrow! Camps for the
Handicapped has bought this farm. We need you to help us
make the camp a reality for the hundreds of children who
would love this experience.

What do we need? Well, we want to build several simple
cabins, each to house eight boys or girls. Our first goal
is to build ten cabins, with the hope of adding others
later. The cabins will be constructed to suit the needs of
physically handicapped youngsters between 10 and 12. Your
contribution can make the dream come true.

Camps for the Handicapped is a nonprofit organization and
has the endorsement of major organizations concerned with
children. Your contribution is tax-deductible as provided in
our present tax laws.

Imagine happy children enjoying outdoor life--working in a
garden, swimming in the pond, playing in the sunshine. Your
company can help make this possible. Your generous help for
other projects in the past has made Wilmington a good place
to live. We know you'll want to be a part of this new
adventure. Your contribution sent in the enclosed envelope
will ensure that _____ Corporation is published in our
honor roll of friends.

Sincerely,

Murray Davis

Enclosure

Example 3
Fund-Raising Letter

Most sales and fund-raising letters are form letters—
letters sent to many people and using exactly the
same wording and format. Although the letters will
be identical, remember that the letter must be written to *someone* originally. With the computer techniques available today, there is no excuse for preparing form letters that make a poor impression on
readers—your potential customers or contributors.

The following guidelines will help you personalize
any form letter you prepare.

Make a Good First Impression. In sales and fund-
raising letters, the first impression is especially important. Your prospect will resist reading the letter
unless you make it attractive. Use good paper. Use a
neat, easy-to-read format, and check for typing errors
and spelling mistakes.

State the Offer Clearly. Your letter should be clear
and direct in describing your offer—a product, a service, or an opportunity to serve the community or
society in general.

```
                    ****Elect Sarah Prouty****
                          Headquarters
                        123 Main Street
                     Bartleby's Landing, MA 02166

         April 18, 19--


         Name
         Address
         City, State, Zip

         Dear _____:

         Ever since the days of Paul Revere and Sam Adams, people in
         our part of the country have taken an interest in the way
         our government is run. Now more than ever we must stand up
         and be counted.

         You can help keep Massachusetts great. We need Sarah Prouty
         as Governor. Her record as Mayor of Bartleby's Landing was
         outstanding. As a Representative, she has voted for all the
         measures that have helped us put this state far ahead in
         education, health, welfare, and commerce.

         You can do something to help elect Sarah this November. You
         know that she is now one of the most respected people in the
         state. Who would be a better Governor? Will you help her?

         All you need to do is send your check in the enclosed
         envelope. If you'd rather make a pledge of support and pay
         it later, that's all right with us. Don't delay, though.
         We need to know you're with us!

         Sincerely,


         Marcia Endicott
         Campaign Manager

         Enclosure
```

Example 4
Fund-Raising Letter

Write with a Positive Attitude. Choose words that have a positive effect. This idea is true for business writing in general, but it is especially important in sales and fund-raising letters. Use positive words like *warmth*, *pleasure*, *convenience*, *comfort*, *security*, *efficiency*, and *profit*. Avoid words like *unfortunately*, *regret*, and *conflict*. These words give your reader a sense of unpleasantness.

Be Truthful. Be enthusiastic, but don't go too far with promises and elaborate descriptions. If a letter sounds insincere, the reader will reject the message.

Be Personal. Even if you are using a rented mailing list, try to keep a personal tone in your letter. Be sure that you know what you can assume about your readers. Don't refer to the future of a family's children if your letter might go to someone who has no children or whose children have finished college. Never misspell the reader's name! Misspelled names always make a bad impression.

See Your Reader's Point of View. Check the effectiveness of your sales letter by looking at the letter as if you had received it. Does the letter offer something you might want to have? Does the offer sound attractive? Would you find it easy to respond to the offer?

18
Worksheets

1. Here is a list of products that might be the subjects of sales letters. For each one, list five adjectives that could be used in writing a vivid sales appeal:

A. a hair dryer

B. a pocket calculator

C. a magazine about food

D. an electronic typewriter

E. a line of greeting cards to be sold in drugstores

F. a new window-cleaning product for home use

G. a restaurant that has been remodeled

H. a set of books for children aged 8 to 12

I. a Game-of-the-Month subscription for electronic games

J. writing paper with engraved name and address

2. For each of the following services, provide three phrases that would be ways of getting attention in the beginning of a sales letter.

A. a checking account that pays interest

B. an office cleaning service

C. a coffee service wagon that will come to offices for morning coffee breaks

D. a nursery school

E. a printing service that offers fast delivery

3. Refer to the sales letter to precede a call or visit (Unit 18, Example 2).

A. Write the letter that might be sent by the manufacturer to pharmacists, persuading them to buy the product for resale in their stores.

B. One of the pharmacists who bought the product for his store is Dr. Kilmer Payne, Sioux Trail Pharmacy, 8811 Marlowe Road, Kansas City, Missouri 64182. Dr. Payne decides to send letters to 200 of his customers, telling them of the product and offering a free sample. Write the letter for his signature.

4. From magazines or newspapers, find an advertisement that has a general appeal. Construct the body of the letters that could be used to sell the product to the following groups:

A. college students

B. women who travel on business

C. new homeowners

5. Find several sales letters that have been sent to you or to someone you know. Analyze them on the basis of the guidelines for personalizing form letters provided in Unit 18.

6. Rewrite this poor alumni fund-raising letter.

DARWIN COLLEGE
Alumni Office
Benton Building
Darwin, New York 12766

February 2, 19—

Mr. Paul Ogden
113 Redwood Avenue
Ganges, CA 98111

Dear Fellow alum,

Its that time of year and we want to begin collecting some money from all the alums to build up the fund this year so that we can show the old college how much our years ther meant to all of us.

If you'll just get out the old checkbook and write us a great big check, we won't have to write you about this matter again (this year) ha! ha!

Be sure to designate your class on the enclosed form. We are having a little friendly (ha! ha!) rivalry between classes.

Looking for your check.

As ever

Lou

Lou Powell
Alumni Secretary

ref

7. The Laurel Trophy Company is located in Preston, Connecticut. This year the company has agreed to be one of the sponsors for the annual Pumpkin Festival. As a part of the company's sponsorship, the president, Amanda Adams, has volunteered to send letters to local businesses asking for donations of merchandise for prizes to be awarded at various events during the three-day festival, October 12, 13, and 14.

Write a form letter that could be sent over Ms. Adams's signature, asking for the desired donations. The address of the Laurel Trophy Company is 122 Bridgeport Road, Preston, CT 06512.

8. Write a letter soliciting funds for any current project that you consider worthwhile. Provide a brief statement telling what kind of readers you expect to reach. In your letter, be sure to explain how the funds will be used. (Suggestions for topics: environmental issues, cultural activities, problems of the poor, assistance to children or to the elderly.)

19
Good Manners Letters

Good manners letters reflect basic thoughtfulness in a business situation. Good manners in business can help ease uncomfortable situations and make strangers into allies.

Often it is helpful to convey good manners in business through written communications—a letter or a memo. This unit will help you prepare good manners letters and memos for the many occasions that arise in business.

BUSINESS MANNERS

Good manners are essentially the same in business as they are in your personal life. Your good manners usually show that you see another person's point of view and want to offer praise, thanks, or sympathy.

These qualities are essential in a good manners letter written in a business setting.

Promptness. If your letter is to convey a message of *caring*, write the letter while an incident is still recent. How often a person intends to write a thank-you letter, waits several days, then several weeks, and finally does not write at all!

Neat Appearance. It may be better to send a messy letter than no letter at all, but you will seem far more considerate if you produce a neat letter.

Naturalness. Certain circumstances seem to bring out formality in all of us. Letters of condolence, congratulations, or appreciation should not sound formal or pompous. In this kind of letter, more than in any other, make every effort to write as you would speak.

Accuracy. Don't put yourself in the embarrassing position of thanking a reader for a gift sent by someone else. In letters offering congratulations, be sure to note the facts correctly. Accuracy in offering or accepting invitations cannot be overemphasized.

APPRECIATION LETTERS

Letters of appreciation or thank-you letters are probably written more frequently than any other kind of good manners letter. Even so, almost everyone misses some opportunities for expressing appreciation.

We have already looked at a letter written to express thanks for an interview (see Unit 17). What are some other situations in business that call for a thank you?

Thanks for a Gift. Many organizations have a fund from which money is taken to provide flowers to those who are ill or bereaved. Special collections may be taken to give wedding gifts and baby gifts. Other occasions for gifts may occur (see Example 1).

Thanks for Hospitality. Doing business often requires that a person travel to other cities or countries. When business associates in other places offer hospitality that makes the visit go more smoothly, write to say thank you. You may find instances of hospitality within your own community. It is always thoughtful to let your host know of your appreciation (see Example 2).

Thanks for Advice. Colleagues more experienced than you may give you helpful advice that enhances your opportunities. If you have sought professional advice of some sort, you might feel special gratitude for the help you received. Who has not remembered some teacher who said just the right words to help? (See Example 3.)

Thanks for Assistance. Often a colleague will help when an emergency arises. Even when the one who helped really had to do it, a thoughtful person will express thanks.

Thanks for Good Work. Everyone likes to be appreciated. Praise and thanks may not take the place of more money or prestige, but most people respond well to learning that their work is appreciated (see Example 4).

21 Woodland Road
Hartford, CT 06192
February 12, 19--

Research Department
Creative Technologies, Inc.
100 Commerce Plaza
Hartford, CT 06192

Dear Friends:

If I had to break my leg while I was skiing in Vermont, I am
so lucky to have good friends like you who care enough to
cheer me up!

The pot of yellow chrysanthemums arrived at the hospital the
third day I was there. They are still beautiful now that I
have come home.

Dr. Grigsby tells me that I'll have a walking cast next
week. I'll probably be back at work before the first of
March.

I really appreciate your thoughtfulness--not just the
flowers, but also your cards and your calls.

Sincerely,

Tony Gillis

Tony Gillis

Example 1
Letter of Appreciation for Gift

Corona Air Lines
8 University Plaza
Minneapolis, MN 55467

June 15, 19--

Mr. Brian Underwood
Plymouth Airways, Ltd.
14 Brewster Road
West Wimbledon
London
SW18 ORL
England

Dear Mr. Underwood:

Thank you very much for your expert guidance as I made my
way around London last week. I'd never have been able to
pack in as much sightseeing with my work without your help.

We are all enthusiastic about the merger plans. All that
remains is to obtain the necessary licensing permissions.

We are setting the wheels in motion today to get the merger
approved. Let me know how everything is proceeding when you
have time.

Cordially,

Winifred Comstock

Winifred Comstock

Example 2
Letter of Appreciation for Hospitality

Pandora Security, Inc.
14 Woodridge Avenue
Scotia, Missouri 64551

February 19, 19--

Mr. Lincoln Foster
Klein, Foster, and Valdez
Certified Public Accountants
92 Elm Street
St. Louis, MO 63199

Dear Mr. Foster:

We have always valued the advice you and your colleagues
have given us. You seem always to go beyond what must be
done, giving your work for us a personal quality.

Never has that special treatment been more evident than in
your recent advice about our liability to our stockholders
in the plans for expansion. We had not thought of the
situation in that light at all. You have undoubtedly saved
us money and much annoyance.

When we see you next week, I expect to have some new ideas
that we think will work. We appreciate your high standards
in advising us.

Sincerely,

Laura De Luna

Laura De Luna
Audit Supervisor

Example 3
Letter of Appreciation for Advice

Interoffice Memorandum

TO: Miss Rebecca Miller

FROM: Larry Afton

DATE: June 28, 19--

SUBJECT: Promotional Materials

The new material has just arrived, and I didn't want to
waste a minute in letting you know that it looks great!
We've never had a better format for the presentation of our
new accessories line.

I especially like the plans you've made for the next boat
show at the Coliseum. This information will help our
dealers plan their schedule for viewing the new items.

Thank you for doing such a sensational job!

Example 4
Memo of Appreciation for Job Well Done

```
                    M E M O

TO:      Martha Brown

FROM:    Steve Vance

DATE:    June 13, 19—

SUBJECT: Conference Committee Meeting

Martha, I just realized that your name was inadvertently
omitted from the meeting announcement that went out on May
24. Somehow I didn't notice that your name was missing. I
didn't find out what had happened until I started to wonder
why I hadn't heard from you yet.

Please accept my apology for the omission. I hope it isn't
too late for you to plan to attend the meeting tomorrow,
June 14, at 2 p.m. in my office. We really need your help
in planning the conference agenda.
```

Example 5
Memo of Apology

Bridges Electronics
552 Ninth Avenue
Detroit, Michigan 48218

```
April 19, 19—


Ms. Sharon Inverness
Wiggins Electronics
12 Wakefield Road
Kansas City, MO 64102-9321

Dear Ms. Inverness:

Congratulations on your recent election as president of the
Organization of Practicing Engineers. I read the announce-
ment in this morning's Detroit News.

Our organization has an interesting year ahead. Under your
leadership I know we will be successful in accomplishing
many of the goals we've been discussing during the cabinet
meetings you and I have both attended.

Since the article in the News is more than just a routine
announcement, I am sending you a copy with this letter. I'm
looking forward to our convention in Colorado in October.

Sincerely,

Mary Anderson

Ms. Mary Anderson
Administrative Director

pd

Enclosure
```

Example 6
Letter of Congratulations

APOLOGY LETTERS

All of us hope to avoid mistakes that cause discomfort or unhappiness to others, but sometimes there are occasions when we need to apologize for something we have done or have failed to do.

You have already considered apologies offered after a client or customer has pointed out a problem (see Unit 16). Other kinds of apology are sometimes needed within an organization. These apologies are usually written as memos.

It may seem obvious to say that a message of apology should contain an apology. Yet such messages often contain only excuses for the undesirable behavior, not an apology for it. If some work is late, apologize for the tardiness. Don't waste space and time on lengthy explanations. If you have forgotten something that has now been called to your attention, express your regrets and avoid placing the blame on someone else.

Not: **The contract was delayed by the Post Office.**

Write: **Please accept my apology for the delay.**

Not: **Your name was omitted from the list of participants because of a computer error.**

Write: **I apologize for omitting your name from the list of participants.**

Whenever you can, offer something more than an apology. For example, an assurance that the reader will appear on the next list might help make the current mistake more tolerable (see Example 5).

CONGRATULATIONS LETTERS

It is a business obligation to congratulate a colleague on a promotion, even if you were the chief rival. It is also likely that you would write a letter to congratulate a business associate on some other occasion—a wedding, a major anniversary, the birth of a child, or an honor given (see Example 6).

Adventurers Unlimited
1837 North Parkway
Memphis, Tennessee 38100-8888

April 20, 19—

Mr. Leslie Windjammer
Rural Route 4
Marketville, AR 72566

Dear Mr. Windjammer:

When we began planning our programs for next season, I immediately thought of asking you to speak at our October meeting on safaris with camera. Many of our members have made camera trips abroad, but so far no one has been to Africa. Your articles in Cameroad and the recent article about you in the Shelby County Gazette have convinced us that we want to hear what you have to say!

Our meeting is at 7:30 p.m., October 14, at the Carmichael Motel, 4495 West Baxley Road, Memphis. We usually have the Cottonwood Room. After the meeting we will serve coffee and cake. If you can come, please plan to speak for about forty minutes. The subject I suggest is "Lighting Problems for African Photography," but you may have alternative ideas of your own.

The club has no resources for paying speakers' fees, but we'll be glad to pay your expenses from Marketville.

Please use the enclosed envelope to let me know if you can be with us. We are all eager to hear you speak.

Sincerely,

Iris Blum

Miss Iris Blum
Secretary

Enclosure

Example 7
Invitation Letter to a Speaker

Rural Route 4
Marketville, Arkansas 72566
April 30, 19—

Miss Iris Blum
Adventurers Unlimited
1837 North Parkway
Memphis, TN 38100-8888

Dear Miss Blum:

Your gracious letter arrived while I was in Canada, and I
received it when I returned yesterday. I am pleased to
accept your invitation to speak to your club at 7:30 p.m.,
October 14, at the Carmichael Motel in Memphis.

I do not usually speak without a fee, but Adventurers
Unlimited has been a help to me in planning some of my
presentations. I am pleased to speak to your group on a
complimentary basis.

If I may, I'd like to change the subject you suggested to
"Photography Problems in Equatorial Regions." I think your
members would be interested to know about some of the
difficulties with heat and humidity I encountered.

Please let me know if there will be facilities for showing
slides of my latest safari. I prefer to bring my own
projector, but I will be grateful if you can provide a
screen.

Thank you for your invitation. I look forward to seeing you
in October.

Sincerely yours,

Leslie Windjammer

Leslie Windjammer

Example 8
Letter Accepting Invitation

Pandora Security, Inc.
14 Woodridge Avenue
Scotia, Missouri 64551

August 8, 19—

Mr. L. R. Stafford
Superintendent
Vickery County Schools
Forge Woods, MO 64001

Dear Mr. Stafford:

Thank you for your letter of August 1, in which you invited
me to be the speaker for your in-service workshop at the
Inkela High School on November 8.

I can well understand that you want a speaker to talk to
your faculty members about security at home and at school.
I wish I could participate, but I am scheduled to be at a
meeting in Calgary, Canada, from November 3 to 7. I don't
think I can return in time to be at your meeting.

If you are interested in finding another speaker on the same
subject, you might call your county Crime Prevention team.
Such groups are usually very helpful in giving information
about improving security.

I appreciate your invitation. Please let me know if the
occasion arises again. I'd like to talk to your group.

Sincerely,

Edgar Spencer Keyes

Edgar Spencer Keyes
Public Information Administrator

Example 9
Letter Refusing Invitation (Good Example)

INVITATION LETTERS

Business invitations are usually related to speaking
engagements or to attendance at luncheons, dinners,
or other meetings. Accuracy is an absolutely crucial
element in invitation letters.

The exact time, the exact place, and complete details
of the event must be given. If you are inviting a
speaker, be sure to give an idea of what subject you
have in mind. Be candid about financial arrangements. If no fee is to be paid, make that clear. If expenses will be paid, say so. A speaker will also want
to know how long the presentation should last (see
Example 7).

ACCEPTANCE OR REFUSAL LETTERS

When you write to accept an invitation, don't just
write "Thanks, I'll be there." Restate the important
facts. Your letter will then show your reader that
you have correctly understood the time, date, and
other details of the event to which you have been
invited. If you have ever made a mistake reading a
date or a time or appeared at one place when you
were expected somewhere else, you will understand
that repeating the important details is vital to the
success of the occasion!

When you accept an invitation, your letter should reflect your pleasure in having been invited. You
should also mention any special equipment or assistance you might require. If you are making a presentation, you might need equipment such as a projector or screen. If necessary, mention any special
requirements for the meeting room (see Example 8).

Sometimes you will have to refuse invitations. The
invitation may come at a time when another event is
scheduled. Sometimes you do not want to accept the
invitation and could not be persuaded to under any
circumstances!

```
Rural Route 4                              42 West River Street
Marketville, Arkansas 72566                New York, NY 10067-0119
April 26, 19--                             September 14, 19--


Miss Iris Blum                             Mr. Jerome Grant
Adventurers Unlimited                      President
1837 North Parkway                         Grant Advertising Agency
Memphis, TN 38100-8888                     441 Madison Avenue
                                           New York, NY 10065-7782
My dear Miss Blum:
                                           Dear Mr. Grant:
I received your invitation to speak at your club meeting
next fall.                                 The sad news about Melissa Durgan's fatal accident has just
                                           reached me. I'll miss her advice about my work and her
You must understand that I receive many such invitations. I    kindnesses in so many ways.
could not possibly go to all the many little meetings with
all the organizations that ask me.        I know that your agency has lost a valuable employee. All of
                                           us who knew Miss Durgan have lost a good friend.
I never speak without a fee, and I see no reason to make an
exception in your case.                    Please let me know if there is any way I can help during the
                                           next few weeks.
I hope you are able to find someone else who will be ready
to accept such an invitation.             Sincerely,

Very truly yours,                          Victor LaRue

Leslie Windjammer                          Victor LaRue

Leslie Windjammer
```

Example 10
Letter Refusing Invitation (Poor Example)

Example 11
Letter of Condolence

When you have to refuse an invitation, try putting yourself in the position of the person who sent the invitation. Normally this process will keep you from sounding as if you are impressed with your own importance. If a reason can be given for the refusal, give it—but be brief. Don't say you want to be asked again unless you really mean it. Sincerity with graciousness is the key (see Examples 9 and 10 for good and bad refusals).

CONDOLENCE LETTERS

Condolence letters occur more often in personal situations than in business situations. However, bereavements sometimes occur within a business organization, and the fact that these letters are extremely difficult to write will not excuse you from writing them.

In a condolence letter, avoid references to religion unless you know your reader will have a favorable response to what you have to say. Such messages

should be brief and need say no more than that you care and that you want the reader to know it (see Example 11).

REFERENCE LETTERS

We have already considered various kinds of letters relating to employment, including letters of reference (see Unit 17). We write letters of reference to support someone else's effort to get a new job or reach some other goal.

Reference letters should be truthful. If you cannot write a truthful letter that helps a job applicant, you should not write the letter at all. A prospective employer may ask specific questions that should be answered to the best of your knowledge. If you do not know some of the facts requested, it is perfectly acceptable for you to say that you do not know about that aspect of the applicant's background (see Example 12).

Ivy College
Economics Department
Churchill Building
Tremont, Delaware 19555

April 10, 19--

Miss Geneva Proust
Director of Field Services
Hector & Sebastian, Inc.
835 Willow Street
Baltimore, MD 21278-6543

Dear Miss Proust:

Your letter brought me the first news that Earle Spruce has
applied to Hector & Sebastian. When I spoke with him last
week, I urged him to send his resume to you. I've been out
of town since then and have not had a chance to talk with
him again.

Earle is a person whom I am pleased to recommend. His work
in my courses--"Introduction to Business," "Business
Economics," and "Economics for the Future"--demonstrated an
innovative approach to the subject. His senior paper was
published in the Darwin Review, a college publication that
is rapidly making a name for itself in the business field.

You can count on Earle's integrity and reliability. He
makes friends easily and shows discretion in business
situations. If I had a position to offer, I would offer it
to Earle without hesitation.

Please let me know if I can be of further help to you as you
make your decision.

Sincerely,

Judith Ganz

Dr. Judith Ganz

Example 12
Letter of Reference

PURCHASED CARDS

You should treat good manners messages with the same degree of seriousness you give to other business correspondence. You can use handwriting for condolence messages and informal thank-you notes, but do not use handwriting for other messages.

The greeting card industry in the United States is very inventive and has provided a card for almost every occasion. If you want to send a card, follow these guidelines:

- Do not use a purchased card to express condolence or appreciation. Write a letter yourself.

- Business invitations should be offered in a letter unless an invitation is formally engraved.

- Use a humorous card when appropriate. Often you can find a card that expresses exactly the right idea for someone who is ill or has had an accident. If humor is appropriate, such cards often serve a purpose that personally written messages could not equal.

Messages of congratulations may sometimes be sent with purchased cards. Try to choose what is suitable. Flowery sentiments may not be as well received as a simpler message would be.

19
Worksheets

1. Suppose that one of your classmates has used your name as a reference on an employment application. Use the name and address of the person who asked you to write a reference letter and write a favorable letter.

2. Gerry Baldwin, Esq., who lived next door to you when you were in high school, has been named Executive of the Year by a well-known national journal, *Business Magazine*. Write a letter congratulating him. He now lives at 16 Stafford Road, Philadelphia, PA 19155. You have not seen him in five years.

3. Rewrite Leslie Windjammer's letter to Iris Blum (Example 8), making it a good letter of refusal for the invitation.

4. You have just learned that your friend and business associate, Annette Duprez, suffered a broken ankle when she fell from a horse during her vacation. She is in the Evergreen Hospital in Gill's Pass, Colorado 80624. Write a letter expressing your concern.

5. Last month Mrs. Wilma Soong attended a business meeting in San Juan, Puerto Rico. Ms. Lila Martinez, of the Sanchez Company, was very helpful in obtaining equipment for some presentations she wanted to make to a meeting of her colleagues. Write the letter that Mrs. Soong could send to Ms. Lila Martinez, Sanchez Company, 162 Calle de San Carlos, San Juan, Puerto Rico 00792. Mrs. Soong works for Whitepage & Blankley Stationers, 777 Allanby Road, Denmark, NC 27890.

6. Rewrite this poorly written letter of appreciation.

1922 Lancaster Road
Baltimore, MD 21278-6543
June 20, 19—

Mr. Henri Casparedis
Hector & Sebastian, Inc.
835 Willow Street
Baltimore, MD 21278-6543

Dear Mr. Casparedis

Please accept this letter as an expression of my appreciation for all that you did on my behalf in regard to my employment at E. J. Goleb Pharmaceuticals in Boston.

The position for which I was making application has been offered to me, and I have decided to accept. I anticipate the move to Boston with satisfaction, since that is my ancestral city and the place of my own birth.

Once again let me say that words cannot express my appreciation for your assistance in obtaining this position.

Very truly yours

Lily Vasquez
Lily Vasquez

7. Last summer David Miller worked for the law firm of Jones & Fudge, 321 Case Circle, Seattle, Washington 98175. After returning to college in September, he learned that one of the partners, Veronica Fudge, has died after a brief illness. Write the letter he would write to Mr. Peter Jones, the surviving partner. While David worked for Jones & Fudge, he did not often see Ms. Fudge.

   David's address is 224 Farmers Hall, Zallion College, Denville, Oregon 97233.

8. Mrs. Karen Rossini is one of your neighbors. She manages her own consulting firm for small businesses. Write a letter inviting her to visit your "Introduction to Business" class to talk about the problems of starting a small business. Her address is Rossini Enterprises, 74 Walnut Street, Rose City, CT 60393.

   Use 778 Willoughby Road as your address, also in Rose City. Your school is Orchard Junior College, Pineville, CT 60588.

Exercises 9–12 are based on activities of the Communications Department of Theta Enterprises in Lexington, Kentucky.

9. You are a trainee in the Communications Department of Theta Enterprises. You and one of your colleagues, Jan Tremaine, were the two candidates for selection to attend a business conference in San Francisco in October. Selection means the likelihood of early advancement in the department. On August 16 Victor Dornitz, the Director of the Communications Department, announced that Jan had been chosen.

   Write a memo to congratulate Jan on her selection.

10. You have been in charge of the committee to plan the annual winter holiday party for the Communications Department of Theta Enterprises. Your committee of employees did an outstanding job, and the party, a dinner and dance held at Reynolds Inn on December 30, was a great success.

    Write a thank-you message to the committee, suitable for use on a bulletin board or in the company's January newsletter. You will want to make clear that the appreciation you express is that of the entire company as well as your own. The employees involved are Sarah French, Mike Baronne, India Jahali, Anna Martinez, Bob Lee, Angus Scott, and Murray Dewitt.

11. The thank-you message described in Exercise 10 appeared in the January newsletter. At once the members of the committee reminded you that Douglas Fitzgerald, whose name was not on the initial list of committee members, had joined the group later. He was very helpful in obtaining and operating the sound and tape equipment needed for dancing. Write an apology memo to Mr. Fitzgerald.

12. *Short Columns*, the alumni newsletter for Abingdon Business Academy, recently published a brief article announcing that Mercedes Novak has been appointed Branch Manager of the Dexter National Bank in Cheyenne, Wyoming. Mercedes was a classmate of yours five years ago at Abingdon. Write a letter to congratulate her on her achievement. You have not been in touch with her since she moved to Wyoming three years ago, but the Abingdon Alumni Office in Chicago was able to give you her address: 505 Forest Trail, Cheyenne, Wyoming 82009.

20
A Business Writer's Workshop

Certain special letters and other written materials are required for planning business activities or conveying information about business developments.

This unit will help you prepare certain kinds of written communications that might be needed in any business:

- Reservations Letters
- Press Releases
- Announcements
- Agendas
- Minutes
- Resolutions
- Telegraphs and Electronic Mail

RESERVATIONS LETTERS

Hotels and motels across the country provide facilities for business meetings. Conference centers provide facilities for conference meetings and also provide rooms, food, and recreation for the participants. Well-known resort hotels are frequently the scene of national and international conventions. These meetings may involve members of professional associations, managers of specific industries, or employees of a single company.

Sometimes a travel agent makes the reservations for company meetings, but planning may be done within the company itself. Any reservations letter should provide complete, accurate details about travel or accommodations. The letter should also provide a way for the reader to respond with additional information or changes (see Example 1).

Often a reservations letter is the written confirmation of arrangements that have already been made by telephone (see Example 2). If you are writing a confirming letter, mention the telephone call at the beginning of your letter:

This morning I spoke with Mr. Paul Chang at your reservations desk and made the following arrangements.

Make clear exactly what accommodations are needed. Tell the number and type of rooms needed, and give the number of people if possible:

We need six rooms, each with two double beds.

Specify the exact duration of the stay:

Our representatives will arrive on April 3 and leave the morning of April 7—a total of four nights.

Give the approximate time of arrival:

Please hold our rooms for late arrival between 6 and 9 p.m.

If you need to arrange for special facilities or equipment, provide all necessary details. Tell the number and size of meeting rooms. Be specific if there is a need for facilities for disabled members of the group:

In addition to lunch facilities for our 24 participants, we want to reserve a meeting room for each morning and afternoon of the three-day conference.

Please ensure that at least one of the meeting rooms is suitable for wheelchair access.

Explain what method of payment you plan to use. Enclose a deposit or indicate willingness to send a deposit if required.

Ask for a written confirmation of the arrangements. As in the case of invitations, a repetition of the details is appropriate:

I would appreciate your sending me a confirmation of these arrangements.

Charlton and Wheaton Enterprises
Hamilton Building, Suite 12
345 Valley Highway
Baltimore, MD 21217-3450

August 21, 19—

Mr. Richard McRae
Reservations Manager
Leones Inn
1567 Peachtree Boulevard
Atlanta, GA 30312-1567

Dear Mr. McRae:

Dr. Melissa Graham, a member of our staff, will travel to Atlanta in November to attend a seminar at the Atlanta Omni Center. Our employees have often stayed at the Leones Inn, and Dr. Graham has asked that I make reservations for her.

Dr. Graham will arrive by car on November 3 and will need a room for three nights. She will check out before noon on November 6. She would like a single room in the Executive Level. The price we usually pay for such accommodations is $150 a night.

Please hold the room for late arrival, probably after 6 p.m. Bill the charges to our BANCOM account, #4512 2123 1230, expiration date 7/——. I understand that valet parking is available for $4.50 a night. Please arrange for Dr. Graham to have that service upon her arrival.

I know your staff will do everything possible to ensure that Dr. Graham has a pleasant stay. I would appreciate your sending me a confirmation number for this reservation.

Sincerely,

Kevin Donnally

Kevin Donnally
Travel Coordinator

Example 1
Reservations Letter

```
August 21, 19--


Mr. Richard McRae
Reservations Manager
Leones Inn
1567 Peachtree Boulevard
Atlanta, GA 30312-1567

Dear Mr. McRae:

I appreciate your help on the phone this morning, when I
made a reservation for Dr. Melissa Graham, a member of our
staff who will be attending a seminar at the Atlanta Omni
Center in November.

As you requested, I am confirming the details of our
arrangements. Dr. Graham will arrive by car on November 3
and will need a room for three nights. She will check out
before noon on November 6. She would like a single room in
the Executive Level. The price you quoted is $150 a night.

Please hold the room for late arrival, probably after 6 p.m.
Bill the charges to our BANCOM account, #4512 2123 1230,
expiration date 7/--. You told me that valet parking is
available for $4.50 a night. Please arrange for Dr. Graham
to have that service upon her arrival.

I know your staff will do everything possible to ensure that
Dr. Graham has a pleasant stay. I would appreciate your
sending me a confirmation number for this reservation.

Sincerely,

Kevin Donnally

Kevin Donnally
Travel Coordinator
```

Example 2
Reservations Letter Confirming
Telephone Conversation

PRESS RELEASES

Press releases are announcements sent to newspapers, news magazines, trade publications, professional journals, and alumni newsletters. Press releases supply recent news about people or subjects that have an appeal to the readers of the publications (see Example 3).

A press release should be written simultaneously with the event it describes or soon after the event takes place. If you are submitting the press release to a daily newspaper, the news will be stale if the event took place several weeks ago.

Generally a press release should contain a specific date. Sometimes, though, it is possible to make the information seem more timely by being less specific about the date. If you have not been able to issue a press release within a few days of a conference or a meeting, mention a general time frame instead of a specific date.

For example, you may have to write a press release for a daily newspaper about an event that took place a month ago. If the event occurred in early September and you are writing in early October, you can avoid giving the exact date of the event and make the press release sound more timely:

Not: **The annual conference was held on September 5.**

Write: **The annual conference was held in September.**

A press release should be as brief as possible, and all names must be spelled accurately. If possible, provide specific details about sources of additional information.

Indicate the end of the press release by typing three number signs (#) after the last line of the text.

Charlton and Wheaton Enterprises
Hamilton Building, Suite 12
345 Valley Highway
Baltimore, MD 21217-3450

FOR IMMEDIATE RELEASE

November 15, 19--

Contact: Ms. Ann Mason

Charlton and Wheaton Enterprises of Baltimore is pleased to
announce that Dr. Melissa Graham of our staff has been
selected to serve as regional coordinator for the new
President's Council on Geographic Linguistics. She will
continue to serve as the language adviser for Charlton and
Wheaton Enterprises. In her new post, Dr. Graham will work
with coordinators from other regions to prepare a series of
guidelines for language instruction in the public schools of
the nation.

Dr. Graham is a graduate of Kelb University in Washington,
D.C. She did advanced research at the Language Institute at
Oxford, England, before receiving her doctorate from Ramsey
University in New York.

#   #   #

Example 3
Press Release

TO: Members of Retirement Banquet Committee

FROM: Elsie Conrad

DATE: August 14, 19--

SUBJECT: Final plans for Banquet for Mr. Joseph Cortez

There will be a meeting of the committee on August 17 at 2
p.m. in the conference room. I hope all members can be
present.

                    Agenda

1. Discussion of Date for the Banquet

   a. October 14
   b. October 19

2. Selection of Gift

   a. Golf Clubs
   b. Workshop Tools
   c. Subscription to Pinevale Theater

3. Selection of Location

   a. Gilbey's Grove Restaurant
   b. Canterbury Tavern
   c. Cherokee Inn

Copies to:

Barry Andrews
Dana Bellini
Lincoln Frazier
Victor Quimby
Adam Scott
Wanda Trimhavner
Miguel Valdez
Alicia Waco

Example 5
Informal Agenda

Agenda for Quarterly Meeting of Board of Directors
April 10, 19--

Board Room, Company Headquarters

   I. Call to order by President Shelby Whitehouse

  II. Reading of the minutes of previous meeting

 III. Reading of reports

     A. Treasurer's report

     B. Hospitality Committee report

  IV. Old business

   V. New business

     A. Selection of site for next year's annual meeting

       1. Denver

       2. Houston

       3. Baton Rouge

       4. Little Rock

     B. Planning for this year's annual meeting in Dallas

       1. Decision on speakers' fees

       2. Announcement of names of new members of
          Nominating Committee

  VI. Adjournment

Example 4
Formal Agenda

Minutes of Meeting of Retirement Banquet Committee

The meeting of the Committee for the Retirement Banquet was
held on August 17 at 2 p.m. in the conference room. All
members were present except Victor Quimby.

The coordinator of the committee, Elsie Conrad, presented
the two possible dates for the banquet to be held in honor
of Mr. Joseph Cortez--October 14 and October 19. Dana
Bellini pointed out that October 14 is the day after a
holiday weekend. After discussion, the consensus was that
October 19 would be a better choice.

Wanda Trimhavner reported on the cost of the three gifts
that had been suggested. The subscription to Pinevale
Theater can be obtained at a discount if the order is placed
before September 15. The group discussed the advisability
of selecting such things as golf clubs and workshop tools.
Lincoln Frazier said that one way of handling either would
be a gift certificate. Alicia Waco, Mr. Cortez's secretary,
said that she thought Mr. Cortez would rather have a gift
that had already been selected.

When Ms. Conrad asked for a vote, there were five for the
theater subscription and two for a gift certificate at
Apollo Sporting Goods. Ms. Conrad asked Ms. Waco to make
arrangements for buying two theater subscriptions.

Miguel Valdez distributed maps showing the location of the
three restaurants we were considering. He also showed us
sample menus. His recommendation was the Canterbury Tavern
because we can have it exclusively. The other restaurants
have enough room, but there would be a parking problem if
other large groups were there. Ms. Conrad asked for a vote,
and Canterbury Tavern was unanimously selected.

There was no further business. The meeting was adjourned at
2:45 p.m.

Respectfully submitted,

Barry Andrews

Barry Andrews

Example 6
Informal Minutes

Minutes of April 10, 19—

The quarterly meeting of the Board of Directors of Specific Drilling Equipment was held on April 10, 19— in the boardroom of SDE headquarters in Tulsa, Oklahoma.

Call to Order   The meeting was called to order at 10 a.m. by the company's president, Shelby Whitehouse. All members were present.

Minutes of Previous Meeting   Secretary Stewart Birch read the minutes of the meeting of January 8, 19—, and they were approved as read.

Treasurer's Report   Treasurer Sally Alvarez submitted the report of the past quarter. There were no questions, and the report is on file.

Committee Reports   Elsie Conrad, Director of the Hospitality Committee, announced that the committee will be meeting during the next four months to plan the retirement banquet for Joseph Cortez, Supervisor of Training Programs. Mr. Cortez plans to retire in October.

Old Business   Board Member Adam Scott made a motion that no old business be discussed at this meeting so that more time could be devoted to choosing the site for next year's meeting. The motion was seconded and approved.

New Business   Mr. Whitehouse presented the names of the four cities under consideration for next year's annual meeting: Denver, Houston, Baton Rouge, and Little Rock. It was pointed out that availability and cost of accommodations would not vary much among the four cities.

Discussion centered on accessibility of each city and on the company's policy of moving from one area of our operation to another for these meetings. Stewart Birch suggested that Houston be reserved for another year, since this year's meeting is in Texas. After some discussion about the accessibility of the

Example 7
Formal Minutes (Page 1)

cities, Valerie Compton made a motion that a vote be taken. The motion was seconded and approved. The vote was taken, and Denver was unanimously accepted.

The new members of the Nominating Committee were announced: Miguel Valdez, Barry Andrews, Lucy Chester, and Morris Day.

Adjournment   Since there was no further business, the meeting was adjourned at 12:30 p.m.

Respectfully submitted,
(Can be omitted)

Stewart Birch
Stewart Birch, Secretary

Formal Minutes (Page 2)

OTHER ANNOUNCEMENTS

Other announcements besides press releases are commonly used in business. These announcements fall into a few general categories.

New Facility Announcement. A business might announce that a person or a business has moved to new quarters.

New Product Announcement. Information on a new product or service might be sent to customers.

Staff Announcement. The hiring of new employees and promotions within a company might be announced.

Employment Announcement. A company might advertise employment positions available. These descriptions might be more detailed than a typical classified advertisement.

AGENDAS

An agenda is a list of the items scheduled for discussion during a meeting. A formal agenda, suitable for formal meetings, has certain specific parts (see Example 4). An informal agenda contains basic information about the subjects to be discussed, but it is usually arranged in a more casual style than a formal agenda (see Example 5). An informal agenda is used for a meeting that is not part of a continuing series of meetings. An informal agenda is also used for regular informal meetings.

MINUTES

Like agendas, minutes may have a formal or an informal framework. For formal meetings based on formal agendas, formal minutes would be presented and taken. For less formal meetings, the minutes can be informal and do not have to follow a parliamentary format (see Examples 6 and 7). When more detailed information is needed about formal situations, consult a book that outlines parliamentary procedures.

RESOLUTIONS

A resolution is the formal statement of the action or the opinion of a group. The style of a resolution is

```
                    Hawthorne Citizens' Committee for Traffic Safety

                                    Resolution

                                Adopted April 4, 19—

            Whereas the short duration of the traffic light at Rosewood
            Avenue and State Highway 42 has been a source of concern to
            many people for the past four years; and

            Whereas numerous attempts have been made to get the city
            government to make some changes in that light; and

            Whereas no steps have been taken to alter the situation; and

            Whereas there was a serious accident on that corner on March
            29; therefore be it

            Resolved, That this committee severely condemn the city
            government for failing to protect the citizens of Hawthorne,
            and be it further

            Resolved, That we recommend to all residents that they use
            the other routes in town until the light is changed, and be
            it further

            Resolved, That copies of this resolution be submitted to the
            City Council and to the Hawthorne TaleBearer.

                                        Respectfully submitted,

                                        Felicia Fillmore
                                        Felicia Fillmore, President

                                        Norman Dooly
                                        Norman Dooly, Secretary
```

Example 8
Resolution

always formal. The resolution may be offered in praise of the work or achievements of an individual or a group. Another use for a resolution is to give a formal statement of the attitude or wishes of an organization (see Example 8).

TELEGRAPHS AND ELECTRONIC MAIL

There are many ways of sending brief messages very quickly. Many companies can transmit messages from one branch office to another through their own computerized electronic mail systems. Some compa-

nies specialize in handling telegraph messages. The exact cost and procedure for such messages vary, depending on the method used.

If you send a telegraph or an electronic mail message, be brief. In telegraph messages, unnecessary words are omitted:

Not: **We are canceling the meeting. You will receive instructions by mail tomorrow.**

Write: **Meeting canceled. Instructions follow by mail tomorrow.**

20
Worksheets

On the following pages you will find information about four companies and some situations that require letters, memos, and other written materials as described in this chapter. Select the company that appeals to you and do all the assignments relating to that company. For additional assignments, select another company from the exercises and follow the instructions provided.

1. E. J. Goleb Pharmaceuticals Inc. is a manufacturer of prescription drugs and drugs sold over the counter. The company also has a small cosmetics line. EJGPI has an extensive research department, and the company handles its own advertising. The address for EJGPI headquarters is 94 Madison Avenue, Boston, MA 02145-1243.

    Donald Koong, Marketing Manager, is planning a meeting of the marketing staff to take place September 10–12. The meeting will be held at the Knoll Haven Inn, 9 Queen Street, Brooksley, Vermont 05666. Preliminary arrangements have been made with the inn through Mr. Calvin Mansfield. The purpose of the meeting is to plan marketing strategy for two new products—AKEGON, a pain reliever; and CROCOGON, a dry-skin cream. In addition to the 12 members of the marketing staff, participants will include Sylvia Bliss, of the Advertising Division, and David Lindholm, Director of Consumer Affairs.

A. Write the letter to Knollhaven Inn, making the final reservations for 15 people and 15 rooms. Mr. Koong has decided that the meeting should run through September 13, with participants remaining at the inn through breakfast on the 13th. Send a deposit of $50 per person, paying by check, and explain that final payment will be made by check upon arrival.

B. At the first meeting, to begin at 2 p.m. on September 10, decisions are to be made about product packaging for both products. The points to consider include the colors for both packages and the size for the skin cream container. Color possibilities are green on white, green on blue, or dark green on light green (Goleb standard colors). The sizes for the skin cream include 2-, 4-, and 5-ounce containers and a possibility of some other size. At later meetings, advertising and test-marketing will be planned.

Write an informal agenda for the first meeting.

C. Write the announcement of the meeting, to be sent to each participant as soon as the final plans have been made. Transportation is being arranged by the company, with a chartered bus leaving from the executive parking lot. Brooksley is about 160 miles from Boston. All meals will be eaten at the inn, which has an excellent reputation. There will be no evening meetings, and all expenses are paid by the company.

2. The Organization of Practicing Engineers has its headquarters at 1420 Phogg Street, S.W., Washington, DC 20099. Ms. Sharon Inverness, of Wiggins Electronics, was elected president of the OPE in April. The Organization of Practicing Engineers' Fifth Annual Convention, to be held in Colorado in October, will be the first convention at which she presides. The organization has 3,500 members, of whom about 400 usually attend the annual convention.

A. The convention will be held at the Greenwood Lodge in Grey Hills, Colorado—about 30 miles west of Denver. Preliminary arrangements will be made from the Washington headquarters. The convention will begin on October 5 and run through October 9. In addition to the professional speakers, Dr. Paul Carmichael, an internationally known electronics researcher, will speak at the gala dinner on October 8. Another feature of this convention will be a tour of the world's largest dephonate plant, where the smallest electric circuits now in use are manufactured.

Write the announcement of the convention plans, to be sent to all members by July 1.

B. The response to the advance information was overwhelming. Ms. Inverness must prepare a letter to Greenwood Lodge, explaining that the number of participants will be 600 instead of the original estimate of 400. Write the letter, to be sent from Ms. Inverness's business address: Wiggins Electronics, 12 Wakefield Road, Kansas City, Missouri 64102-9321. Greenwood Lodge requires a deposit of $25 a night for each person. Date your letter August 10.

C. The previous president of the Organization of Practicing Engineers was Benjamin Gold, president of United Systems and Circuits in Minneapolis. He also was the founder of the OPE and served as president for two terms—six years. The members of the executive council meet before the gala dinner to draft a resolution of appreciation to Mr. Gold. The secretary of the council is Ms. Lucia Katz. Write the resolution.

D. In his speech, Dr. Carmichael announces that he has discovered a substance that will take the place of dephonate and will make possible many advances in electronic technology. There were no reporters at the dinner since it was supposed to be a fairly routine speech. Write the press release Dr. Carmichael would approve for immediate release. (Add any details you want about where the new substance was discovered, where it is being kept, and what it is called.)

3. The annual Furniture Showcase, a dealers' exhibit for furniture buyers, is scheduled for April 13–18 in Roanoke, Virginia. Anderson's Department Store, which has large downtown stores in seven Southern cities and smaller stores in twenty shopping malls, plans to make arrangements for its 27 buyers to attend the Showcase. Anderson's home office, Grove Street at Tenth Avenue, Atlanta, GA 30376-8510, will make the reservations for the entire group. Accommodations will be in various hotels and motels. Anderson's staff always stays at the Hopewell Inn. One of the new exhibitors this year will be Rosewood Antiques, 458 High Point Plaza, Greenhaven, NC 28766.

A. Write the letter to the Hopewell Inn, 8890 Darthwood Road, Roanoke, VA 24099. Reserve 27 rooms and a hospitality suite for April 13–18. Since Anderson's has used this inn for many years, Hopewell no longer requires a deposit from the store. Ms. Kelly Beaupre will sign the letter as Furniture Department Coordinator.

B. Write an announcement from Rosewood Antiques to be included in all showcase folders distributed at the exhibit. Rosewood is a dignified old firm.

C. Ms. Beaupre plans to hold a meeting before the beginning of the showcase to explain to Anderson's buyers that this year they should concentrate on the kinds of furniture that each individual store sells best. She wants their ideas on what type of furniture should be featured—French, Spanish, Danish, Early American, or Italian—and also what kind of seating furniture will sell best—sofas, love seats, chairs, or modular units.

Prepare an informal agenda for her meeting.

4. Canterbury College in Middle Springs, Ohio, has an enrollment of 12,000. In October Dr. Pamela Argosa will be installed as the president, the fifteenth in the 130-year history of the college and the first woman to hold the position. Middle Springs has a resident population of 60,000 and is about 30 miles from Cincinnati.

Dr. Argosa will be inaugurated at a formal convocation at which representatives of about 150 colleges will take part in the academic proceedings. Colleges around the country have been invited to send their representatives to participate.

Among those who will attend are four of Dr. Argosa's college classmates: Dr. Jerome Baldwin, now president of Hector & Sebastian, Inc., Baltimore, MD 21278; Mrs. Barbara Sharpless, a partner in Melton & Sharpless Realtors, New York, NY 10055; Helga Alberich, a credit manager for Anderson's Department Store, Atlanta, GA 30376; and Dr. Michael Lopez, head of the English department at Winston University in Grover, Kansas 65110.

A. Each of the four friends from college days has accepted the invitation and has asked the college to make arrangements for accommodations in Middle Springs for the two days and nights of the convocation. Write a letter informing any one of them that you have made the reservations at Chesterfield Lodge, 2218 Kessler Road, Middle Springs, OH 45311. Each participant is to make his or her own arrangements about deposits and billing. Explain that the festivities will begin on October 21 with a luncheon. Sign the letter with your own name.

B. Prepare the official announcement of Dr. Argosa's selection. She is succeeding Dr. David Brixton, who has taken a job with the State Department. Dr. Argosa attended Canterbury College, majored in history, later received a master's in economics from Royal College in London, and then received her doctorate from Winston University in Kansas. She is married to a famous writer of science fiction, Kenneth Harwood, and they have three daughters, Jill, Jan, and Julia. Her latest job was as head of the Economics Department at Darwin College in Darwin, New York. She is well known for her work in consumer economics.

C. Write the letter from Dr. Lopez confirming his reservations at Chesterfield Lodge.

21
Reports

Letters and memos are usually written for specific readers or for small groups who are known to the writer. Reports, on the other hand, are less personal. The writer expects that the report will be read by people other than the ones to whom it is originally submitted. For that reason, the report is usually written in an impersonal style, with few first-person or second-person pronouns.

When you write a formal report, or a long report of any kind, you should follow certain basic procedures. The steps in the preparation of such a report often require written notes. For a brief report the steps may not be as clearly defined or as consciously followed, but certain processes are common to the preparation of all reports, regardless of length or formality.

PURPOSE OF REPORTS

The first step in preparing a report is to determine its purpose. For a brief memo, a routine progress report, or any other short, informal writing, the purpose is usually so clearly understood that it is unnecessary to state the purpose in writing before you begin gathering information.

For longer reports, take time to formulate your purpose in writing before you begin. If the report is one you *want* to write—one that deals with a subject in which you have great interest or from which you expect beneficial results—it should be easy to determine the purpose. Because your involvement is immediate, you can state in writing or have in mind exactly what you want to accomplish in the report.

If the report is one you *must* write—one that deals with a subject for which you lack enthusiasm—it may be more difficult to determine the purpose. You may even wonder why the report is needed. In such circumstances, it is even more important for you to be able to state the purpose of the report before you begin—not your purpose, perhaps, but that of the person who assigned it to you. Once you have recognized that purpose, it becomes much easier to decide what should be included in the report.

ORGANIZATION

Keeping your purpose in mind, you begin the second step—collecting the facts you need. A helpful procedure is simply to make notes of the things you consider important. Often one fact leads to another question, and you may find that you need some information that is not already available. You may have to check files or consult references.

When you have listed the facts you plan to use, you are ready for the third step: arranging the facts in the order that will make your report effective. For a lengthy or formal report, this step requires a formal outline. For a brief report, it is usually enough to make a quick arrangement of facts in the order in which you want to use them. In either case, choose a writing plan that suits the subject of your report.

Chronological Order. If you choose to organize based on time or occurrence, you could begin with the earliest events and move to the latest. There are some instances in which you might want to state the present situation and then give the background.

General Statement Followed by Supporting Details. This method works well for situations that involve explanations.

Series of Facts or Ideas Followed by Conclusions. This method is usually effective for writing recommendations.

Series of Facts in Order of Importance. The items in the report may have varying degrees of importance. You can decide how best to arrange them to emphasize the most important points. Usually the most important point should be saved for last.

Sometimes a particular topic will have an order all its own, not fitting any categories.

Once your outline or plan is clear, you can determine what additional facts you need to complete your explanation or back up your recommendation. You may discover that you have some information that does not belong with the rest of your material. If that information is important to your report, you will need to revise your plan of organization to include it. If the information is not important, omit it. The quality of a report decreases when unrelated or unimportant material is included.

INTRODUCTION AND CONCLUSION

When you have an outline of all the material you intend to use in the order in which you plan to use it, then you are ready to write the introduction and the conclusion. An introduction sometimes gives the reason for the report, and it sometimes gives a broad definition of a problem:

> **During the staff meeting on April 14, a question arose about the extent of the damage to the warehouse in last month's fire.**
>
> **Breaches of security have been occurring at plants like ours all over the country.**

These sentences could be developed further to serve as introductions to informal reports. The purpose, the facts, and the plan of your paper will determine what kind of introduction you need.

The conclusion of your report can be written when you write the introduction. If your facts and their arrangement have led to a conclusion that is not stated elsewhere, the final paragraph (or paragraphs) should give that conclusion. When you write the conclusion just after you write the introduction, you can be sure that the connection is logical and that the conclusion is not merely a summary of what you have already written in the introduction.

Working from your outline, prepare a draft of the report. In many organizations there is a format that your final draft must follow. Refer to a company style guide or to existing reports in your organization for format requirements.

Often a final draft is submitted for approval before the report takes its finished form. For specific handling of such things as graphs, charts, and tables, consult a manual of style.

When you have completed your report, be sure that every word contributes to the accomplishment of your purpose. As you read and evaluate the report in the light of your purpose, you should see well-developed, clear, and well-organized ideas. These qualities show that you have achieved your goal.

SHORT REPORTS

When preparing short reports, try to make the material as easy as possible for your reader to understand.

Recommendations. Usually recommendations are a report of suggested ways to handle a problem or to change a situation. Such a report should begin with a brief *statement of the problem* or *description of the situation*:

> **Many customers are having difficulty understanding our new credit policy. To lessen the confusion that has resulted from our recent changes, here are some steps we might take.**

Next, provide a *list of steps* or *recommendations*. Usually a numbered list is easier to read than a narrative.

Conclude a recommendation with a *final statement of what you expect*:

> **Following these procedures will eliminate the misunderstandings among our customers.**

Explanations. The reason for writing explanations might involve explaining how something works or why something does not work. An explanation should include a brief introductory statement, an itemized list of procedures or reasons, and a final statement.

An explanation of why something did not work might begin like this:

> **The payroll checks for the marketing division were not ready on Tuesday morning as they should have been. This is what happened:**

Many other situations call for explanations. In an explanation keep in mind that you need some sort of introductory statement. Include an introduction even if the report is being submitted at the request of your supervisor.

Also keep in mind that itemized lists of steps or reasons can make the material easier to read. Finally, be sure that you have a strong concluding statement:

Not: **I hope this explains what you wanted to know.**

Write: **These were the events that caused the problem.**

Status Reports and Progress Reports. Reports on the status or progress of a project are written after the project has been started. The information you report is determined by what has happened. Such reports usually do not include a history of the project, since your readers already know that.

For example, your department might have the responsibility of reviewing the files on product claims to determine what kinds of problems have been the most prevalent over the past three years. Your report does not have to explain why you are conducting the review, since the reason would have been established before the assignment began. A status or progress report should show what has been accomplished since the last report, what difficulties have arisen, and what you expect to do next.

Periodic Reports. A periodic report is part of a series of reports submitted at regular intervals. The weekly report and the monthly report are the most usual types. You might have a weekly report of the number and type of consumer requests, a monthly report of the figures for sales. The quarterly and annual reports published by corporations for their stockholders are a type of formal report.

Brief Reports for the Record. Even when we use oral communication, such as telephone calls, interviews, or conferences, we need at least a brief written record of what happened:

In our telephone conversation, Mrs. Soong made these points:

FORMAL REPORTS

A formal business report is similar in many ways to formal reports for academic purposes. Though a formal report is not written in the exact style used for history or English reports, a formal style is usually appropriate.

Language. In most business writing, the warmth that is achieved by an informal style is important. In report writing it is preferable to use a more formal, impersonal style. Use pronouns like *it* and *they*, or, better still, use nouns. In general, avoid second-person pronouns:

Not: **As *your* use of electric power has increased . . .**

Write: **As *customers'* use of . . .**

Or write: **As *the* use of . . .**

Contractions are another mark of informality. Try to avoid them in formal material.

Even with a formal style, you should still avoid using passive verbs when you can find a graceful way of writing in the active voice:

Not: **These programs were initiated in January.**

Write: **These programs began in January.**

Although the first-person singular pronouns (*I*, *me*, and *my*) are not a good idea in formal writing, plural first-person pronouns referring to a company are often useful:

Our customers demanded better control of security, and we have been able to supply it.

Organization. A formal report is usually long enough to require headings. Those headings are like signposts, telling the reader what each section contains. The headings will vary with the content.

If a report is long, a table of contents should be placed at the beginning and followed by an introduction. Some formal reports also contain a summary, which is a digest of the contents of the body of the report.

Within the body of the report, headings should be included to help organize the material. Some typical words used in headings are these:

History   Background   Problem   Reasons

Most reports contain a formally stated conclusion. Sometimes the conclusion is a deduction or suggestion based on the facts given in the report. Sometimes the conclusion is simply a generalized restatement of the material.

Documentation. Citing authorities and sources for your information requires documentation. You should cite your sources within the text in footnote format, and you should supply a bibliography, or list of sources, at the end of the report.

For detailed information about the format for footnotes and a bibliography, consult a manual of report writing style. A brief summary here of basic requirements will serve as a quick reference.

A bibliography is an alphabetical list of references. Each type of reference has a particular citation form, but generally the author's name comes first (last name, then first name). The title of the work cited comes second, and information about the publication comes next. Page numbers, if appropriate, are given

49 Bellevue Road
Chicago, IL 60678
January 10, 19--

Mr. Albinoni Millo
Director, Channel 16
321 Woodward Highway
Lawrence, Ohio 41234

Dear Mr. Millo:

Here is the report you and I discussed when we met last
September. As you requested, I used all the students in
Camden County as my research base, rather than a mere sample
from each school.

The data in this report should provide just the material you
need for the development of your series on geography. I
learned much from my studies, and I enjoyed the project. Not
all freelance assignments are as interesting as this one.

I am enclosing the three copies you requested. For the next
three weeks I am going to be on temporary assignment in
Salisbury, North Carolina. If you want to talk with me about
the report, you can reach me at 704-555-0191 or by mail at
the Salisbury Inn, 405 North Beacon Street, Salisbury, NC
28141.

Sincerely,

Margot Lukas

Margot Lukas

Enclosures: Three Copies of Report

Example 1
Cover Letter for Report

at the end of the citation. In the case of dated publications (magazines, journals, and newspapers), the date is considered part of the title of the publication. Here are some examples of types of entries in a bibliography:

- **Book with one author**
  Bishop, Hildegarde. *Meteorology for Today*. New York: Bixby Publishers, 19--.

- **Book with more than one author**
  Coriander, Benjamin, and Paul Lee. *Climate*. Chicago: Alwich, Inc., 19--.

- **Book with editor (part of book)**
  Evans, Timothy, ed. "Snow and Sleet." *Essays on Weather*. Baltimore: Rohmer Company, 19--, 46–70.

- **Newspaper article (author's name not known)**
  "Climate Becomes an Asset." *Minneapolis Journal*, June 14, 19--, 16.

- **Magazine article with author's name**
  Katowski, Vernon. "Mapping Our Weather." *Scientific Adventures*, June 19--, 81.

There are many other reference sources—pamphlets, speeches, interviews, and unpublished manuscripts. The important thing to remember is that the point of the bibliography is to show the source of your information. The order of material within each entry should always be roughly the same, and the author's name should always come first, if it is known. The date and the name of the publisher are also important parts of your source.

Footnotes are used to cite sources within the report. Footnotes may appear at the bottom of the page on which the reference occurs. Increasingly, writers place footnote information within parentheses where appropriate in the body of the report. This method eliminates the need to rearrange footnotes every time a report is changed.

Sometimes endnotes are used—footnotes listed on a separate page at the end of the report. For the technicalities of writing footnotes and endnotes, a report writer's manual is invaluable.

Two basic facts about the form of footnotes and endnotes may be helpful. Remember that the author's name is written in normal order and that the note refers to the single page used, not to all the pages in the source.

TRANSITIONS

Certain words and phrases can be used to show the relationship between the ideas of one paragraph and those of the next. These expressions should be used sparingly and should be varied. Beware of the pompous-sounding *firstly*, *secondly*, *thusly*, and *more importantly*. Instead write *first*, *second*, *thus*, and *more important*. Vary the position of transitional phrases in the sentence so that every paragraph in your report doesn't begin with the same kind of word. (However, do not sacrifice clarity!)

Here are some useful transition words and phrases:

next	**furthermore**	**then**
in contrast	**similarly**	**in summary**
likewise	**as a result**	

LETTERS OF TRANSMITTAL

When you have completed a report, you are ready to deliver it to your reader or readers. A letter of transmittal, or cover letter, goes with the report to summarize the work you have done and explain why you are sending it (see Example 1).

A letter of transmittal can be simple and informal. Notice that Example 1 gives an explanation of when the writer will be available for additional information.

Many situations require reports. For almost any kind of report, however, certain techniques are valuable:

- Determine your purpose and make everything you write fit that purpose.

- Make an outline so that you will be sure to include all the items you need.

- Develop your ideas in a logical order.

Examples 2 and 3 show a sample title page and first page of a report.

Prepared for Albinoni Milo, Director of Channel 16 News

By Margot Lukash
January 9, 19—

Example 2
Title Page of Report

Television 16, represented by its director, Albinoni Millo, is preparing to develop a series of programs designed to increase the geographic knowledge of students in the five high schools of Camden County. This study was prepared as a first step in planning the series.

Participants

All students in the five Camden County high schools will participate in the series:

Cadwell High School	850 students
Dexter Academy	600 students
Forstman High School	900 students
Hodges Preparatory School	645 students
Montrose High School	1,382 students

Procedures

A survey testing general geographic knowledge was prepared. The survey included basic facts about United States geography and implications that can be derived from those facts. It also included basic facts about world geography and implications derivable from those facts.

Example 3
First Page of Report

21
Worksheets

1. Choose any subject that interests you and prepare a bibliography consisting of one book, two magazine articles, and one newspaper article.

2. Write a letter of transmittal to go with your report on possible uses of a new fiber, denisilk, when you send the report to the chairman of your division, Mr. Harvey Allegheny. He asked you to write the report.

3. Choose any procedure that you know well and write a brief explanation for someone who is not familiar with the procedure. (Simple activities such as building a fire, making a pie, or driving in snow are good to use.)

4. As one of the managers of a medium-sized shopping mall, you believe it would be to the advantage of all concerned if the mall remained open only two evenings a week (Thursday and Friday) instead of the six now scheduled (every evening except Sunday). Write your recommendations to the mall council, showing how you think the limited business hours would benefit the stores, their employees, and the customers.

5. Write the introduction to a report to the employees of Hector & Sebastian about the possibility of changing from the U. N. Risk Company to Athenia for health insurance. You've found that Athenia has advantages because it gives dental, pharmaceutical, and maternity coverage that is superior to that of the other company.

6. You are a member of the staff of the Human Resources Department of a large corporation. You have just taken part in a meeting between Jewel Morris and one of the employees under her supervision, Susan Philips. Ms. Morris brought up several complaints about Ms. Philips's work, including habitual lateness, frequent personal telephone calls, and occasional bickering with other employees over such things as air conditioning and ventilation. Ms. Morris has pointed out these problems to Ms. Philips before. On this occasion she wanted your presence so that the oral reprimand would get official attention. Ms. Morris has told Ms. Philips that she will work with her to correct the difficulties, but that if the problems persist, Ms. Philips will be dismissed at the end of a three-month probationary period.

Write a brief summary of the meeting for your records.

Part Four
Other Forms of Communication

In this book we have been looking at business writing—an activity that always requires conscious involvement. No one can write or read a letter, memo, or report without being aware that communication is taking place.

Other forms of communication are not always composed deliberately but are the result of our simply *being there* in the presence of other people. Others talk and we listen. We answer and they listen. We perceive and interpret many nonverbal impressions. Because these unwritten communications usually involve very little planning and are often interpreted subjectively, we tend not to think of them as activities at all. We forget that speaking and listening are skills that can be developed.

In the next three units, we shall consider the ways we communicate with the spoken word and with nonverbal messages. Get ready to practice those communications skills that do not involve writing.

Because the activities of talking, listening, and communicating without words are interrelated, the assignments for the three units are grouped together at the end of the last unit.

22
Oral Communication

All written communications are permanent. Once words are put on paper, they may be copied, filed, and retrieved. The written communication stands as proof of itself, available for others besides the reader or readers to whom it was originally addressed. Oral communications do not have this permanence, but they form an essential part of business communications.

Like written communications, good oral communication involves skill with words. Vocabulary plays an important part, as do good pronunciation and enunciation. Another important factor—beyond the skills used in writing—is the attitude that can be conveyed by tone of voice and even by silence. This unit will help you build strong oral communications skills.

SPEAKING STYLE AND VOCABULARY

There are entire courses on the subject of speech; college degrees are based on various aspects of the subject. We are not concerned here with the study of speech or with the techniques of public speaking. We shall look at these aspects of oral communications only as they relate to the everyday activities of most people—the daily routine of "I talk, you listen; you talk, I listen; they talk, we listen."

In all your oral communications, try to avoid "empty" words and phrases that detract from what you are saying:

Not: **I want to, you know, get like a job in the electronics field.**

Say: **I want to get a job in the electronics field.**

Not: **The program was, I mean, interesting, but it was like too long for most people to enjoy.**

Say: **The program was interesting, but it was too long for most people to enjoy.**

Somehow it is easier to keep our vocabulary within a normal, natural range in speech than it is in writing. Even so, we do have a tendency to slip into pompous language when a situation seems to require formality.

Good advice to a writer is "Try to write the way you talk." To a speaker, the advice might well be "Try to speak the way you talk." No one would suggest that business language should be slang or baby talk, but neither is it a good idea to rely solely on long words and a formal style:

Not: **We assure you of our intentions to remedy the situation.**

Say: **We'll take care of the problem at once.**

Pronunciation. Take care to use standard pronunciations of the words that are in your vocabulary. When you begin to use a new word, be sure that you are pronouncing it correctly. Listen to other people, and listen to yourself. If you realize that the rest of the world pronounces a word differently from the way you do, consider the possibility that you are wrong. Check the dictionary to be sure.

Be careful to say all the syllables that should be pronounced. We hear announcers say "the Prezdent" and "guvmint," and we probably know what they mean. However, there really isn't any excuse for leaving the listeners to fill in the missing syllables.

TELEPHONE BASICS

The telephone dominates the office just as it can dominate the home. Before we consider specific telephone situations, review the following guidelines for receiving and making telephone calls.

Receiving Calls. Always keep in mind that to the person on the other end of the conversation, your voice alone conveys your message. Aside from good enunciation (clear speech), correct pronunciation, and acceptable intonation or emphasis, your voice also conveys an *attitude*.

Impatience, boredom, and hostility are not appropriate attitudes to show toward toward a customer, a client, or any other business associate. These attitudes are audible even when the words you speak are pleasant. Imagine this sentence spoken by some-one who is annoyed at having to answer the phone:

Good morning, may I help you?

Even if you have answered the telephone dozens of times and found it necessary to repeat the same rou-tine information to the callers, remember that for each caller his or her call is special. Anyone who calls your business is entitled to your interest and your courtesy.

When receiving telephone calls, be sure to answer promptly. If answering the telephone is a normal part of your job, have a clear understanding of the accepted procedures in your office. You should know what greeting your company prefers—*hello*, *good morning*, or simply the name of the organiza-tion. You should also know what other information you should give—your department name, your name, or your boss's name.

Often a secretary needs to find out the name of a caller before transferring the call to the appropriate person. There are various ways of obtaining this in-formation without saying "Who is this?" A courteous question will usually get a response from the caller:

May I have your name, please?
Who shall I say is calling?

Do not say *"Whom* is calling?" *Who* is the only ac-ceptable form for the subject of *is calling*.

It is also important to understand how to operate the telephone equipment. If answering the phone is not a normal part of your job, find out how to put callers on hold and how to transfer calls before you begin receiving calls.

Making Calls. To avoid the delay and annoyance of repeating information, be sure you have the ap-propriate person or department before you begin to explain what you want:

I'd like to speak with someone who can tell me about airline schedules to Montreal.

If you know the name of the department, just ask for it:

I'd like the order department, please.

Once you have the person or department on the line, be willing to identify yourself:

My name is Al Florentine, and I'm calling to find out your charges for boarding dogs.

TELEPHONE USES

The telephone has many valuable uses in business.

Placing an Order. Many national firms now have toll-free numbers that cut the cost to the customer of placing orders by telephone. Before you make a call to place an order, be sure that you have all the in-formation you need—the same facts you need when you place an order by mail:

- The name and address of your company
- Information on exact item or items you want to order
- The method of payment to be used
- Special instructions about shipping
- A written record of the order for reference

Receiving an Order. When you receive an order by telephone, you have an excellent opportunity to re-sell the customer on your company. When you take an order, you owe your customer the same things you would give in person or in a letter:

- Complete attention
- Courtesy
- Helpfulness in taking the order

Often the person taking the order records the order by computer as he or she takes it. Sometimes the or-der is written on an order form. In any case, a record of the order must be made at once.

Making Inquiries. Be prepared to give enough information at the beginning of the call to ensure that you reach the right person. An inquiry call, like an adjustment request, is pointless unless it is di-rected to a person qualified to handle it. Begin with a statement or a question that will cause your call to be transferred to a suitable person. Then present the inquiry clearly and courteously.

Study the following examples of opening questions and appropriate follow-up statements.

Example A. **May I speak with someone in the re-search department please?** Your call is transferred to Dr. Rosemary Whitehall in Research. **Dr. Whitehall, I am Lee Patterno of the Greenville Historical Soci-ety. In April we'll have a display on gemstone arti-facts, and we are looking for a speaker to discuss the chemical tests that are used to establish the ages of such relics. My friend Jeremy Blackstone sug-gested that you might be willing to speak to us.**

Example B. **Could you connect me with someone who can give me information about tides along the Virginia-Carolina coast?** Your call is transferred to Errol Pickens, a staff member of the government agency you have called. **Mr. Pickens, my name is**

Garrett Mitchell. In June I'm planning a shell-hunting trip to the Virginia-Carolina coast, and I'd like to know the low tide times during that month.

Answering Inquiries. Providing intelligent answers to telephone inquiries is a superb way of building goodwill for your company. Too often a potential customer is given no information, is given the wrong information, or is made to feel that the inquiry is an intrusion. The responder misses an incomparable opportunity to build goodwill.

Study the following examples of situations in which a telephone inquiry can be used to build goodwill.

Keith Guilen has called a home improvement store to ask how to take the measurements for wallpaper in a room at his home.

> *Not:* **When a customer buys paper from us, we send someone to measure. Otherwise we can't help you.**
>
> *Say:* **There are a lot of factors that affect the amount of wallpaper you'll need. That's why we like to send someone to do the measuring after you select the paper. Why not come down to the store and let us show you our sample books?**

College freshman Laura Ortega has locked her keys in her car at a shopping mall. She telephones the service station where she usually buys gasoline and asks if someone can help her.

> *Not:* **We're busy with customers, and I don't know when we can get to you.**
>
> *Say:* **Can you wait for about an hour? Everyone is out of the shop, but someone should be back within an hour. If you're in a hurry, you could try (name another station or give some other suggestion).**

Asking for Adjustments. When you want to complain about poor service or a poor product, making a telephone call may seem like the best idea. In practice, however, such calls are often disappointing because the person who receives the call may not have the background information to produce a satisfactory response. Whenever possible, send a letter before you make the call. Then, when you call, you can refer to the letter as a guide. Written requests give the receiver an opportunity to look into the matter, obtain the necessary facts, and make a decision based on more solid information than can be obtained from most phone calls.

Making Reservations. As in the case of placing orders, be very sure of what you want before you place a call to make reservations. In the case of restaurant reservations, you'll need the following information:

- Date and time
- Name of persons for whom reservation is being made
- Number of persons in the group

Be sure to ask about any special requests for members of the group for whom you are making reservations, such as facilities for handicapped persons or availability of smoking or nonsmoking areas.

Verify credit card acceptability by asking what credit cards are accepted, rather than asking about any specific card.

In the case of travel and hotel reservations, you'll need the following information:

- Date of arrival and departure
- Name(s) of person(s) for whom reservation is being made
- Exact accommodations desired

Have credit card information available, if necessary, to guarantee your reservations.

There are many other business situations that require the use of the telephone. In general, keep in mind the following guidelines when conducting business by phone.

First, let your voice reflect an attitude of helpfulness and friendliness. If you are placing an order or asking for help, try to assume that the person on the other end of the conversation *wants* to help you. If you are receiving the call, go out of your way to be positive in your response.

Second, be as sure of your information as you would be for written communications.

Third, remember to make a written record of the transactions you handle by telephone.

EMPLOYMENT INTERVIEWS

Another important use of oral communications in business is in the employment interview. The interview is a vital part of the employment process. Most employers allow the interview to carry heavy weight in any hiring decision. Effective oral communications contribute to creating the right impression in an interview.

Prepare for the Interview. Before the interview, learn as much as you can about the organization where you seek employment. Knowledge about a company and its competitors will increase your confidence in your ability to talk with your interviewer.

Speak Clearly and Accurately. Of all times, the interview is the time to be meticulous about such things as grammar, pronunciation, and vocabulary. Be sure that your voice is loud enough to be understood.

Be Yourself. Naturalness is an asset. Use words whose meaning or pronunciation are absolutely clear to you. If you are well-informed about what questions might be asked, you will be prepared to talk in a natural way.

Let Your Interest Show. Be sure that your answers reflect your interest in the job. If you answer simply *yes* or *no* without giving other information, you will give the impression of boredom, if not surliness.

Do Not Talk Too Much. Volunteer the kind of information that relates to the position involved, but do not give irrelevant details of your personal life. Do not ask the interviewer personal questions, and do not wander far from the purpose of the interview.

Some aspects of the interview are based on nonverbal communications, a subject that will be considered in Unit 24.

INFORMAL OCCASIONS

It would be difficult to give specific guidelines for the times when employees talk with each other in unstructured situations, such as during lunch or coffee breaks or while riding to work together. In general, however, it is a good idea to steer clear of office gossip and to avoid saying anything you would not want everyone in the office to know.

Informal oral communication also takes place when an employee talks with co-workers in a structured situation like a conference, a meeting, or a seminar. Good group participation requires that the members of a discussion take some responsibility for the success of the activity. As you take part in a meeting or any kind of discussion group, keep the following guidelines in mind.

1. Express your ideas. The leader will have set up some framework for the discussion, and usually the success of the discussion will depend on the participation of the members—their contribution of opinions and relevant facts. The meeting would not be taking place if the leader didn't want and need the ideas of the group.

2. Be respectful of the opinions of others. Be attentive when others are speaking. Keep an open mind so that you are able to learn from what your co-workers say, even when you have strong ideas of your own. Try not to take sides until you have heard the facts. The role of the listener will be considered further in Unit 23.

3. Try to imagine yourself in the role of the person directing the activity. When an opinion is requested, be ready to offer yours. It is just as discourteous to remain silent during a group discussion as it is to try to dominate the discussion. There may be times when the leader is someone you don't especially like. You may be tempted to show your dislike by refusing to cooperate in the discussion. In business situations, the leader is *in charge*, and members of the group should not attempt to bypass that person's authority in any way.

4. If the group is to reach a decision of some sort, offer your ideas and listen to the ideas of others. Then, when a decision is reached, be prepared to support it. It is a sign of immaturity to keep silent during a discussion and then complain about the decision later.

SPEAKING TO A GROUP

Sometimes it is necessary to make an oral report to a group or to submit an oral presentation of your own. Even without training in public speaking, you can do a creditable job:

- Be prepared with the material you need. If you are going to use handouts, be sure they are available in adequate supply and that their appearance is professional.

- Familiarize yourself with the material so that you are not merely reading aloud from text that is in the hands of your listeners.

- Be 100% sure that you can pronounce correctly any words that you will be using. Be especially careful with the names of people and places.

Formal speech-making is a specialized form of oral communications. Speech-making involves techniques of speech writing, public address, and salesmanship. For the casual speaker, one who has not had special training for such situations, keep the following suggestions in mind.

- If you are using a microphone, be sure it is turned on and adjusted to a suitable height for you.

- Be brief. No one ever complains that a speech is too short! Brevity almost always shows that you have organized your material in such a way that your presentation is clear and concise.

- Resist the temptation to use the cliche "A funny thing happened." A serious business speech is enhanced by wit and by humor, but comedy "one-liners" are really inappropriate.

The value of good oral communication cannot be overestimated. It is well worth your time and effort to learn to use spoken language well.

23
The Positive Listener

Almost everywhere we are surrounded by noise. Sometimes that noise is organized, and we call it "sound." In the midst of constant noise, we become conditioned to focusing on what we want to hear—or even to focusing on our thoughts—and we are able to ignore everything else. Students can sit in a classroom, apparently attentive to a teacher, and actually not hear anything that is said. Parents may "listen" to a child's recital of the day's activities—and not hear a word. And who has not "listened" to a weather report and failed to hear any of it?

We sometimes think of listening as a passive occupation—we think that listening is merely the absence of any other obvious activity. Yet when we list the traits we seek in a friend, we often say that we are looking for a person who is a "good listener." In this unit we shall look at some of the activities involved in positive listening and examine some ways in which we can improve our listening skills.

LISTENING SKILLS

It is usually impossible to shut out extraneous noises in our environment. There are sounds of traffic, airplanes, dogs barking, and running motors of everything from lawn mowers to electric typewriters. Music is always around us, too—music from radios, television sets, and stereo players and piped-in music in stores, offices, factories. These sounds are so much a part of us that it would seem odd to be without them.

Because we are so accustomed to a certain level of background noise, we need to develop some techniques that will turn us into conscious, deliberate listeners when listening is our role in the communications process.

LISTENING TECHNIQUES

A few useful techniques will help you improve your listening skills.

Prepare for Listening. Whenever possible, prepare yourself for positive listening by reviewing material you know will be discussed or explained. Such a review enables you to follow the train of thought of a speaker more easily and allows you to prepare questions about points you have trouble understanding.

Another advantage of advance reviewing is to become familiar with some of the vocabulary of a subject. Imagine how difficult it would be to listen actively to a speech made in a language that you did not understand. Becoming familiar with the vocabulary of a subject increases your ability to understand what a speaker is saying.

Concentrate on Listening. Planning is not always possible, of course. Much of the listening we do is not in a formal context, as with a lecture, sermon, or speech. We may be listening to directions or explanations given by members of our families, by supervisors, or by co-workers. To improve this kind of listening, avoid distractions. Concentrate on the activity of listening and look at the speaker. Looking at someone who is speaking to you is more than simple courtesy. If you are looking out the window, you may see something that attracts you. If you are turning the pages of a book, cleaning your eyeglasses, or searching your pockets or handbag for a pencil, your attention is diverted from the activity of listening.

Organize While You Listen. Follow the ideas that are being presented. Think about what is being said and try to see the connections as the speaker moves on to the next point. In the case of a formal speech, the speaker is likely to be following an outline. Try to enumerate the points.

Take Notes. In some situations it will be useful, possibly even necessary, to take notes. Notes should not include every word spoken. As you select what you write down, keep in mind the purpose of the notes. Students sometimes get into the bad habit of writing down everything that is said during a lecture. Try not to let the activity of taking notes replace the activity of listening. Notes are useless if there is no order to them.

When taking notes, remember that you need not write down something you are sure you already know. For example, when the speaker is someone you know well and have heard many times, you do not need to identify the notes with the speaker's name, title, and background. In other circumstances you might need that kind of identification.

Listen, Then Speak. In an informal context, such as a meeting or conversation, the roles of speaker and listener shift frequently. When you are listening, try to concentrate on the listening role. If you are thinking only of what you want to say as soon as you have a chance, you will not hear the speaker at all. When you are the speaker in these situations, make your comments appropriate. Since a conversation is a two-way exchange, what a speaker says should reflect what has already been said. *Non sequiturs* are remarks that do not logically follow what went before. Non sequiturs may be humorous, but they do not reflect good listening habits.

LISTENING IN BUSINESS SITUATIONS

For most of us there are numerous listening situations that represent entertainment in our personal and social lives. We enjoy films, plays, and musical events. We watch programs on television for information and for entertainment, and we want to listen. In a business context we are seldom looking for entertainment, but we do seek information. In a business situation (or a school situation) we are often part of a captive audience—individuals who cannot easily walk away from a particular situation. Listening skills are important in many business situations.

Telephone Listening. In Unit 22 we considered various uses of the telephone in business. When taking orders by phone, the listener must be sure to get the right information. One persistent problem in placing orders by phone is the likelihood that a name of a person, a company, or a street will be misspelled. A misspelling of a city like Cincinnati, Albuquerque, or Philadelphia is embarrassing, but a misspelling of a street name—Norwood instead of Garwood, for example—can prevent the delivery of an order. The person who takes orders by telephone must be meticulous about the spelling of names.

Responding to inquiries and arranging for reservations also require careful listening. A reservation made for the wrong name, the wrong occasion, or the wrong time is quite useless and will cause unpleasantness.

Listening to a Speaker. In many business situations a speaker may give valuable information that listeners must remember. It is not always possible to take notes. Many speakers provide handouts. However, a positive listener is able to absorb much information directly from the speaker, keeping in mind the special listening skills of avoiding distractions, looking at the speaker, and organizing while listening.

Listening at a Meeting. In most business meetings the leader is not the only one who speaks. The leader presents the subject and gives some information, and then other members of the group have a chance to speak. As a member of a group at a meeting, you have an opportunity to practice active and positive listening. While another person is talking, you should resist the temptation to think about what you want to say. Careful listening helps ensure that your comments will be relevant to the discussion.

Listening in a Small Informal Group. Everyone knows someone who simply talks too much! Whether in a personal or business context, we have a tendency not to listen at all after someone who talks too much has been speaking for a while. Of course we know that the problem is not caused by poor listening, and that it can be solved only by the person who is talking. How do we handle the listening side? Probably the only positive, active thing to do is to give the same kind of attention you would give in other circumstances. (In a social situation the "overtalker" is likely to lose popularity. In business, if your supervisor is the talker, there is not much you can do except to listen attentively and courteously.)

Listening to Instructions. Whether instructions are given in person or by tape, be sure that you can visualize just what is expected of you. If you have taped instructions of how to handle a piece of correspondence, play them over to aid your understanding. If instructions are given in person, ask questions so that you know just what to do.

Careful listening, positive listening, even creative listening—however you think of the listening activity, be aware that it is an activity, not just the absence of any other occupation. Listening well will give you insight into what others are thinking. Listening carefully and noting what you have heard can keep you from making mistakes.

24
Communicating Without Words

Writing, reading, talking, and listening—all these activities
are forms of communication that require words. One other aspect
of communication merits our attention—communication without words.

In this unit we shall look at some of the ways we communicate
nonverbally and consider how we can improve our ability to send
effective nonverbal messages.

Nonverbal communication includes all the ways we send messages to others without words. Much of our nonverbal communication is rooted in psychological motivation. Books have been written about the various ways that we transmit messages by our use of color and by our gestures. On a simple level, when the traffic director holds up a hand, most of us understand *stop*, just as we recognize that same message from a red light.

These messages without words are the most nebulous of all our means of communication. They are easily affected by subjective interpretation. For example, this situation could be misinterpreted:

Sarah and Ann are both at a party. Both are very near-sighted. Ann wears glasses, but Sarah does not. Bob talks with Sarah, who moves closer to him. Later he talks with Ann, who moves away slightly.

Bob will be making a mistake if he thinks that Sarah is seeking closeness with him and that Ann is rejecting him. Both are merely trying to see him clearly.

Color associations are also easily misinterpreted. Some people consider black clothing depressing, a sign of mourning. To others, black clothing indicates glamour and mystery. A person might wear black clothing for one of many other reasons or for no particular reason at all.

In business situations we should be aware that nonverbal communication can influence our message. Most messages involve the use of words, but nonverbal communication does affect the message—sometimes by enhancing it and occasionally by contradicting it. Almost always our nonverbal messages are ways of letting our attitudes show—attitudes toward ourselves, toward specific situations, and toward other people. Always be careful about drawing firm conclusions from purely nonverbal signals.

ATTITUDE TOWARD OURSELVES

Although there might be several reasons for any nonverbal message, we do show how we feel about ourselves in some simple physical ways.

Posture. A person who walks, stands, and sits with a straight back and who holds his or her head high shows confidence. In contrast, a person who hunches over and always looks down seems defeated, even furtive. Actors and actresses use slumping posture in roles where they want to appear old. Much can be said about the health benefits of good posture. The message it gives about a person's self-confidence is another real benefit.

Voice. A clear voice that is loud enough to be heard gives the impression that a person is comfortable in a situation. A weak voice or a voice that is too loud reflects insecurity. How loud one's voice should be is sometimes determined by the circumstances in which one is speaking. For example, you may have to speak more quietly than usual if you have to interrupt a meeting to give someone a message. Your low voice would not mean you are unsure of yourself.

Clothing and Appearance. You show confidence when your appearance reveals that you have respect for yourself. In contemporary business, cleanliness is basic to self-respect. For both men and women, the standards are high. A disregard for the latest fashion in clothes or in hair styles may not reflect a low self-image, but an inappropriate outfit or an untidy appearance will convey the idea that one does not care enough about one's self to bother.

ATTITUDE TOWARD SITUATIONS

No matter how secure we may be, all of us encounter situations in which we feel threatened or frightened. In other situations, we feel in control.

We cannot completely separate how we feel about a situation from how we feel about ourselves. There are, however, some ways in which we clearly give nonverbal messages of our attitudes toward a situation.

Promptness. In business, being on time has great value. Wasting time also wastes money. Tardiness indicates poor planning and lack of effective organizing skills. Being habitually late also suggests a dislike for an activity. Throughout our lives we show a tendency to be on time for the things we want to do, even if we are late for everything else. The child who just can't be on time for school or for an appointment with the dentist is likely to be quite prompt about leaving for a picnic. When we are reliable about time in business, we convey a message of our confidence and of our liking for a situation.

Procrastination may also be a nonverbal message that we feel uncomfortable about a project or that we feel threatened by it. Someone who is uncertain of how to begin an assignment may delay, while someone who is enthusiastic about it will start as soon as possible.

Unsuitable Behavior. In a situation, such as a meeting, in which listening and speaking are involved, those who are uncomfortable about the circumstances may indicate that discomfort without saying anything at all. Such nonverbal messages include sighing, fidgeting, and looking at the clock or at a watch. Yawning is an involuntary action, but doing so openly is a display of bad manners. Such an open display of bad manners is a nonverbal message that the meeting is source of threat.

Often a person will deliberately behave in ways that call attention to a lack of interest, believing that such action reflects poorly on the person in charge of the meeting. In reality, though, the poor impression is made by the person who is displaying nonverbal signs of boredom.

Mannerisms. In any interpersonal contact, there are opportunities to observe others and to be affected by such things as facial expressions, movements of hands, and other minor physical activity that takes place during face-to-face encounters. Distracting physical movements include scratching one's head, rubbing one's eyes, and removing and replacing eyeglasses. These activities reveal nervousness about a situation.

Inappropriate Clothing. How we dress can give a nonverbal statement of our attitude toward a situation. We quickly recognize that wearing extremely casual clothing for a formal occasion is a sign of lack of respect for the event. On the other hand, a person who overdresses is also showing a disregard for the occasion. If a situation is clearly designated as a work session in which the people involved will be doing physical work, those who attend dressed for a more formal situation are revealing a lack of regard for the instructions.

ATTITUDE TOWARD OTHERS

The clues we give of our attitude toward ourselves and toward situations are often part of the clues we give of our attitude toward others. Usually in the way we show our attitude toward other people, there is another dimension—we expect some response.

Intrusiveness. As our society requires more people to live and work very close to each other, we run into more ways in which our behavior *intrudes*—that is, enters another's life without invitation. With such intrusive behavior we may also *obtrude*—that is, insist upon calling attention to ourselves.

In the small space of an office, men and women may be both intrusive and obtrusive in their use of perfumed cosmetics. This nonverbal message should be a pleasant one, but when the fragrances are overwhelming, the message can be interpreted as an intrusion into the lives of other people. The person who uses too much fragrance seems to be saying to others, "You have to accommodate *my* choice."

The way we use our voices also reflects our attitudes toward the rights of others. For conversational purposes, a voice that is loud enough to be heard by those included in the conversation shows that the speaker wants to welcome the listeners. On the other hand, a conversation held in a voice loud enough that uninvolved people are forced to listen shows that the speaker is willing to intrude on the privacy of others.

Accepting the Role of Others. In many business situations, we must operate with someone in a position of authority. It is standard for the various levels of management to function as authorities in business situations. While all employees must accept the authority role *openly*, there are subtle ways in which individuals can show a lack of acceptance. These signals are usually nonverbal because spoken resistance to authority is likely to bring repercussions. Notice the unspoken signals in this situation:

Mrs. Kingsley is the director of the Human Resources Department. She had called a staff meeting for 9 a.m. on March 23. That day an emergency arose that made it impossible for her to be at the meeting. She wanted the meeting to proceed, and she called Sam Halston, another member of the department, and asked him to conduct the meeting.

Sam is one of four equals on the Human Resources staff. He reached the conference room and told the other three members that Mrs. Kingsley would not be present and that she had asked him to conduct the meeting. Barbara Lutwell left the room to get a cup of coffee, which she brought back into the conference room. Jim Cook opened his briefcase, took out some papers, and studied them throughout the meeting. Adam Upshaw announced that he would have to leave at 9:15 because he expected an important telephone call.

Not one of the staff would have openly said to Sam, "I do not accept your authority to conduct this meeting." Each of them, however, gave a nonverbal message of a lack of acceptance by doing what they would not have considered doing if Mrs. Kingsley had been present.

Sometimes the person in authority shows an inability to accept the role of those in subordinate positions. The inability to delegate authority or to leave a person to handle his or her own responsibilities is a nonverbal clue of a lack of confidence. Consider the nonverbal clues in this situation:

Katie Lopak has overall charge of a company conference that is to be held at headquarters in May. Jason Lindquist has been assigned the task of finding accommodations for the 115 visiting participants. Courtney Whitman is responsible for planning the schedule for the three-day event, and Anna Ortiz has been asked to prepare the program for the printer.

If Ms. Lopak has delegated authority properly, she will check periodically to make sure that her three assistants are carrying out their responsibilities, and she will offer help if they need it. However, she will not take on any of the tasks she has delegated. She might ask Mr. Lindquist if he has secured all the spaces needed, but she will not tell him to send 12 people to Franklin Lodge and 10 to the Sunrise Motel. Within the group it might be necessary for Ms. Whitman to ask Anna Ortiz when she must send the program to the printer, but it would not be appropriate for Ms. Whitman to bypass Ms. Ortiz and deal with the printer herself.

Stereotyping. In current business situations it is extremely important that the rights of individuals be respected. No person should automatically be treated as part of a stereotyped group. Legal action to enforce individual rights may be taken when those rights are abridged by verbal means, written or oral. More subtle infringement of rights may occur nonverbally, through such actions as designation of office space, placement of desks, or preferential assignments.

Those who base their behavior on stereotyped assumptions are likely to be embarrassed when their assumptions are proven to be incorrect. To others they appear insecure, needing to prove their own superiority at the expense of those who are disabled, those who are members of ethnic minorities, those who are from different regions of the country (or different countries), those who are older, or those who are in any way different.

Remembering Names. One of the most useful kinds of nonverbal communication is the ability to remember the names of people. The apparent lack of this ability is so widespread that no one takes serious offense when names are not remembered. We all hear people say, "I just can't remember names."

Since not many people make the effort, the positive message that goes with remembering is a great advantage. It is worthwhile to develop a good system for remembering names and for using the correct ones in business situations. Aside from taking a memory course, how can you develop such a system?

First of all, remember that the human brain works somewhat like a computer—it cannot give back to you any information that was not put in! When you meet someone whose name you want to remember, be very sure to get the name right in the first place. The correct spelling and pronunciation will help you fix it in your mind. If you think you heard "James Thomas" when the man you've met is actually "James Thompson," you will not remember the name accurately. Take time to be certain. If the name is unusual, ask how to spell it. Pronounce the name and ask if you are saying it right. If you talk with the person for a few minutes, try to use the name at least once. (Don't overdo it.)

Concentrate on any clues that will help you recall the name the next time you see the person. Obviously, the color and type of clothing will *not* help if you have to remember at some future date. You cannot hope that Mr. Gray will always obligingly wear a gray suit. Remembering that Ms. Brown has brown eyes is not very useful because many other people have brown eyes. Some helpful clues might be established if Mr. Gray reminds you of a friend named

Gary, or if Ms. Green tells you that she lives on Kelly Avenue. Any valid memory association you can make is helpful, and often the unusual connections will stay with you longest.

The nonverbal message you give by remembering names and details about other people is a powerful one. You are communicating to those other people that they matter to you—that they are important. When you consider the great advantage you have if you are able to remember names, you will recognize that *learning* to remember is worth the effort.

OTHER NONVERBAL MESSAGES

There are, of course, many other kinds of nonverbal messages. One way in which we show all our attitudes is by facial expression. The value of a smile has been mentioned so often that we tend to think of it as a cliche—yet the value is still there. Facial expressions reflects how we feel about the situation, ourselves, and other people. Just as with other nonverbal messages, there are times when the immediate interpretation is not valid. A frown may be an expression of disapproval, but a frown could also be a response to bright sunlight or to a headache.

Another nonverbal message that reflects all our attitudes involves making eye contact with those in our presence. Looking a person in the eye as we speak is considered by many to be a sign of honesty. It is certainly a sign of attention, and in most instances it conveys a message that is flattering to the receiver. People who have the ability to make others feel important by giving full attention make a point of sending positive nonverbal messages.

Nonverbal communication must always be considered from two sides—the messages we are receiving and those we are sending. We should take care not to draw conclusions based solely on the nonverbal aspects of messages from others. We should also take care that what we are "saying" nonverbally is consistent with the deliberate message we convey with our words. At times, "mixed messages" can produce serious difficulties.

We are careful when we write, and we must give similar thought to each aspect of business communication. Clear, concise writing, thoughtful speech, and appropriate nonverbal messages produce the effective communication so important in business.

22–24
Worksheets

1. List five words that you hear often whose meanings are not completely clear to you. Look them up so that you are prepared to use them properly.

2. Here are some possible ways you might answer the telephone for your supervisor, Miss Rita Graham. Evaluate them on the basis of the information they provide for the caller, the image they provide of your company, and the ease with which you could make such an answer:

   A. Good morning.

   B. This is Miss Graham's office.

   C. Hello.

   D. This is (your name). May I help you?

   E. Yes? What can I do for you?

3. Think of at least three situations in which you need good listening skills. For each one, explain what difficulties you might have to overcome to be able to listen well.

4. When you describe a person as a good listener, what do you mean?

5. List five words from the Spelling Reference List (see Appendix) whose pronunciations are difficult for you. Use the dictionary to find the correct pronunciation.

6. Plan what you would say if you were placing an order by telephone for 12 reams of your company letterheads with the printer who has been printing them for many years. You want them charged to your open account and delivered by messenger as soon as possible.

7. Think of the most recent social conversation you had. What were some nonverbal messages you received? Can you think of any such messages that you were sending?

8. List all the ways you can think of in which positive nonverbal messages may be given.

9. Write a memo explaining what you consider the most important elements in good business use of the telephone. Address the memo to the members of the Marketing Department of Fillmore Box & Carton Company.

10. Read the following account of an employment interview. Identify the mistakes made by the applicant.

    Cadwell Electronics is planning to hire several secretarial employees who will have the opportunity to advance as administrative assistants. Ms. Staci Munro is an applicant, and Ms. Deirdre O'Hara is the interviewer.

    O'Hara: Come right in, Ms. Munro. Did you have any trouble finding us?

    Munro: No, I already knew where this office was because me and my sister used to ride our bikes past here.

    O'Hara: Please sit down. I see from your resume that you have just left a position with Carlisle Industries. Did you enjoy your work there?

    Munro: Well, I did at first, but after a while I realized that my supervisor just didn't like me. She kept picking on me because I was late a lot.

    O'Hara: I see. Why do you want to work for us?

    Munro: This company has a reputation for good benefits, like, you know, vacations and insurance and everything. Do you mind if I smoke?

    O'Hara: Go right ahead. There's an ashtray on the bookcase. Tell me about your career goals, Ms. Munro. What do you want to be doing in five years?

    Munro: Well, I hope to have like a good supervisory job with one of the really big electronics firms. Not that this one isn't like, you know, good, but I want to go to the top.

    O'Hara: I see. You are expected in the Testing Department in a few minutes for our preliminary test battery.

    Munro: I hope it don't take too long. I promised my friend I'd meet her for lunch.

11. Certain foreign terms occur in regular use in our everyday speech. You should not use words you can't pronounce or understand. Use a dictionary to find pronunciations and definitions of each of the following:

potpourri	hors d'oeuvres	vichyssoise
faux pas	cachet	elan

12. Some words are frequently mispronounced, and other have more than one acceptable pronunciation. Consult a dictionary to find the correct pronunciation for each of the following words. If two pronunciations are acceptable, decide which one you will use.

again	frustrated	harass	herbal
height	often	salmon	statistics
similar	valet		

13. You are the secretary to Luis Hernandez at Mendoza Manufacturers in Columbus, Ohio. He has decided to take a management team to make a surprise inspection trip to the factory in Shepherd, Pennsylvania. He wants to leave tomorrow, May 3, and stay three nights in Shepherd at Green Willow Inn. Accompanying him will be Georgia Douglas, Frank Maloney, and Lee Soong. You've already arranged for the company plane to provide transportation.

Plan what you would say when you call Green Willow Inn to make the reservations for Mr. Mendoza and his management team.

14. Make a list of the questions you would ask a job applicant if you were an interviewer. Assume that the applicant has just completed extra training after high school to prepare for a secretarial position.

---

15. At a management seminar today, you met several people. You expect to see these people again at a second session tomorrow. You want to make a good impression by remembering their names, where they work, and the location of their companies. Study the business cards you collected from these people at the meeting, and be prepared to answer questions about them.

912-555-0111

Barbara DeLoach
Bulldog Tractors
333 Forsyth Road
Macon, GA   31216

Lucy's Pet Food
1110 Wisconsin Street
St. Paul, MN   55123

Skip Dowell
Research Chemist
612-555-1777

Artwell Inks Incorporated
344 Balak Highway
Chicago, Illinois 60617

Camden O'Rourke, Personnel
Telephone: (312) 555-1872

AMERICAN ENVELOPES

88 Carteret Drive

New Brunswick, NJ   08904

Bill Hightower   Telephone: 609-555-4985
President   Fax: 609-555-3472

Appendix

200 WORDS OFTEN MISSPELLED

absence
absolutely
accidentally
accommodate
accountant
accumulate
achievement
acknowledge
acoustics
acquire
acquittal
adequately
adjacent
administrative
advisable
anonymous
apology
approval
approximately
authority
believe
beneficiary
boulevard
budget
buoyant
calendar
cancel
carefully
catalog
chief
commitment
commodity
comptroller
concede
confusion
congratulate
conscientious
consensus
conspicuous
contiguous

convenient
correspondent
courageous
courtesy
curriculum
deceive
decision
deductible
definitely
description
desperate
develop
disastrous
disbursement
discrepancy
discretion
efficiency
eligible
embarrass
eminent
emphasize
environment
equipped
etiquette
exaggerate
exceed
exorbitant
extension
facsimile
familiar
financial
foreclosure
foreign
forfeit
fortieth
forty
fourteen
frivolous
fulfillment
functional

government
grammar
grateful
greatly
grievous
guarantee
guidance
guilty
handkerchief
harass
height
hindrance
immediate
imminent
inconvenience
incurred
indebtedness
intention
interpret
interrupt
irrelevant
itinerary
jeopardy
judgment
judicial
knowledge
laboratory
legitimate
leisure
lenient
liaison
license
likelihood
lucrative
maintenance
manageable
memento
mileage
miscellaneous
misspelled

monopoly
mortgage
necessary
nineteen
ninetieth
ninth
notable
noticeable
obsolete
occasional
occupancy
occupant
occurrence
offered
omission
opposite
parallel
partial
perhaps
permanent
persevere
personnel
persuade
pharmaceutical
precede
privilege
procedure
proceedings
proprietary
pursue
quantity
questionnaire
receivable
recognition
recommendation
referring
registration
responsible
restaurant
safety

schedule
sensible
sensitivity
separate
similar
sincerely
success
successfully
summary
superintendent
supplement
surprise
suspense
suspicion
tariff
tenant
their
thorough
transferred
transmittal
tyranny
unanimous
undoubtedly
unprofessional
usage
utility
utilize
variable
variety
verification
vocabulary
volume
voluminous
weird
whether
wield
withdrawal
withhold
yield
zealous

MAIL AND DISTRIBUTION SERVICES

The Postal Service offers four classes of mail.

First-Class Mail includes written or typed matter, bills and account statements, and all materials sealed against postal inspection. Most daily business correspondence must be sent First Class.

Second-Class Mail consists of newspapers and magazines that have been officially entered at the post office as Second-Class Mail. A record of that entry must appear on each magazine or newspaper.

Third-Class Mail consists of circulars, booklets, catalogs, and merchandise. Each individual piece sent Third Class must weigh less than 16 ounces. Two categories of Third-Class Mail exist: bulk and single piece.

Fourth-Class Mail (also called Parcel Post) consists mainly of merchandise. Packages weighing 16 ounces or more are sent Fourth-Class. When the Fourth-Class rate is used, any parcel—either sealed or unsealed—may be opened for postal inspection.

These mail and distribution services are available.

Special Delivery. An envelope or parcel for which the Special Delivery fee has been paid will be given speedy handling in transit and will be delivered by special messenger. Special Delivery service is available for all types of mail.

Special Handling. This service, available for Third-Class and Fourth-Class Mail, provides quick handling, dispatch, and transportation.

Express Mail. The post office offers guaranteed overnight delivery for an extra fee. Insurance is included at no extra charge.

Registered Mail. Registered Mail is used to send valuable documents or articles through the mail. The sender pays a special registry fee and receives a receipt. The addressee is required to sign for the mail upon its delivery. For an additional fee, the sender will get a return receipt for any registered article.

Certified Mail. This service provides for a record of delivery at the post office of address. At an additional cost, a receipt is sent to the sender. Only First-Class Mail is accepted as Certified Mail. Certified Mail cannot be insured, but special delivery is available.

Insured Mail. First-, Third-, and Fourth-Class Mail can be insured. The sender obtains the insurance by paying a special fee at the post office and is given a receipt. The fee varies with the amount of insurance.

C.O.D. First-, Third-, and Fourth-Class Mail may be sent collect on delivery (C.O.D.). For a fee, the post office will collect the amount due and forward it to the sender. The C.O.D. service fee includes insurance.

Money Orders. Money orders are a safe and convenient way of sending money through the mail. The fee varies with the amount of the Money Order.

Mailgram. This post office service, offered in conjunction with Western Union, is a way of sending a message quickly and with impact. The Mailgram will arrive the next business day in a distinctive format.

Couriers. Independent businesses also provide delivery service. Within cities, couriers offer same-day delivery. Overnight delivery or second-day service is available between cities.

Facsimile. Many companies use facsimile, or fax, equipment to send documents to their destination in minutes. A fax machine scans the document to convert the image into electrical impulses. These impulses are transmitted by telephone lines to a receiving machine, which prints the document.

STATE AND TERRITORY ABBREVIATIONS

This list provides the name of each state and territory followed by the postal service two-letter abbreviation. Use the abbreviation whenever you are typing an address with a ZIP Code.

If you are writing a state name by itself or without a ZIP Code, spell out the name.

Alabama	AL	Kentucky	KY	Ohio	OH
Alaska	AK	Louisiana	LA	Oklahoma	OK
Arizona	AZ	Maine	ME	Oregon	OR
Arkansas	AR	Maryland	MD	Pennsylvania	PA
California	CA	Massachusetts	MA	Puerto Rico	PR
Colorado	CO	Michigan	MI	Rhode Island	RI
Connecticut	CT	Minnesota	MN	South Carolina	SC
Delaware	DE	Mississippi	MS	South Dakota	SD
Dist. of Columbia	DC	Missouri	MO	Tennessee	TN
Florida	FL	Montana	MT	Texas	TX
Georgia	GA	Nebraska	NE	Utah	UT
Guam	GU	Nevada	NV	Vermont	VT
Hawaii	HI	New Hampshire	NH	Virgin Islands	VI
Idaho	ID	New Jersey	NJ	Virginia	VA
Illinois	IL	New Mexico	NM	Washington	WA
Indiana	IN	New York	NY	West Virginia	WV
Iowa	IA	North Carolina	NC	Wisconsin	WI
Kansas	KS	North Dakota	ND	Wyoming	WY

TIME ZONES AND AREA CODES

Use this map to determine the time and area code in the location you need to dial.

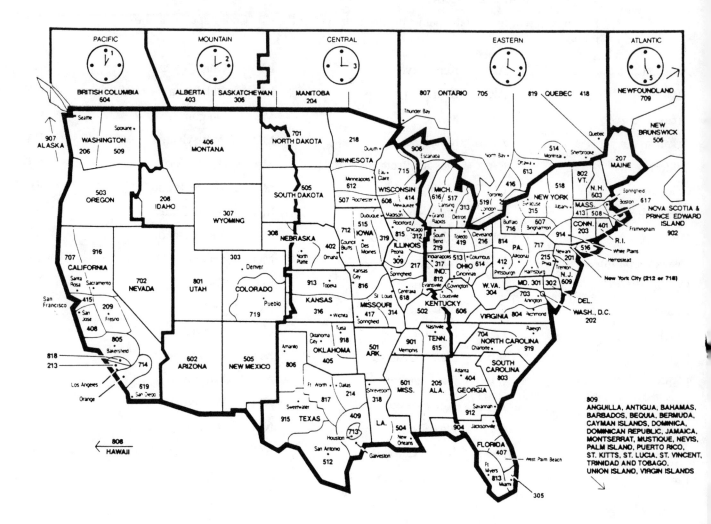

MILITARY TIME

Many businesses use military time, in which the hour is given according to a 24-hour clock. Instead of going back to 1 after the noon hour, the hours continue to count 13, 14, 15, 16, and so forth, up to 24 hours in a day. All morning (a.m.) times are the same in standard and military time. To convert any afternoon or night (p.m.) time, add that time to 12. For example, 5 p.m. is 1700 hours on the 24-hour clock, and 1 p.m. is 1300 hours.

GLOSSARY

Agreement—consistency in using singular or plural forms for nouns, verbs, and pronouns

Almanac—annual reference work that contains short summaries and tables of useful information

Atlas—reference work containing maps and other information about geography

Blind advertisement—classified advertisement that gives a convenience box number rather than the name of the advertiser as a return address

Cashier's check—a check purchased from a bank, not written on an individual depositor's account

Certified check—a check written by a depositer and guaranteed payable by the bank before the check is offered as payment

Cliche—an overworked expression

C.O.D. (or **c.o.d.**)—shipping terms in which all charges are paid on delivery, including cost of merchandise and shipping charges

Complimentary close—the final words preceding the name of the writer (*Sincerely, Yours very truly,* etc.)

Consumer—one who uses a product or a service for noncommercial purposes

Courtesy title—the title that precedes a name (Miss, Mr., Ms., or Mrs.)

Executive-size paper—paper that measures $7\frac{1}{4}$ by $10\frac{1}{2}$ inches (also called monarch)

Extension—figure on an order form or an invoice that shows the total cost of a given quantity of an item ordered

Facsimile—method of transmitting and receiving documents over telephone lines

F.O.B. (or **f.o.b.**)—shipping term followed by **shipping point, destination,** or the name of a city that tells the location at which the quoted price is valid

Heading address—the return address used on a letterhead or plain paper for business correspondence

Human resources department—the department responsible for hiring and training new employees (also called **personnel office**)

Inside address—the address of the receiver of a letter, written at the beginning of the letter

Invoice—an itemized list of articles shipped on an order (sometimes an invoice serves as a bill)

Letterhead—stationery imprinted with an organization's name and address

M—the Roman numeral for 1,000, used as a symbol for 1,000 units of anything

Monarch-size paper—paper that measures $7\frac{1}{4}$ inches by $10\frac{1}{2}$ inches (also called **executive**)

Nonverbal communication—messages given and received without the use of words

Official title—the title that designates a person's position or function

Parallelism—connecting or separating items in a series so that each item has a similar structure and value

Parcel post—regular package delivery through the United States Postal Service

Prospect—a potential customer

Re (or **in re**)—a way to begin a subject line; the Latin phrase for *in the matter of*, not an abbreviation for *regarding*

Ream—500 sheets of paper, regardless of the size of the paper

Reference initials—lowercase letters that indicate the initials of the typist of a letter

Resume—a detailed summary of qualifications for employment

Salutation—a way of beginning a letter by naming the reader, usually preceded by *Dear*; sometimes just *Ladies*, *Gentlemen*, or *Ladies and Gentlemen*

Standard-size paper—paper that measures $8\frac{1}{2}$ by 11 inches

Thesaurus—a reference work used to find words of similar or opposite meanings

Verbal communication—any communication that uses words, either spoken or written

Watermark—a faintly visible design, legible only from the front, on good letterhead paper

INDEX

Abbreviations
  academic degrees, 57
  courtesy titles, 56
  in company names, 57
  states, ZIP Code, 57, 213
Acceptance
  of invitations, 175–176
  of invitations, examples, 175, 176
Acknowledgment, of orders, 91–92
Advice, consumer
  regarding credit, 116
  regarding rights, 133, 134–135
Agendas
  formal, 185
  formal, example of, 184
  informal, 185
  informal, example of, 184
Agreement
  nouns with pronouns, 4
  nouns with verbs, 4, 5
  pronouns with verbs, 4, 5
Almanacs, 40, 215
Announcements, 185
Applications
  for credit, 116–118
  for credit, form, example of, 116
  for credit, letter, example of, 117
  for employment, form example of, 152
  for employment, letters, 152–154
  for employment, letters, examples of, 153, 154, 155
Atlases, 40, 215
Attention line, 57
  placement of, 57

Behavior, in business, 205–208
Bibliography, 193–194
Blind advertisements, 153
  replying to, 154, 155
Block Style, 51
  examples of, 52, 53
Body, of letter
  dynamic entrance, 79
  graceful exit, 80
  logical development, 79–80
Bond paper, 73

Cash, not sending by mail, 91
Checks, types of, 90
Cliches, 13–14
c.o.d. shipment, 89, 215
Collection letter series, 124
  example of, 125, 126
Collect shipment, 89, 215
Color, for letterhead paper, 73
Complimentary close, 58, 215
  placement of, 58
  punctuation with, 51
Concise writing, 11
Condolence letters, 176
  example of, 176
  natural language in, 171
Confidentiality, 118, 119
Congratulations letters, 173
  example of, 173
  natural language in, 171
Conjunctions
  correlative, 4
  in faulty sentences, 4

Consistency
  of tense, 6
  of verb forms, 6
Consumer advice
  regarding credit, 116
  regarding rights, 133, 134–136
Consumer inquiries, 97–99
  response to, 107–108
Copy notation, 59–60
  placement of, 59
Credit
  letters applying for, 116–118
  information requests, 118
  letters granting or refusing, 118–120
  responses to information requests, 118–119

Date, correct form, 55–56
Date, necessity of, 55
Date, placement of
  in Block letter, 51, 55
  in Modified Block letter, 51, 55
  in relation to heading address, 55
Dictionaries, 39
  to verify pronunciation, 39
Direct-mail selling, 166–167
Directories
  business, 41
  city, 41
  telephone, 41
Dynamic entrance, in letter, 79

Employment
  application form, example of, 152
  application form, filling out, 151–152
  application letters, 152–154
  application letters, examples of, 153, 154, 155
  interviews, 160, 201–202
Enclosure notation, 59
  placement of, 59
Envelopes
  addressing, 75–76
  appearance, importance of, 74
  quality of, in relation to letterhead paper, 74
  size of, 74
Etiquette, books of, 41
Express shipment, 89
Extension, 87, 215

Finish, of paper, 73–74
f.o.b. shipment, 89, 215
Folding letters, 74–75
Footnotes, 194
Form letters
  guidelines for writing, 107
  used in inquiry responses, 107
  used in sales letters, 166–168
Fund-raising letters
  appeals in, 165
  examples of, 167, 168
  forms, 166–168
  organizations using, 165
  purpose of, 165
  style of, 165–166

Graceful exit, in letter, 80
Gratitude
  as basis for letter, 171
  letters of appreciation, examples of, 172

Heading, for two-page letter, 60

Inquiries
  consumer, 97
  consumer, examples of, 98, 99
  from one organization to another, 98
  from one organization to another, examples of, 100, 101, 102
  in-house, 99, 102
Inquiry responses
  in-house, 109–110
  requirements, general, 107
  style for, 109
  to businesses, 109
  to consumers, 107–108
Inside address, 56, 215
Invitation
  example of, 174
  letter of, 175

Letter, folding to fit envelope, 74–75
Letter formats
  Block, 51
  Modified Block, 51
  two-page letter, heading, 60
  Simplified, 53
Letterhead paper
  color of, 73
  finish of, 73–74
  quality and weight of, 73
  size of, 74
Listening
  in business situations, 204
  techniques, 203–204
Logical development, in letter, 79–80

Mail, classes of, 212
Memorandums (memos)
  formats, examples of, 68, 69, 70
  simplified format, 69–70
  standard format, 67–69
Memory, ways to improve, 207–208
Memo sheets, weight and size of, 74, 99
Minutes
  formal, 185
  formal, example of, 185
  informal, 185
  informal, example of, 184
Modified Block Style, 51
  example of, 54
Modifiers, placement of, 5–6
Money orders, 91

Names, remembering, 207–208
Naturalness
  in speaking, 199
  in writing, 13, 24–26, 171
Nonverbal communication, 205–208
Numerals, in street addresses, 56

Official titles
  in inside address, 56
  in typed signature line, 58, 59

Order forms
  example of, 88
  how to fill out, 87
Order information, complete, 88
Organizing techniques, 31–34
Outlines
  parallel structure in, 4, 32
  examples of, 31, 32, 33

Paragraphing, 33–34, 80
Parallel structure
  in outlines, 4, 32
  in writing, 3–4
Parcel Post, 90, 215
Paper, quantity, terms for, 73
Positiveness, 23–24
Postal Service abbreviations, 57, 75, 212
Press releases, 183
  example of, 184
Proofreading
  importance of, 39
  symbols, 42
  techniques, 43–44
Punctuation
  mixed, in letters, 51, 52
  open, in letters, 51, 53
Purchase orders, forms, 87
  examples of, 88

Quire, of paper, 73

Reams, of paper, 73, 216
Reference initials, 59, 216
Reference line, 58
Reports
  documenting information used in, 193–194
  organization of, 191–192, 193
  purpose of, 191
  style of, 193
  submission of, 194
  types of, 192–193
Reservations letters, 181
  example of, 182
Resignation letters, 161
  example of, 162
Resolutions, 185–186
  example of, 186
Resume, 155–156
  example of, 157, 158–159

Sales letters
  appeals in, 165
  examples of, 166, 167
  guidelines for, 165–168
  types of, 165
Salutations, 57, 216
Shipping charges, 89

Signature block, 58–59
Simplified style, 53
  example of, 55
Speaking
  before groups, 202
  during interviews, 201–202
  on telephone, 200–201
  style of, 199
Specific writing, 11–12, 24
Statement, of account, 119
States
  ZIP Code abbreviations, 75, 213
Subject line, 58, 69
Substance, of paper, 73
Superscription, 74

Telegraphic messages, 186
Telephone, use of, 87, 200–201
Tense, of verbs, consistent, 6
Thank you letters
  examples of, 172
  reasons for, 171
Thesaurus, 40, 216
Transmittal letters, 194
Transitions, 194

Watermark, 73, 216
Weight, of paper, 73
Words frequently misused, 12–13